IN DEEP WATER

How People, Politics and Protests Sank Irish Water

Michael Brennan

MERCIER PR

For my family –
Siobhán, Daragh, Jessica and Mark

MERCIER PRESS

Cork

www.mercierpress.ie

© Michael Brennan, 2019

ISBN: 978 1 78117 658 0

A CIP record for this title is available from the British Library.

Printed and bound in the EU.

CONTENTS

Part One

JOBSTOWN

1

THE JOBSTOWN REVOLT

There had been no public announcement that Tánaiste Joan Burton would be visiting the local education centre in Jobstown for a graduation ceremony on the morning of 15 November 2014. But the protesters had been told about it by some of the sixty graduates because a small number of them were unhappy about getting their certificates from Burton.

It was just a month after the introduction of water charges nationwide in a country which was in the midst of a deep recession. Contractors around the country were installing meters, at a rate of over 30,000 per month, in order to measure how much water people were using. The protests against water charges were growing.

The word about Burton's impending arrival in Jobstown spread through postings on the Facebook pages for water charge protesters. The most influential page was 'Tallaght Says No', which had been involved in organising protests against water meter installations on the fringes of Tallaght. It posted a message at 8.56 a.m.: 'Joan Burton will be attending an event at An Cosán next to Mary Mercer Centre Kiltalown, Jobstown this morning. Event starts 10.30 and we believe she will be there about 12 noon (unless she bottles out like she did yesterday for her event in Blanchardstown)'.[1]

The news was spread by other protesters living in the local area on their own personal Facebook pages: 'Dear Joan the phone Brutal. If you have the neck to turn up in my home town of Jobstown today just want you to know I've a hangover and I'm in a bad mood,' wrote one protester on Facebook.[2]

The protesters were going to ensure that Burton's visit to a graduation ceremony in Jobstown would be an eventful one.

There had been warning signs of growing unrest over water charges in Jobstown. Two weeks earlier, there had been an anti-water charge rally of 8,000 people in the Tallaght and Jobstown area as part of a nationwide Right2Water protest. There had also been a confrontation during the local elections between a young Labour council candidate and a husband and wife involved in the anti-water charge campaign. The YouTube clip of Carole Purcell and Martina Genocky had gone viral. Carole and her husband, Ken, lived just around the corner from the education centre where Joan Burton would be. They were going to be there.

The Facebook pages of the water charge protesters began appealing for a good turnout outside the local education centre. But despite these warning signs, local gardaí had no advance intelligence of the protest. They did discuss the possibility of a protest taking place, but only one garda inspector, one sergeant and three rank-and-file gardaí were assigned to go to An Cosán.

By now, some of the protesters were on their way from housing estates in the vicinity of the local education centre. Anti-Austerity Alliance TD Paul Murphy wanted to be there, but he was delayed by a meeting. He had been elected to the Dáil to represent Dublin South West in a shock by-election victory just a month before. He had been arrested four times in his short political career for being involved in protests. He was stuck at a meeting of the Socialist Party's national committee in their Thomas Street headquarters in the Liberties that morning. 'Those are important meetings and meetings you shouldn't miss,' said Murphy.[3]

It was coming up to the lunchbreak. Murphy knew the Jobstown protest had been due to start, so he discussed it with a few other party members. They agreed that he should go. 'I think I grabbed the megaphone from the office and I headed out. I drove there by myself,' he said. Just like a plumber would bring his toolbox to work, the megaphone was a 'tool of the trade' for political activists like Murphy.

Jobstown had originally been created to rehouse families from the slums in the inner city and remains one of the poorest areas in the state. It is twenty kilometres from Dublin city centre. The unemployment rate among men at the time of the protest was forty-nine per cent. Around sixty-one per cent of families were headed by a lone parent.[4] It had a food bank operated by Crosscare on the grounds of the parish church. Demand for the bare necessities – tea, sugar and pasta, frozen food, chilled foods, vegetables, toiletries and washing powder – was constant. But it always soared during the summer holidays – when children were not getting their free school meals – and in the run-up to Christmas – when parents were under extra financial pressure.

Burton had a habit of turning up late for events. She had been due in

Jobstown at 11.30 a.m. This time, she was ten minutes late. Around fifteen protesters had managed to assemble across the road and chanted the slogans of the anti-water charge movement as her car passed them. 'No way, we won't pay.'

Burton noticed them but thought little of it. She had gone hiking in Jobstown as a child and had friends in the area. Nothing had happened when Burton visited flooded houses in Jobstown in 2011–12, which had required state funding to refit them. It was the same six months earlier when she'd visited An Cosán (the Pathway) education centre, which had been set up fourteen years earlier. The centre had a 'one generation' solution – get people in Jobstown into third-level education to boost their own prospects and their children's.

Burton got into the robing ceremony in An Cosán without incident. Normally, the full graduation ceremony would have taken place in the centre, which had been funded with a IR£600,000 grant and a free site from South Dublin County Council. But with sixty students graduating this time, there was not enough space. So Burton and the students would have to walk eighty-five metres down a pathway to the Church of St Thomas the Apostle, which was big enough to host the graduation ceremony.

By now, the group of protesters had more than doubled and they were shouting slogans outside the front door of the centre. An Cosán's chief executive, Liz Waters, came outside to appeal to the protesters to stop ruining the occasion for the graduates. 'It's their day,' she said. A female protester responded: 'I don't care. Tell her [Burton] not to come out to us.'[5] Waters bowed her head in disappointment, turned on her heel and went back into the centre.

Burton had a small team of her own people with her in Jobstown. There was Karen O'Connell, her special adviser, who had driven up in her own car from a Labour Party event in Portlaoise. She had joined the Labour Party while studying in University College Dublin (UCD). Chatty, gregarious and intelligent, she was a popular member of the party. She was also utterly loyal to Burton, whom she had worked for as a parliamentary assistant. O'Connell knew what protests were like. During her student days she had travelled to Rossport in Mayo to protest against the construction of Shell's Corrib gas terminal and its underwater sea pipe. O'Connell stood outside the doorway of An Cosán, waiting for Burton to come out.

The gardaí on the scene advised Burton to use her state car and garda driver to make the eighty-five-metre journey to the church. The protesters started chanting 'Out, Out, Out' and 'Traitor, Traitor' as the first graduates emerged in their black caps and gowns at 11.50 a.m. Then the protesters changed the chant to 'Bring her out', as it became clear that Burton was still inside the building.[6]

Burton decided to walk with the graduates. She knew that there were protesters assembling, but she was not worried about them. She was determined to carry on with the function. She was accompanied by Senator Katherine Zappone and her wife, Ann Louise Gilligan, who had set up the centre in Jobstown.

A staff member at An Cosán started to clap the graduates in an attempt to encourage them as they walked out past the protesters. Karen O'Connell immediately joined in. So too did a garda standing beside her. Gradually, the protesters clapped too, as it dawned on them that their chanting might be getting to the graduates rather than Burton. 'Well done, lads,' shouted one of them.[7]

The protesters starting booing and shouting when Burton emerged behind the last of the graduates. O'Connell quickly moved to her side, as did her plain-clothes garda protection officer. The protesters pursued them along the footpath. They surrounded Burton as she walked and some of them were sticking phones in her face. The officer in charge, Garda Inspector Derek Maguire, told two of the gardaí on duty to move in front of Burton so they could force their way through. Some protesters shouted abuse at Burton: 'Labour scum', 'Traitor' and 'Joan, you're a liar.'

Burton noticed one of the protesters in particular – a tall teenager wearing a blue tracksuit top with white stripes. That was Jay Lester (fourteen), who lived a five-minute walk away in an estate in Brookview. He was not involved with any political party but had been active in his area, campaigning for a children's playground. He was motivated by issues like unemployment and homelessness. 'That's what influenced me to get up off my arse and get involved,' he said. Lester recorded Burton as she walked along the pathway to the graduation ceremony in the Church of St Thomas the Apostle. 'Talk to us, Joan; talk to us, Joan,' he said. Lester said he was there to ask questions: 'I wasn't there to antagonise somebody.'[8]

Another protester held up a poster which had an uncomplimentary reference to the Woman of the Year award Burton had been given by *Irish Tatler* magazine two weeks earlier. It said: 'Woman of the Year? Traitor of the Decade.'[9]

By this stage, it was clear that the water charges were the main issue on the minds of the protesters. 'No way, we won't pay' was the loudest chant, followed by 'Shame on you, shame on you.' One woman called Burton a 'bloody traitor', while another protester shouted: 'You're not welcome in Jobstown.'[10]

Some of the protesters had their children with them. One woman pushed a buggy alongside Burton with a young child in it. By now, Burton and O'Connell were hemmed in by protesters. They included Frank Donaghy, a retired construction worker (seventy-one) from Derry. He lived around four kilometres away in the Alpine Rise estate in Tallaght. A member of the Anti-Austerity Alliance, he had been buying petrol that morning in the Applegreen station in Jobstown and had spotted the protest outside An Cosán. He wandered over and joined in.

Burton was an easy target because she was making such slow progress down the footpath. She was hit by a small object on the back of her neck. She thought it might have been a small ball. It was actually a plastic water bottle.

Then she was hit by a red water balloon on the right side of her face. She flinched from the impact and the water soaked her white jacket and the bottom of her hair.[11]

Burton checked briefly with her garda protection officer and then carried on walking. Her aim was to look as calm as possible rather than show the protesters that she was actually frightened. Then a female protester made a mocking remark: 'Where's your phone, Joan?' Burton had once accused the water charge protesters of having 'very expensive phones'. Now she was being filmed by multiple smartphones.

Ann Louise Gilligan and Katherine Zappone each put their right hand up in the air to appeal to the protesters to clear the path for Burton. Burton and O'Connell got through a gate into the grounds of the Church of St Thomas the Apostle.

Inside, Burton took off her soaked white jacket and O'Connell gave her a loan of hers. She dried her hair with a tissue, which another person had given her, and tidied herself up as much as possible before her speech to the graduates.

It was around 12.25 p.m. and Paul Murphy had just arrived at the protest with his megaphone. He and the other protesters waited outside the church for Burton to re-emerge. 'We need people on the other side as well because she can get out over the other side,' said one female protester.[12]

2

GETTING OUT OF THE CHURCH

Garda Inspector Derek Maguire could see that there were already protesters gathering near the state car Burton had been granted as Tánaiste. So using it was no longer an option. Maguire decided instead to sneak Burton out through a side entrance to an unmarked garda car, a grey 2006 Toyota Avensis.

The driver of the patrol car, Detective Garda Gavin Cooke, had been on drug patrol before he got an urgent call to get to the church. He and his colleague tried to get in through the main entrance to the church at 12.05 p.m. The protesters blocked them. Their car might have been unmarked, but it was a familiar sight around the Jobstown area – and the protesters recognised it. They started to shout: 'Rats', 'Traitors' and 'Shame, shame, shame on you.'

Detective Garda Cooke rolled down the window and told the protesters to move aside. They let the car through. But Cooke had no idea that the Avensis was going to be used as a getaway vehicle. He parked it facing the wall of the church, which meant it would have to be reversed out.

The graduation ceremony was still going on. It was now 12.30 p.m. Burton did not know the time because she never wore a watch. Having finished her speech, gardaí told her to leave immediately, before more protesters arrived. They brought her through the sacristy, the room where the priest gets ready for mass, and opened the side door leading to the waiting car outside.[1]

There were now around fifty people outside the front of the church – twenty men and the rest were women and children. They had a clear view of both the side entrance and the Avensis car lined up beside it. They rushed up to the car as soon as they saw Burton and O'Connell get into the back seat. 'Here she is, here she is,' they shouted.

Now the position of the car facing the wall of the church became a problem. The protesters got there within nine seconds. The car could not be reversed because it was surrounded. The protesters banged on the car windows and shouted, 'Shame, shame, shame on you.' Then the chants became more abusive towards both Burton and O'Connell, with the words 'bitch' and 'cunt' being used.[2]

The banging on the windows became more intense. One of the protesters tried to take the air out of the tyres of the trapped patrol car and to pull off the wing mirrors. All the gardaí at the scene rushed to the car to try to move the protesters out of the way. Katherine Zappone became deeply concerned for Burton and O'Connell's safety. She called 999.

More protesters arrived. The banging on the windows continued. Burton said some of the protesters were very wild. 'They were banging on the car, they were screaming and shouting. And some people were just completely carried away,' she said.[3] O'Connell started crying. She was petrified and Burton tried to calm her down. The two of them put their arms around each other. One woman banged repeatedly on the windows and shouted that she wished Burton would die. She was beside herself with rage.

The protesters started to shake the car back and forth. Burton's main fear was what would happen if the protesters got the main car doors open. 'Are they going to drag us out? And all the time I kept looking – where are we going to run to?' she said.

Garda Cooke had locked the doors from the inside. Burton's full-time garda driver, Barry Martin, stood outside beside one of the back doors to prevent anyone from opening it.

Burton could not believe the number of young children in anoraks and hoodies who were wandering around the protest. She wondered where their parents were. 'There were little kids around. There was no harm in them. There was just a lot of excitement and a lot of noise. I think had they [the protesters] any sense of responsibility, they would have sent those children home,' she said.

Then Burton spotted Paul Murphy, who had been elected to the Dáil just a month earlier on an anti-water charge ticket. He was standing around the back of the car. He had a megaphone and was chanting slogans through it. Burton had only met Murphy before on a radio panel and did not know him well. But O'Connell did because they had attended UCD at the same time. Both were involved in student protests in the college, as well as protests in Rossport against Shell's gas refinery. Murphy knew O'Connell enough to say hello to during his college days. But he did not recognise her in the car alongside Burton.[4]

Some of the protesters started singing: 'You can stick your water meter up your arse.' Paul Murphy, still at the back of the garda car, did not join in the sing-song. But he got going for the next familiar protest chant. 'They say cutbacks – we say fight back.'

At this stage, Burton and O'Connell had been trapped in the car for about ten or fifteen minutes. Detective Garda Cooke revved up the engine to warn everyone that he was going to reverse. But Paul Murphy and four other protesters sat down on the ground behind the back of the car. 'Joan Burton's in the car. There's a surge of the crowd towards the car. People are standing up. It's me who sits down first. It was my experience that it's a much more controlled situation if people are sitting down. It's much more clear that people are peaceful protesters. They are sitting down,' he said.

Paul Murphy said his sit-down tactic was inspired by his experience in Rossport, where protesters used to do the same in front of gardaí. He spoke briefly to another sit-down protester called Michael Banks, who had set up the 'Brookview Says No to Water Meters' Facebook page against water charges. They had never met before. Banks told Murphy that he had voted for Sinn Féin's Cathal King in the recent by-election.

Frank Donaghy, the retired construction worker, was another of those sitting down at the back of the car for several minutes. He rapped the back of the car and chanted, 'No way, we won't pay.' He later said, 'It was a sit-down protest. People have been doing it for years. I think it's fairly legitimate.'[5]

Another person sitting down behind the garda car was Scott Masterson, who worked as a delivery courier. He was a member of the republican socialist party Éirígí, which had been involved in protests against the household charge and now water charges. Masterson got up shortly afterwards and stood at the back of the car. He shouted at the gardaí beside him: 'Tell her to get out and answer our questions.'[6]

Karen O'Connell was filming the protesters from inside the car, using her smartphone. As another rendition of the 'You can stick your water meter up your arse' chant came to an end, she captured one protester making a rude and vulgar gesture. 'Up your arse, Joan,' the protester said. As the chanting continued, one of the gardaí in the car told O'Connell sympathetically: 'Bet you're glad you came in to work today?'

'I chose to be here today,' she responded.[7]

Garda Inspector Derek Maguire had seven gardaí under his command at this stage, but they were outnumbered by around fifty protesters who were surrounding the car, and up to 100 more milling around in the church grounds. He called for urgent assistance through his garda Tetra radio unit. The garda command and control unit in Harcourt Street started to dispatch gardaí from other garda divisions around the Dublin region.

Inspector Maguire then issued a direction to the protesters under Section 8 of the Public Order Act, which gives gardaí the power to clear people from an area if they are posing a risk to the safety of others. He told them to move back from the car, desist from what they were doing and leave the area in a peaceful manner. However, Maguire's warning to the protesters to leave the area had to match the legally required wording of Section 8 of the Public Order Act. It did not, so it had no force in law.[8] The protesters stayed put. Maguire spoke to Paul Murphy, but he later said the TD did not respond to him.[9]

The water charge protesters were using their smartphones to film every second of the discomfort of Burton and O'Connell inside the car. They had discovered that uploading videos of their protests was a potent political weapon. It allowed them to publicise their actions to a much greater audience. It was also a way of 'shaming' their enemies – Irish Water contractors, gardaí and politicians – and getting a reaction. If their targets snapped and retaliated, then it would get even more views online.

But there was also a deeper purpose. Every new video showed that the government and the gardaí were powerless to stop the water charge protesters from doing what they wanted – stopping water meter installations, blocking roads, blocking the gates to Leinster House. And now their smartphones were recording the Tánaiste of the country stuck in a garda car, unable to get out of Jobstown.

Burton and O'Connell were in complete darkness at times because the protesters covered all the windows with their placards. Burton was becoming increasingly frustrated. She took out her own iPhone and started recording the protesters herself.

Gardaí tried to pull back the protesters out of the way of the car so that it could reverse back, but they were outnumbered. A female detective sergeant was hit on the back of her head with an egg. Jay Lester, the teenage protester from Brookfield, held the megaphone for a woman who appealed to young people in the crowd to stop throwing things at the gardaí. 'The gardaí were being pelted by stuff, which isn't right. Everyone in the protest wasn't happy about that. They weren't part of the protest,' he said.[10]

Councillor Mick Murphy of the Socialist Party, a veteran protester, was also becoming concerned about what was happening. He suggested to gardaí that they should move Burton out of the car and back to the church she had come out of. 'Give her sanctuary in the church, it is the only place she will be safe,' he said.[11] Paul Murphy said that it was an attempt by his party colleague to provide a way out. 'They were stuck, like, and they had a problem,' he said.[12]

But Inspector Derek Maguire was worried about the safety of Burton and O'Connell if he tried to move them out of the Avensis car. He decided to wait for reinforcements to arrive before he came up with a new plan.

At around 1 p.m. gardaí tried to drag Paul Murphy away from the back of the unmarked garda car by pulling on his black jumper. It went up around his neck and he grimaced in pain. Mick Murphy pulled it off him in case he would choke. 'Animals,' shouted a female protester at gardaí. Another protester in a blue top lay down on top of the now bare-chested Paul Murphy to stop gardaí from dragging him away. 'That's a TD you're mishandling there,' shouted another man.[13] The irony that gardaí were trying to rescue another TD who had been hit with a water balloon and subjected to personal insults was lost on him.

Gardaí were called 'dirtbags' and 'tramps'. A female garda with a blonde ponytail, who was trying to pull Paul Murphy away from the car, was singled out by one female protester. 'Look at the woman. Watch what you're doing, you fucking bitch. I'll kill you what you did [sic],' she screamed.

Inspector Maguire gave the order to gardaí to pull back. 'Everyone calm down,' he said.

'You started this – this was peaceful till you started dragging people out of it,' responded a protester.

The protesters linked arms to stop the gardaí from pulling them away from the back of the unmarked garda car where Burton and O'Connell were. Then another water balloon was thrown and it hit a garda on the head. Some of the protesters called this behaviour out. 'Stop it. Stop throwing them,' said one. 'Calm the fuck down,' said another. 'Don't throw fucking anything,' said another.

Paul Murphy was still bare-chested on what was a cold November morning. 'Where's your shirt, Paul?' asked one of the protesters. Councillor Mick Murphy did not want to see him left like this for the rest of the protest. He took off his coat and gave the cardigan he was wearing underneath to Paul Murphy. The TD put that on, but he eventually got his own jumper back from Mick Murphy, who had been handed it by a garda.

Superintendent Daniel Flavin arrived on the scene at 1.30 p.m. and took over as the commanding officer. He believed it was time to move the two women from the car because there was a risk to their safety. He thought about moving them to a nearby building. But he was afraid that would lead to a siege situation, with the protesters moving to surround the building.[14] He decided to bring up a garda jeep instead. Inspector Maguire came up to the back window of the car to pass on the news to Burton and O'Connell. They were going to have to run through the crowd to get to the garda jeep.

3

GETTING OUT OF THE CAR

Inspector Maguire ordered gardaí at the scene to form a human cordon around Joan Burton and Karen O'Connell once they got out of the car, so that they could be moved into a garda jeep parked at the church gate which leads onto the main road. At around 1.36 p.m. Maguire went back to Burton and O'Connell in the car. It was time to move.

The protesters surged forward when they saw that the two women were getting out of the car. One protester grabbed the collar of O'Connell's coat. The roaring and shouting became more intense. 'Come out and face the people, you're a fucking disgrace,' shouted another protester towards Burton.

'When we got out of the car, the guards surrounded us, and the crowd charged the guards. I think it was probably a very frightening experience for the gardaí as well. They were very badly treated,' said Burton.[1]

Garda Sergeant Michael Phelan was hit on the back of the head by a can of Red Bull as he tried to help Burton move from the car to the jeep.[2]

Burton was terrified that she was going to fall while she was moving along a narrow passageway between the two lines of gardaí. Inspector Maguire was in front of her, walking backwards. He repeated: 'Look at me, look at me, look at me' to try to keep her focused. Burton could feel her left shoe starting to come off. She was afraid that she would not be able to run away from the protesters if she was wearing only one shoe. 'Don't worry about your shoe,' said Maguire.[3] Burton managed to stoop down and get it on again. She was able to get into the garda jeep that was parked at the gates of the church. It had taken ten minutes for her and O'Connell to walk the thirty metres from the Avensis car to the jeep.

Garda Cooke, the driver of the unmarked Avensis car, had followed after Burton and O'Connell. He took up a position beside the jeep. A man ran up and punched him on the side of the head.

Some of the protesters tried to close the entrance gate to the church yard to prevent the jeep from leaving. Gardaí shoved them out of the way. In the crush of bodies, a female garda was stuck between the gate pillar and the jeep. A person in the crowd pulled her forward to get her to safety. A garda helped a female protester up off the ground, after she had been knocked over accidentally by another protester. A male protester called him a 'woman beater', a 'coward', a 'bully' and a 'uniformed scumbag'.[4]

Paul Murphy was one of the first to get to the front of the jeep after it got onto the road outside the church. He sat down in front of it and invited other protesters to do the same. Children on the street tried to block the jeep themselves, copying the adults. The crowd was growing all the time. Some of the protesters outside the jeep started shouting abuse at Burton again: 'Cunt.' 'Bitch.' 'Let's just petrol bomb them all out of here,' shouted one protester. There was a female garda standing at the front passenger side of the jeep. She later complained that two men continuously pushed up against her.[5] The sit-down protest in front of the jeep lasted ten minutes. Then the protesters got up and started walking slowly ahead of it instead.

The main chants from the protesters were loud and repetitive: 'No way, we won't pay.' 'From the rivers to the sea, Irish water will be free.' 'Labour, Labour, Labour, out, out, out.' But Burton did not pick up all the chants. Her hearing had been badly damaged by an ear operation that went wrong when she was a child. She would say herself that she was not good at hearing people in noisy places.[6]

The protesters were momentarily distracted by the garda helicopter over-head. The Eurocopter had come from its base in Baldonnel Airport, just six kilometres away, and was filming the scene below from 1,500 feet using its broadcast-quality, high magnification digital camera. The jeep had only moved a few metres beyond the church gates with a force of at least twenty gardaí in yellow high-vis jackets surrounding it. The direction of travel was back past An Cosán to the roundabout, which would provide an exit to the Tallaght bypass.

One protester kept putting his foot in front of the front wheel of the garda jeep to prevent it from moving. He shouted that the jeep was going over his foot. He banged the front windscreen and cracked a small hole in it. People stood up on the railings outside the houses across the road to get a better view of what was going on.

In the hour Burton and O'Connell had now been inside the jeep, it had only moved around thirteen metres, even with a human cordon of gardaí surrounding it. Burton was trembling with fear because the crowd outside were shouting and banging on the sides of the jeep. As a distraction, she picked up a copy of *The Irish Times* from the floor of the vehicle. It had an article about Michael Collins and how the IRA attacks he organised were described as 'outrages' and 'dastardly crimes' by the *Irish Independent*. 'I remember saying to myself: Okay, what would Michael Collins have done?' said Burton.[7] She also thought of the advice from family members who had served with the Defence Forces in the Lebanon about keeping cool in a crisis. 'The one thing in those types of protest is to try to stay calm, try to keep smiling, try not to look frightened. The more frightened you look, the more dangerous things potentially get,' she said.

Burton had no idea how many of the protesters were from Jobstown itself. But from the back seat of the jeep, she could see some of the locals standing outside their houses off the Fortunestown Road. Some of them gave her a thumbs up. Burton took it to mean they sympathised with her.

By now, Burton was stiff and cold. She was worried in case she needed to go to the toilet. One of the gardaí in the jeep told her: 'Don't worry, adrenaline will take care of it; you won't need a toilet.' Her only daughter, Aoife, a lawyer, rang her. Public Expenditure Minister Brendan Howlin, who had heard what was going on, also phoned to speak to her for a few minutes.

'It was a very, very unsavoury situation for two women to be trapped like that. What was going on around them was unacceptable. I just wanted to express support and solidarity,' Howlin said.[8]

At 2.30 p.m. Paul Murphy and Mick Murphy decided to have a discussion with the Jobstown protesters about bringing it to a conclusion. 'It was on our initiative. We weren't happy with what was going on. We decided this had to end at a certain point,' said Mick Murphy.[9]

Paul Murphy picked up his megaphone on the road outside the An Cosán centre. A large group of protesters were blocking the road in front of the garda jeep holding Burton and O'Connell. He asked the protesters to be quiet for a minute while he outlined two potential courses of action. The first was to march in front of the jeep for half an hour to the Tallaght bypass. Paul Murphy checked his watch on his left hand to see what time that would be. That would have Burton leaving at 3 p.m. 'Right. And the other option is that we just keep her here. Okay?' he said.[10]

Paul Murphy proposed having a speaker for each of the two options, followed by vote on what to do. 'Who wants to speak for stay?' he asked. A female protester took the microphone from him. 'I, as a resident of Killinarden, am proposing that we keep Joan here. Keep her here. Joan Bruton [*sic*] is on our turf now and she is staying until we say,' she said. There were cheers from the crowd around her, which included children.

Then Paul Murphy brought up his party colleague Mick Murphy to speak in favour of letting Burton go in half an hour. Mick Murphy said he did not think that staying – keeping Joan Burton where she was – was an option.

'If we decide to stay what is going to happen is, the garda will push through,' he said. 'Now, we can live with that but there are a lot of young fellas here, there is a lot of potential for argy bargy and I have to say that is not really what we came for, right?'

A protester shouted back at him: 'That is what they came for,' referring to the gardaí.

Mick Murphy said that he was proposing to allow the jeep carrying Burton to get to the bypass by 3 p.m. 'That's twenty minutes. That's what I propose we do. And then we let her off. We've done what we came to do. That's what I am arguing,' he said.

There was another woman talking about keeping the protest going until 3.30 p.m.

Paul Murphy took back the loudhailer and came back in. 'So people know the two different arguments. So are we ready for a vote on it? Okay?' he asked.

He had to fend off a young boy who tried to grab the loudhailer from him. Then he put Mick Murphy's proposal to the crowd first. He put up his hand and so did Mick Murphy and a few others. Then he asked for votes on the proposal to stay at the protest. More hands went up and there was a big cheer. But it was hard to see how many.

Paul Murphy decided to hold a second vote. 'Most people genuinely didn't vote either way on that. Can people actually vote? Be prepared to vote whatever you want, it doesn't matter, I am going to do whatever people decide,' he said. He put Mick Murphy's proposal to slow march Burton out by 3 p.m. 'Looks about twelve people,' said Paul Murphy. 'All those in favour of staying?' he asked. More protesters put their hands up again than had voted for the slow march. 'Okay, I think staying marginally has it,' said Paul Murphy.

One protester in blue jeans and a black jacket had been filming the entire discussion about what to do on his smartphone. At one point, he captured the garda helicopter hovering directly overhead.

By now, an acclaimed war photographer had arrived on the scene. Crispin Rodwell, from Surrey in England, had got a call from the news desk of *The Irish Sun* to ask him if he would go out to photograph the Jobstown protest. He made it over quickly from his home in Rathmines in south Dublin. He got up close to the jeep, in the middle of the protesters and the gardaí.

While the gardaí were shocked by the intensity of the protest, Rodwell did not find it intimidating. He had seen much worse before, having started taking pictures of the Troubles at the age of nineteen. He had captured some famous riot images, such as British Army troops under gun and petrol bomb attack in west Belfast. And he had taken a photograph on the day of the IRA ceasefire in August 1994 that was used in newspapers around the world. It showed a young boy throwing a ball up against a red-brick side wall of a house. The wall had a slogan on it in white letters – 'Time for Peace'.[11]

Rodwell took pictures of Joan Burton stuck inside the jeep, reading the newspaper and making phone calls. Then one or two eggs were thrown at the windows of the jeep. That gave him another element to photograph. He zoomed in close again. A male teenager, aged around fifteen or sixteen, suddenly stuck up his middle finger at Burton while she was talking inside the jeep on her iPhone. Rodwell's lens was zoomed in so tightly on the jeep window that it just captured the upturned middle finger of the teenager's hand.

'It was fleeting. It was fortuitous. It was a stroke of luck for me, to be honest,' said Rodwell. 'I had lots of other pictures of Joan looking somewhat anguished, but the added component of the egg on the window and the finger made it into a whole different piece.'[12]

Rodwell knew that his photo now had an element of rebellion in it. It became the defining photo of the Jobstown protest – and it later won him the award for Irish news photograph of the year.

4

GETTING OUT OF THE JEEP

Joan Burton and Karen O'Connell were cold, hungry and thirsty. They could not see much through the windows of the jeep. There were lengthy silences between them. But they laughed about the woman who was protesting in her leopardskin pyjamas with a leather jacket on top when they had had to run through the garda cordon from the Avensis to the garda jeep. Being seen in your pyjamas was a no-no in middle-class areas, but 'pyjama girls' who wore them all day long were common in working-class areas. Some saw it as laziness. But sociologists described it as a statement of defiance by women who felt excluded from society.

The female garda in the jeep mentioned how she had three children. The joke in the jeep was that being stuck for hours in Jobstown 'must seem like a day off for her'.[1]

At one point, O'Connell heard a protester outside the four-by-four shouting about cuts to breakfast club funding. 'They said we cut funding to breakfast clubs. We didn't,' she said.[2] Burton had actually increased the funding for breakfast clubs during her time as minister, and basic social welfare payments had not been cut. But there had been huge cuts during the recession to the annual grants given to organisations in the Jobstown area. An Cosán had been forced to put its staff on unpaid leave to balance its books.

Burton could still see children roaming around in the middle of the protest from inside the jeep. She wondered what was going to happen to them, with no parents or bigger brothers and sisters in sight. She told O'Connell that it would be a good idea to get this message out on social media. 'What you should do is go on social media and say it was just shameful, all the little kids that there were, and no one minding them or looking after them. They were just free to roam the streets,' she said.[3] O'Connell decided against it.

The protesters were still walking slowly in front of the jeep. The jeep's driver, Garda Gary Farrell, repeatedly stopped and started the engine because it was moving at a snail's pace down the Fortunestown Road. Inspector Derek

Maguire again attempted to direct the protesters to move out of the way of the jeep so it could get to the N81 Tallaght bypass junction. They kept walking defiantly in front of it.

From his vantage point in the sky, the garda helicopter pilot told the gardaí on the ground that the jeep should reverse to make more progress. There were protesters in front of the jeep but not at the back. 'If they went backwards they'd probably get back quicker y'know,' he said.[4]

But Garda Gary Farrell in the jeep told his superiors that he could not reverse because he had 'no vision'.[5] His windows were blocked due to the presence of gardaí and protesters all around. He was relying on gardaí outside the vehicle to direct him.

The garda public order unit – better known as the riot squad – arrived to try to move the protesters out of the way. They were wearing their standard protective gear but with baseball caps on their heads rather than helmets, which is known in the force as 'soft cap' mode. They deployed in a V-formation in front of the jeep at 2.55 p.m. and started to move the protesters off the road.[6]

The tension escalated. Some of the protesters shouted: 'We were slow walking her out.' Others called the gardaí 'scum'. A group of protesters quickly sat down in front of the jeep, with their arms interlocked. Paul Murphy was among them. The public order unit hauled the protesters out of the way of the jeep. But as soon as they did, others took their place. There were too many protesters to handle. The jeep, which had been inching forward, came to a complete halt.

Superintendent Daniel Flavin ordered all armed gardaí at the scene to stand down because the situation was so dangerous. The command was relayed over the garda radio system: 'No one should be going near the public order incident if they're armed.'[7] The last thing gardaí wanted was for a protester to get shot.

Garda Brian Boland, who had just arrived on the scene with the public order unit, found it to be the most hostile incident he had attended during his twelve years responding to such call-outs. He recognised Paul Murphy TD sitting down in front of the jeep and he tapped him on the shoulder. He tried to build up some rapport with him by congratulating him on his by-election victory. Then he told Murphy that the protest had gone on for two-and-a-half hours. The political point had been made. The situation was now getting dangerous. Murphy responded by saying he was entitled to engage in civil disobedience as a form of protest. 'How can we resolve this issue?' asked Garda Boland. Murphy said there could be further discussions if the garda public order unit was pulled back. He got up from his position in front of the jeep to have a meeting with the senior gardaí at the scene. He told them that if the public order unit was removed, he would try to get the crowd moving again.[8]

Paul Murphy got his megaphone and asked the crowd of protesters to take part in a slow march ahead of the jeep to let it reach the Tallaght bypass in return for the withdrawal of the public order unit. 'If they withdraw the public order unit, will we let her go?' he asked. Paul Murphy, Mick Murphy and the majority of the protesters voted for the slow march.

At around 3.03 p.m. Superintendent Flavin withdrew the public order unit to the grass verges of the road. There was a round of applause from the protesters.[9] The unit had been deployed for less than ten minutes.

Paul Murphy said that it would have been a huge error had gardaí tried to use the unit to clear protesters off the Fortunestown Road. 'At some stage, some sense kicked in, being forced to deal with the reality that protesters have rights. There were 500 people here on the street,' he said.[10]

Gardaí walked in front of the jeep so that it could edge forward. But they were shoved and pushed and had their caps knocked off. Missiles of all shapes and sizes rained down on them – coins, cigarette lighters, placards and even branches of trees. Some protesters held up their placards to shield the gardaí around the jeep from the hail of coins. Burton's garda protection officer, Barry Martin, who was walking alongside the jeep, was pelted with eggs. The yolk ran down over his jacket.

Superintendent Flavin leaned in against the rear window of the jeep to talk to Burton. 'We'll get you out, you'll be all right; we're going to go out to the main road,' he said.[11]

Burton heard a woman shouting at her. 'Are you proud of yourself that there's children still starving with hunger in our country over fucking you?'[12]

The jeep made painfully slow progress because the road ahead was thronged with protesters. Frank Donaghy was walking well ahead of the jeep, carrying a banner that said: 'Tallaght, we won't pay'.

But then the pace started to pick up. At 3.22 p.m. the crew of the garda helicopter hovering overhead saw that the jeep was making good progress. 'She's only another 100 metres, not even 50 metres, from the Tallaght bypass. There's no pushing, shoving or anything … The jeep could have went backwards ages ago, but they seemed to not want to do that. There's no hassle, really …'

'Roger, she's still not out of there?' asked a garda in the ground control unit.

'No, no, she's still not out. Could be here another 20 minutes, half an hour anyway,' the garda helicopter crew member replied.[13]

Burton was also listening to the radio communications between the helicopter and the garda driver in the jeep. She laughed because she could not believe it might be possible to escape by driving the jeep backwards.

O'Connell was very tired and frustrated after over two hours of being stuck inside the jeep with no sign of the protesters moving away. She was not known for using bad language. But this time she did. 'This always happens at the end of protests. The fucking dregs decide not to finish it,' she said.[14]

'There'll be more, loads more of them out on the road,' Burton replied.

Burton felt even more nervous than before, given the presence of some angry young men who looked a lot tougher than some of the people who had been there earlier. Most of the women and children on the protest had left by that stage.

The gardaí heard a protester on a loudhailer shouting: 'We are going to march her out of Tallaght.'

Gardaí had believed the deal was that the protesters would disperse once the jeep got to the N81 Tallaght bypass junction, which the Jobstown Inn was located beside. It didn't happen. The jeep turned left at the junction but stalled again after 100 metres due to the size of the crowd on the road.

Garda Boland, the man who had congratulated Paul Murphy on his by-election victory, approached him again. He asked him to use his influence to get the jeep out of Jobstown. But Paul Murphy felt that he was not in control of the crowd.[15]

Paul Murphy said he and Mick Murphy had tried to shape the protest by introducing chants, organising marching and negotiating with the gardaí. However, he pointed out: 'There wasn't a plan because it wasn't our protest. We didn't have control. We didn't have the capacity to march out there and say, "This is what we're doing."'[16]

By now there were 100 gardaí on the scene in Jobstown and over 500 people out on the street. Gardaí believed that any 'perceived leadership of the protest had removed themselves from the area'.[17]

At 3.24 p.m. garda control called for back-up from any units 'that might be doing traffic duty or anything'. One garda got back to say he could not go to Jobstown because he was on duty alone. Garda control asked him to go anyway because 'things are very tight on the ground'.

Superintendent Flavin decided to make one last attempt to get Burton and O'Connell out safely. The plan was to move Burton and O'Connell to separate garda patrol cars, which would pull up behind the jeep. At 3.45 p.m. gardaí formed a cordon around the jeep and positioned other members in front of the protesters so they would not see the doors being opened. At this stage, Burton knew the drill before she was even told it by the gardaí on the scene. When they opened the door of the jeep, she ran.

A crying O'Connell got out the other door and ran as well. She was petrified. The crowd surged forward again, with some of the protesters giving chase.

'Shame on you, Joan, shame on you, you're a fucking disgrace,' shouted one protester.

'There they go, there they go, get the cunts,' shouted another.[18]

Burton was bundled into the back of one garda squad car, O'Connell got into another, and both sped away from the scene.

Their three-and-a-half-hour ordeal was finally over. They were driven to garda headquarters in the Phoenix Park, where they got to have a cup of tea and access the toilet facilities.

Burton said she was glad that nobody had been hurt or injured. 'I think the gardaí showed extraordinary forbearance. There were suggestions that other police forces in other parts of the world might have handled it much more rapidly. But in that case, there would have been a much higher risk of people being injured,' she said.

Around fifteen minutes after Burton's departure, a young father threw a rock through the rear window of a garda car. Gardaí later said he got 'carried away' during the protest and the two-and-a-half-year sentence he received for the act was suspended.[19] Several garda patrol cars were damaged after being hit by objects and 'kicked by protesters'.[20]

One garda was left with a suspected broken thumb and a female garda sustained a toe injury.

What had just happened on the streets of Jobstown was that the protesters had won a decisive battle. One of the country's most senior politicians had been held up for over three hours. The gardaí had been egged, jostled and humiliated. And the government's authority had been badly undermined.

The roll-out of water charges had raised tensions to levels not seen before in Irish politics. Water metering had turned Irish Water into a visible symbol of austerity outside the doors of most homes in the country. What was supposed to have been the 'last ask' of a weary population had backfired on the government.

It could all be traced back to a chance encounter that Enda Kenny had had at Charles de Gaulle Airport in Paris nine years earlier.

Part Two
WATER SOURCE

5

THE SOURCE OF IRISH WATER

The creation of Irish Water arguably began when Enda Kenny bumped into an Irish economist at a check-in desk in Charles de Gaulle Airport in Paris in 2005.

Andrew McDowell had been visiting the Organisation for Economic Co-operation and Development think tank in Paris and was catching an Aer Lingus flight home to Dublin. He spotted Kenny in the queue and started talking to him about his fears about the economy. Another party leader might have made his polite excuses and turned away, but one of Kenny's strengths was that he liked talking to people. McDowell was a descendant of Eoin MacNeill, the minister for finance in the first Dáil, and grew up in a strong Fine Gael family in Donnybrook, Dublin.[1] A tall, thin man, polished and self-assured, he had clinical blue eyes that hinted at his determination to pursue ideas he believed were right. He had a warning for Kenny. There was a problem with the economy that hadn't been seen yet.

McDowell was the chief economist of the state's economic analysis unit, Forfás. He had also been writing reports for the National Competitiveness Council, warning that things were not as good as they seemed. But at the height of the Celtic Tiger boom, no one was listening.

The encounter was useful for Kenny because he was looking for an angle on the economy that he could use to make some headway as the leader of a Fine Gael party that had shrunk to just thirty-one TDs in the 2002 general election. But he was also impressed by McDowell. Kenny called McDowell on the phone a few months after their airport encounter and offered him a job as Fine Gael's director of policy. McDowell had not been politically active before, but he would later say that it was a 'wonderful opportunity to bring ideas and advice into practice'.[2]

McDowell took up the job in 2006. From his time as the chief economist of Forfás, he had a good relationship with Richard Bruton, Fine Gael's policy director. Now he was reporting directly to him.[3] Under the McDowell–Bruton policy engine, Fine Gael came up with a series of new ideas that it would later implement when it finally got back into government. One was the notion of an 'Action Plan for Jobs', which turned out to be a success in government; another idea was a policy of Dutch-style universal health insurance, which turned out to be a flop. Paschal Donohoe described McDowell as a 'walking policy machine'.[4]

The Irish economy went into a deep recession in 2008, with the collapse of the Celtic Tiger property bubble leading to a sharp rise in unemployment, emigration and government borrowing. The state banking guarantee in September 2008 put the state on the hock for the toxic property loans held by the Irish banks. Watching on from the opposition, McDowell knew that Fine Gael would have to cut back public spending to balance the books if it got into government. However, despite these inevitable cutbacks, he realised the party still needed to show that it had a way of increasing spending on infrastructure like rural broadband, water and the electricity grid. So, in 2009, McDowell devised a new policy. Under this policy there would be a new organisation that would have control over the country's powerful semi-states, including the ESB, Bord na Móna and Bord Gáis. The state could only borrow so much without breaking the EU's financial rules. But the new organisation would be able to fund spending through a stream of consumer charges, instead of through the government. All this spending would be 'off the books'.

McDowell offered his policy staff a few free pints if they could come up with a name for the new quango. A young Fine Gael staffer called Paul O'Brien suggested 'New Economy and Recovery Authority', which won the prize. 'NewERA', as it became known, was born.

Part of the NewERA policy was to set up a new water company. McDowell himself came up with its very simple name – Irish Water. It was a temporary name, which he thought would be changed. But it stuck. Under his plan, Irish Water would raise €4 billion for new water infrastructure spending. It was a way of providing jobs for the tens of thousands of construction workers who were losing their jobs amid the recession. Instead of building houses, they could be employed to replace leaking water pipes and to build new water and wastewater treatment plants. It was very clear that the money would come from introducing water charges. 'Any borrowing will be repaid through charges on consumers,' the policy said.[5] But it was more than just charges. Irish Water was due to take over the water system that was being run by the separate city and county councils.

One of the people McDowell had consulted about this was John FitzGerald, the economist and Economic and Social Research Institute (ESRI) researcher. He had served on the review panel for the establishment of Northern Ireland Water in 2007 and had a good understanding of how water services worked.

Water services in Northern Ireland had been run by individual councils until 1973, when they were centralised in the North's Department of the Environment. In the Republic of Ireland, in contrast, they were still being run inefficiently by thirty-four separate county and city councils. There were three times more staff in water services in Ireland than in Scotland, yet the water system in Ireland was worse. Under NewERA's plan, water services would be provided by one body alone and the number of staff would be slashed.

The plan was launched with great fanfare by Simon Coveney, who was Fine Gael's spokesman on the environment at the time. His view on the need for a single water company had been influenced by personal experience of water outages in Cork city when the Inniscarra dam flooded a key city water treatment plant in December 2009.

There were some connections between the water supplies of Cork City Council and Cork County Council. But there were not enough, in Coveney's eyes. 'We had crazy situations where we had flooding in Cork city which essentially wiped out water supplies for half the city, despite the fact that 100 yards away there was a pipe that Cork County Council was managing water in, and we couldn't tap into it,' he said.[6]

There were multiple local authorities across the country doing their own thing on water. 'All had their own separate budgets on water. Some local authorities investing heavily. Other local authorities hardly investing at all. We had forty per cent of the water in pipes leaking into the ground as a result of that,' Coveney said.

Coveney believed it made sense to set up Irish Water and give it the money to pay for new water infrastructure by bringing in water charges. 'This idea that water is free is a fantasy. It's not free, it costs us a bloody fortune. We know that. It's just a question of how we pay for it,' he said.

The NewERA policy was put into the Fine Gael election manifesto in full.

The party went into the 2011 general election promising to introduce water charges and to set up a new company called Irish Water.

The influence of Andrew McDowell was to become even stronger once Fine Gael entered government following that election. He was no longer the man bumping into Kenny in the airport queue. He was made his chief economic adviser and had constant access to the Taoiseach in Government Buildings. 'Enda listened to Andrew,' said one Fine Gael cabinet minister.

6

A GREEN LIGHT FOR WATER CHARGES

The ground for Irish Water had already been prepared by the only TD in history who was a former cuckoo-clock salesman. John Gormley did that job while travelling in Europe to earn money to pay for his college fees at UCD. His other jobs prior to his becoming a Green Party politician included spells working as a scaffolder, a coal miner and a carpenter.

Gormley hoped one day to get an opportunity to implement Green policies in government but was to spend ten years as an opposition TD in the Dáil first. He was particularly exercised by the issue of water pollution. He grew up in Limerick, where he could swim in the River Shannon alongside salmon, pike, bream and perch. 'And that river subsequently was destroyed by pollution. That to me is shameful, and the focal indictment of us as a species that we would allow things like that to occur,' he later told *Village* magazine.[1]

Gormley's long-term goal was to introduce water charges. He believed the money raised could be spent on stopping the flow of raw sewage into seas and rivers, and fixing the massive leakage of water from the system. But when Gormley's Green Party went into government with Fianna Fáil for the first time ever in 2007, water charges were out of the question because Fianna Fáil would not countenance them. So, as the new environment minister, he started with small steps. He made it mandatory to install dual flush toilets in all new homes and offices to save water. It got very little publicity, but it saved millions of litres of water. Gormley said his wife once overheard an American tourist talking to her friend about the dual flush toilets. '"They've got these funny toilets over here, a small button and a big button. And you press …" She was explaining all of these things and she just found it hilarious.'[2]

As the economy worsened and the Fianna Fáil–Green government became more precarious, Gormley seized on the chance to renegotiate the programme for government in 2009. It was an opportunity to introduce water charges and other seemingly impossible Green policies. He was coming from a position of strength because Taoiseach Brian Cowen knew the government would collapse if the Green Party pulled out. As a result, Gormley got everything he asked for, including the introduction of water charges. 'It was an extraordinary renegotiation. Our agenda was basically put through. Everything we wanted,' he said.

Fianna Fáil's decision to sign up for water charges was an astonishing U-turn for a party which had opposed them as recently as the 1997 general election. But Gormley said that it was not difficult to get Fianna Fáil to agree to water charges by 2009. 'I didn't have to do much persuasion whatsoever. Fianna Fáil can be quite an expedient party. They felt with us there was an opportunity to set things right because it was certainly the right thing to do,' he said. The fact that the state's finances were now in the red due to the collapse of the economy was another motivating factor, of course. But the Greens were at least satisfied that households would now be paying directly for the water service through charges, rather than letting the state foot the bill.

Minister for Finance Brian Lenihan announced that water charges were on the way in his budget speech in December 2009. 'The Renewed Programme contains a commitment to introduce a system of water metering for homes. Preparations are underway. Water charges, when introduced, will be based on consumption above a free allocation,' he said.[3]

Gormley's coup in securing government agreement on water charges got relatively little attention. Most of the media coverage was on the proposed ban on stag hunting, which Gormley had also managed to wrangle out of Fianna Fáil during the renegotiation of the programme for government. 'That got a lot of publicity but because that's the way the media works. But it was by no means the most important thing,' said Gormley.

He carried on by bringing his water charges memo to cabinet in September 2010. It showed that households would be facing bills of around €330 per year. 'The application of the proposed free allowance of forty litres per person per day would result in an estimated average household bill of €330 per annum,' it said. But there was further correspondence from officials which stated that the average water charges bill would rise to €500 per year when the cost of paying for the water meters and the upgrade of water infrastructure 'over time' was included.[4]

There were no objections recorded from any Fianna Fáil ministers, including the then education minister, Micheál Martin. The target date for the start of water charges was January 2014.

Gormley's memo was vague on what should be done to help people who could not afford to pay annual water charges of €500. He said he intended to have a scheme to reduce the risk of water poverty because he did not want people on low incomes avoiding showers and baths and going back to the poor hygiene of the 1940s and 1950s. 'I was always very aware of the fact that one of the few luxuries – if you want to call it that – that poorer people have is running water, where they can have the shower, they can have high levels of hygiene. I don't believe it's right that you deprive people of that,' he said.

Gormley believed that bringing in metering would get the public to reduce their water usage. The notion of a fast roll-out of one million meters also began with him. He wanted to have a 'significant proportion' of the meters installed within two to three years. 'I felt very confident about our stance. I looked at all of the issues that I felt were looming. I felt that if we had dealt with all of those issues, we wouldn't have opposition,' he said.

One of those issues was privatisation. Gormley anticipated that there would be fears that water charges would lead to the privatisation of the water service, as had happened in England. He was also getting feedback from other government departments saying that there were people in the Department of Finance in favour of privatisation. 'I immediately went to cabinet and said, "We need a referendum on this." I could see immediately which way this was going to go. I was right,' he said. But the referendum plan was later dropped after objections from the Department of Communications that it could be complex, contentious and time-consuming.

Gormley got cabinet approval for his water charges plan on 15 September 2010. Two months later, Ireland was forced to request an international bailout. The public finances were so bad and the banking crisis so severe that the state was no longer able to borrow on the international markets. The European Commission, the European Central Bank and the International Monetary Fund agreed on 28 November 2010 to provide €67 billion in loans for the Irish bailout programme – but only as long as the government kept meeting its targets. They became known as the Troika, named after the Russian carriage drawn by a team of three horses harnessed abreast.

But as Gormley pointed out, the water charges plan had been agreed before the Troika ever arrived. 'It's very important that people get the facts right. This was our initiative. It predated the Troika,' he said.

The Troika did, however, like Gormley's water charges plan because it was a further opportunity to broaden the tax base. It went into the bailout deal with the government agreeing to 'start charging in 2012/2013'. The memorandum of understanding with the Troika stated: 'we are also planning to move towards full cost recovery in the provision of water services'.[5] That phrase was significant because it meant that over time water charges would rise until households and businesses were paying the full €1.1 billion annual cost of the water service.

However, the man who conceived of the water meters would not get the chance to install them. Gormley and all five other Green Party TDs lost their seats in the general election on 25 February 2011. 'The problem when you're in the middle of a recession, for our government to engender goodwill was always difficult because we were making huge cuts and introducing terrible taxation,' said Gormley.

The introduction of water charges was now up to the incoming coalition government of Fine Gael and Labour. And the job would be given to a politician with a big personality.

7

BIG PHIL

When Phil Hogan was eight years old, a JCB digger arrived in his village. It was driven by Chris Maher, who had been given the job of delivering the first piped water scheme for the village of Tullaroan in Co. Kilkenny. Maher dug a thirty-two-foot borehole to get a supply of water and then dug trenches for pipes to supply houses and farms, including the homestead of Fine Gael Councillor Tom Hogan.

'I had a few lads working with me. I paid my own lads and the group scheme paid me,' said Maher.[1] That was in 1968. From then on, the local households would club together each year to cover the cost of pumping up the water and piping it around. Therefore, from an early age, Big Phil knew about paying for water.

Hogan's father, Tom, a hard-working Fine Gael councillor, always wanted to make it to the Dáil. But he never managed to overtake the local Fine Gael TD Kieran Crotty, a skilful politician who also had the advantage of being located in Kilkenny city, whereas Hogan was eight miles outside it. Tom Hogan subsequently transferred his own ambition to his son. He used to tell people that Phil would be elected to the Dáil some day.

When Tom Hogan died after a long illness in 1982, Phil Hogan replaced him on the council. He later told the *Kilkenny People* that his father had influenced him. 'Certainly. We worked very closely together, and even today I sometimes ask myself what he would have done in the same situation,' he said.[2]

Hogan always stood out because of his towering presence, coming in at six foot five inches. But he had that vital ability in Irish politics: to remember people's names and faces and where they were from. On top of that, he could figure out the angles of who wanted what and who could deliver it.

As a councillor, Hogan was hard-working and politically savvy. But he complained that roads and services in Kilkenny were generally better before Fianna Fáil had abolished the rates on private houses in 1977, which used to fund county councils. 'This has diminished the power of local authorities,' he said in an interview with the *Kilkenny People* in 1985. He also backed the council's policy of charging for water, which had been introduced to fill the gap left by the abolition of domestic rates. 'I think water rates should stay,' he said. Hogan also liked the idea of metering households but noted that it would cost IR£720,000 (€914,000) to have meters installed in every house in the county. 'The fairest way is to pay for what you get – it costs the county council millions to provide and maintain these services,' he said.

Hogan had the reputation of a young man in a hurry, determined to fulfil his father's wish for him to be elected to the Dáil. He ran in the 1987 general election in Carlow–Kilkenny, but sitting Fine Gael TD Kieran Crotty held on to his seat.

Hogan went for the Seanad immediately afterwards.[3] He was in thirteenth place after the first count, with just nine seats up for grabs. But then he got a huge number of transfers from Sean Garland of the Workers' Party, resulting in him becoming a senator.[4]

The Seanad was often referred to as a nursery for up-and-coming politicians like Hogan, as well as being a retirement home for ageing ones. Hogan made good use of his new position. Within two years he succeeded in getting elected to the Dáil.

Hogan's first big break in politics came when he was appointed as a junior minister in the 'Rainbow Coalition' between Fine Gael, Labour and Democratic Left in December 1994. The news was greeted with joy in Kilkenny, which had not enjoyed a minister of any kind for two decades.

Hogan lasted just seven weeks, however, as one of his staff leaked part of the budget to the *Evening Herald* newspaper. At that time, the budget was not widely leaked like it is now. Hogan accepted responsibility and resigned. RTÉ News broadcast a report of Hogan reading an *Irish Times* report of his resignation at a table in Buswells Hotel. 'No, I don't regret it. I'm very much at ease with myself today,' he said.[5] In fact, Hogan never forgot it. He would mention regularly to people how he had to resign over what he saw as a trivial matter. It would take him another sixteen years to get back into a ministerial office.

Hogan was a politician who was more feared than loved. He helped Enda Kenny to defeat the leadership heave against him by Richard Bruton in

2010 and was director of elections for the 2011 general election. Kenny then appointed him as environment minister when Fine Gael swept into power.

Once in power, his biggest job was to bring in a household charge and water charges. In his first months in the Department of the Environment, Hogan considered wrapping them into one single charge to make it easier to collect them. This would have basically been a return of the domestic rates system that had been in place until Fianna Fáil abolished it in 1977.

Hogan had a meeting with officials in his department about the potential 'synergy' between household charges and water charges in April 2011.[6] But that plan never came to anything. The feeling was that the household charge and water charges should be separate.

Hogan told the Institute of International and European Affairs in November 2011 that he had been 'studying and thinking' about his water reforms long before the bailout programme. 'We have to get this right. And we get one shot at it probably in our lifetime to get it right. So there are big decisions to be made,' he said.[7]

He had the clear backing of his Taoiseach – a person who had grown up without running water.

8

WATER IN THE WEST

In 1948 Henry Kenny and his wife bought a farmhouse in the parish of Islandeady in Co. Mayo.[1] When their son Enda was born in 1951, the house had no electricity and there was no running water in the house or toilet. The drinking water came from a well on their land. In summer time the well would often dry up, so Enda Kenny would have to go to a neighbouring well for water instead.

There was no running water either in Coranool National School when Kenny started there at the age of four-and-a-half in 1955. He and the other pupils used a 'dry toilet' in an outhouse, which was emptied out once every year. A classmate at the time, Martin McLaughlin, said the contents of the toilet were usually spread out in the neighbouring fields. Due to the lack of running water, Kenny and the other pupils used to wash their hands and faces in a nearby stream after playing football in the school yard. McLaughlin said running water and flush toilets were considered to be luxuries in the 1950s, when most pupils in the area were emigrating to find work. 'There was no difference between at home and at school. There was no water and no toilets at home, so the expectations for people were pretty low,' he said.[2]

Kenny's experience of living without running water in his youth certainly made him conscious of the value of it when he got into politics. His father, Henry, had been a TD for twenty-one years before he died from cancer in 1975. After Enda Kenny won the subsequent by-election, much of his constituency work involved lobbying for funding for the roll-out of group water schemes and getting a proper water supply for Castlebar.

The town had managed to get its first ever foreign direct investment in the form of Travenol Laboratories in 1972. But the company was struggling to operate on the town's poor quality water supply. A new pipeline was built especially for the factory in 1975 to take water from a local lake. But that was not good enough either; other potential businesses were looking elsewhere because of the town's poor water infrastructure. 'Castlebar loses out because of poor water supply' was the headline in the *Western People* newspaper on 1 October 1977. The article complained that a 'large male-employing industry' had gone elsewhere due to the shortage of water.

At the time, Castlebar not only had a poor water supply, it also had no wastewater treatment plant. There was a bacon factory in the town that used to employ 700 men in peak season, killing pigs, and cattle as well. All of its waste water went straight into the Castlebar river. The river's water used to turn red due to the blood of the pigs. Then there was the stench of raw sewage. It all amounted to a toxic cocktail flowing into the River Moy, killing salmon at the country's prime fishing spot in Ballina. According to the *Western People* report, Kenny believed that it was a 'disgrace' that a town the size of Castlebar should be discharging raw sewage into a stream that was incapable of carrying it. It was no joke for the people downstream, particularly in summer time, he said.[3]

At that time Mayo was almost entirely dependent on group water schemes, with public water supplies only in the main towns. McLaughlin said people in rural areas went to the ends of the earth to get water. 'They did everything in the world and they went to enormous expense. They tried to harness rivers, they bought pumps, they harvested water off sheds and houses and roofs,' he said.

One of the simplest ways of getting water to an area was to install a parish pump. They were installed by councils who had used drilling machines to dig down as far as 300 feet to access underground rivers and springs. A pump would be placed at the bottom to get the water up.

McLaughlin spent a lot of his early years repairing the parish pumps as part of his work for Mayo County Council. 'If they were out of action for a day, they'd be on to the council straight away. They used to be queuing up with asses and carts and buckets at the parish pump,' he said.

The parish pumps are now historical artefacts, well maintained in the local parish colours by tidy towns committees. But they were really valuable in a much poorer Ireland.

There was a breakthrough in 1979 when a new water treatment plant was built in Tourmakeady to extract water from the 22,500 acre Lough Mask and pump it to Castlebar. The new public water supply in Castlebar was connected up to the parish of Islandeady, three miles away, in 1984. Until then, the Kenny family had been relying on a pump they had rigged up to take water from their well.

When the new water supply arrived, the annual water bill for households in Islandeady was IR£70, which increased to €90 with the advent of the euro. But there were no such bills for the 'townies' in Castlebar, who were also getting the same water supply from the Lough Mask scheme. Mayo County Council agreed to abolish the charges in the early 2000s to end what the locals saw as discrimination.

The threat of domestic water charges in Islandeady receded then, at least until Enda Kenny became Taoiseach. But he was going to have to convince a man who had fought against water charges for his entire political career, if they were going to once more come into effect in Islandeady, and the rest of Ireland.

9

GOING AGAINST THE TIDE

For five decades after independence, the British system of paying for water through domestic rates had survived in Ireland. Then Fianna Fáil promised to abolish them in the 1977 election campaign to win back power. Taoiseach Jack Lynch's government kept that election promise. Sinn Féin's environment spokesman, Brian Stanley TD, has described the abolition of local rates by Fianna Fáil as a classic example of populism. 'It might have won them 106 seats but they destroyed local government. All governments since haven't done much to repair that,' he said.[1]

Then the Fine Gael–Labour coalition government brought back water charges in 1983. The resistance in Dublin was so strong that they were not imposed there. There was a serious protest in Waterford city in 1989, where three water contractors carrying out water disconnections on households who had not paid their charges were held hostage for eight hours. The *Munster Express* reported that the men had been leaving the Lismore Park estate in the city when they were intercepted by several women and a man in a wheelchair. 'The van was trapped on a grass verge and the air let out of at least one of its tyres. Gardaí rushed to the scene but, as the afternoon wore on, more and more people surrounded the van, making it impossible for the contractors to either drive away or escape on foot,' the newspaper reported.[2]

A ring of gardaí put themselves between the van and the angry crowd, which grew to an estimated 1,000 people. None of the contractors were harmed, but they were trapped in the van from 3 p.m. to 11 p.m.

During this time, one of the ardent opponents of the water charges was a young Workers' Party politician called Eamon Gilmore. When he was running for the Dáil in the 1987 general election, he told voters that he had been the first councillor in the country to call for the abolition of water charges.[3] In 1997 he distributed a leaflet with an image of him walking his dog on the beach. It described him as an outstanding public representative and listed 'the abolition of water charges' as one of his achievements.[4]

Gilmore had developed a reputation as a shrewd, hard-working politician who was a tireless advocate for the marginalised in his Dún Laoghaire constituency. And he was proud of his record in not accepting any of the cash bribes in brown envelopes that were on offer from developers for rezoning votes. His 1989 election leaflet said, 'We buy our homes and the developers buy the big parties.'[5]

His political career after that would involve a long spell in the Workers' Party, then setting up a breakaway party called Democratic Left and then merging it with the Labour Party. Throughout all of this, he held onto the Dáil seat in Dún Laoghaire that he had first won in 1989.

Gilmore's hostility to water charges remained constant. When Fianna Fáil's finance minister, Charlie McCreevy, said he was in favour of re-introducing water charges in 2003, Gilmore was quick to condemn him. 'Any move to reintroduce water charges would be a further regressive back-door taxation on Irish households,' he said.[6]

But Gilmore's time as Labour's environment spokesman from 2002 to 2007 did have an influence on his thinking. He learned about the problems of leaking pipes and raw sewage being discharged into seas and rivers. Water charges were a way of getting the money to fix those problems. And if people were given meters, so they could be charged only for what they used, he felt that could be acceptable.

Gilmore was elected as leader of the Labour Party in 2007 and he now had to decide what his and his party's policy was on water charges.

As the recession worsened, in a Dáil debate in October 2010 Gilmore floated the idea of supporting water charges once every house in the country had a meter.

It looked like he was preparing Labour for government. His likely coalition partners, Fine Gael, were in favour of water charges. And water charges were included in the Troika bailout programme.

But in the months leading up to the February 2011 general election, Gilmore's views on water charges hardened again. When some in the party suggested that it made sense for people to pay something for their water supply, Gilmore and Pat Rabbitte shot them down. 'The sort of stuff they [Gilmore and Rabbitte] were saying was "We'd be crucified if we did it. Any government would be mad to introduce that,"' said a Labour source.

The Labour election manifesto in 2011 ultimately said that the party 'does not favour water charges'. Labour's Brendan Howlin said during the election campaign that it made no sense to spend hundreds of millions of euro metering a leaky system. 'We are not in favour of water charges, we don't believe in a flat rate and you couldn't meter everybody within years,' he said.[7]

Towards the end of the campaign, Labour was panicking that Fine Gael was going to get an overall majority. It ran an infamous 'Tesco' ad about the 'Every Little Hurts' that Fine Gael had in store for voters. It included a €238 water charge illustrated by a dripping tap.[8] The poster helped to turn back some of the momentum. Fine Gael got seventy-six seats. Labour got a record tally of thirty-seven.

Afterwards, Gilmore led the party into a coalition government. But he now had a problem. In the programme for government, Gilmore agreed to bring in water charges, even though he knew it would be politically toxic, particularly given that Labour had campaigned against their introduction. 'We were in a colossal economic mess. There was no easy way of doing it,' he said.[9]

The programme for government commitment reflected Fine Gael's desire for water charges and Gilmore's desire to have a metering programme and a free allowance. 'The objective is to install water meters in every household in Ireland and move to a charging system that is based on use above the free allowance,' it said.[10]

Gilmore insisted on getting a metering programme in place prior to the programme's introduction. The previous water charges in Dublin in the mid-1990s had been flat charges. The householder paid the same bill regardless of how much or how little they used. Gilmore believed that water meters were fairer. He did not want to bring in water charges until every possible home was metered. And he also thought that it would be possible to bring in a large free allowance for households, which would result in low water-charge bills. It was clear that some in Labour thought that the metering could be a valuable stalling tactic. It would take years, which meant that water charges could be put on the long finger.

But this time it was different. The latest memo negotiated with the Troika at the end of 2011 stated that the government would carry out an assessment about transferring water services to a new utility company 'with a view to start charging in 2012/2013'.[11] Furthermore, the Troika were demanding monthly updates on every government commitment – including water charges. Labour's Brendan Howlin, who was now public expenditure minister, also had to meet the Troika, along with Finance Minister Michael Noonan, every three months. Each inspection visit would last a week. Basically, the government was in thrall to a very big moneylender.

Howlin said he was always mindful that the Troika 'could squeeze us' if they were not happy. 'They demanded progress and they released money to us on the basis of our achieving the designated checklist. So we couldn't just say – we're not doing that. And in terms of water charges, there was a very, very demanding timeline,' he said.[12]

Over time, the government did persuade the Troika to change some aspects of the bailout programme. The €1 per hour cut to the minimum wage was restored and the target for the sell-off of state assets was dropped from €5 billion to €3 billion. But dropping water charges was never broached. 'There would have been an extraordinary battle to change an entire policy platform,' said Howlin. He said water charges were not the biggest issue facing the government in any way at the time. 'Our economic survival was at risk,' he said.

The work to set up Irish Water continued. A leader was needed and there was a confident Corkman who believed he was up to the task.

10

THE MAN FOR THE JOB

The new government of Fine Gael and Labour, under the long and threatening shadow of the Troika, needed a strong leader to deliver a project as complex as Irish Water. Someone like ESB founder Thomas McLoughlin.

Born in Drogheda, McLoughlin went to London in 1922 and joined the German firm Siemens-Schuckert as a young engineer. While working for the company in Bavaria, he saw how a network of hydro-electric plants was powering an entire rural region. 'To this area I went and studied for myself on the spot, always with the query in my mind – why not so in Ireland?' he later wrote.[1]

McLoughlin came home in 1923 and set about persuading the newly founded Irish Free State government to set up a new hydro-electric plant on the River Shannon to deliver electricity to the entire country. The state's infrastructure had been shattered by the Civil War and the government had no money to pay for the preliminary surveys required. As author Brendan Delany recorded, McLoughlin took out a personal overdraft from a bank manager in Limerick to fund them himself. His plan was evaluated by an independent international team of four experts appointed by the government. They backed it. Then McLoughlin persuaded the government that it needed to set up a state company to deliver the project rather than rely on a private company.

The legislation to set up the Electricity Supply Board (ESB) was passed in 1927, with McLoughlin as the first managing director. He delivered the Shannon scheme in Ardnacrusha with the help of Siemens, subsequently providing affordable electricity to towns and villages throughout the country. And in the 1940s and 1950s, he drove the final part of his plan – the electrification of rural Ireland. Under his leadership, the ESB built up a reputation for public service, efficiency and a community connection.

That was what Irish Water needed to do as well. And the government turned to a former ESB man to deliver it.

John Mullins grew up in a council house in the working-class suburb of

Knocknaheeny in Cork city. His father was a painter-decorator and money was often tight. 'You mightn't have had your bus money on a Thursday,' he later recalled.[2] He qualified as an engineer from University College Cork (UCC). It was said there were two types of Cork people in his line of work: the engineers who wanted to stay at home joined Bord Gáis, a Cork-headquartered company, while those who had the ambition to travel further afield joined the ESB, which was based in Dublin and had an international wing. Mullins went for the ESB. He would later say that he got a 'very fine career foundation' there.[3]

Like the ESB's founder, Thomas McLoughlin, Mullins also worked abroad. He was employed by PricewaterhouseCoopers (PwC) in London to work as a consultant with West of Scotland Water Authority and Yorkshire Water. While employed there, Mullins saw at first hand how these companies had managed to reduce their leakage rates in their pipes from fifty per cent to twenty per cent, although it had taken fifteen years of investment in pipe repairs. Ireland was still stuck with a leakage rate of forty-nine per cent.

One of the jobs Mullins did for Yorkshire Water was to install a modern asset management system from IBM called Maximo.[4] He realised that in Ireland there were no modern computer systems to track the condition of the pumps, valves and sensors in water and wastewater treatment plants. Instead, there were thirty-four councils, each trying to keep track of their water assets. 'For a small island, having thirty-four different systems was inefficient,' said Mullins. He found that the British water companies had good records of all their water and sewage networks. 'Britain had gone through all this. They had digitised all of their records and that had taken a long period of time. But did anyone know the condition of the water assets in Ireland? They were very, very flaky,' he said.[5]

Due to the disorganised nature of the water system, there was no figure for the length of sewer pipes in Ireland. And there were areas where there were no records at all of the locations of water pipes. That became a problem in Carrick-on-Suir in Tipperary, for example, when the local council water technician died suddenly. He had memorised the entire water network and had always been able to fix any problems. It was only after his death that it emerged that Carrick-on-Suir's water network had never been recorded on paper.[6]

After his time with the ESB and PwC, Mullins got first-hand experience of the Irish water system when he joined National Toll Roads in 2002. It owned Celtic Anglian Water, which operated water and wastewater treatment plants on behalf of the county councils. Then, in 2007, he was appointed chief executive at Bord Gáis Éireann. It had a strong Cork identity, having been set up in 1976 to bring ashore the gas from the Kinsale gas field. But even though Mullins was from Cork, he was seen within Bord Gáis as an 'outsider' because he had gone to the ESB.

One of Mullins' big actions during his tenure as chief executive was to take on the ESB at its own game. Bord Gáis bought a new customer billing system, so that it could supply electricity as well as gas. When he told Padraig McManus, the ESB chief executive and a good friend, about his plan, McManus did not seem too worried. That made Mullins more determined to make a success of it.

He and his staff put a lot of planning into the project, which was the called 'The Big Switch'. By 2009 it was ready. In the space of seven months that year, 200,000 people changed their electricity accounts from the ESB to Bord Gáis.

Mullins was also someone who knew how politics worked. He had been president of Fine Gael's youth wing in the 1990s, where he put together alternative budgets with a future minister for finance, Paschal Donohoe. He put his name forward to run for Fine Gael in a Cork North Central by-election when he was in his mid-twenties but was beaten in the selection convention. Enda Kenny had even asked him to run for the Seanad in 2002, but he missed out.

When the new Fine Gael–Labour government came into office in 2011, Mullins could see that the future of Bord Gáis was in doubt. The Troika wanted the state to sell off €3 billion of assets to speed up the repayment of the bailout loans. Bord Gáis's retail arm was on their 'for sale' list. That meant that Bord Gáis was under threat. It would be back to just owning and operating the gas network. But Mullins spotted an opportunity to diversify into a new area that he knew well. Water.

He started telling the government that Bord Gáis had the expertise to issue water charges to the nation because it was already doing it for gas and electricity. And it also had the information technology systems that he had first seen in England. Mullins said they would provide an accurate picture of what the water network was like.

'Why did you need an asset management system? Because we didn't have one. Because the condition of the assets wasn't even recorded,' he recalled.[7]

Mullins had also already overseen an upgrade of 1,200 kilometres of the Bord Gáis gas pipe network in Dublin, funded by the company's income from gas customers. But leaking water pipes did not pose the same threat to people's lives. They were left alone, for the most part. Mullins knew how bad the water pipes were due to a lack of funding from government to upgrade them. 'We do need to fix our leaks and we do need to ensure that we have a system that's ready for the twenty-second century, because what we have is a nineteenth-century system for the twenty-first,' he said.

Mullins could roll out catchy phrases like that because he was a natural communicator. The stereotypical engineer is someone who is good at building the bridge but poor at telling people about it. He was very comfortable dealing with the media, which was a rarity in Bord Gáis.

'The culture in Bord Gáis was extremely inward-looking. It was: "Keep the head down, don't say anything." There were some good people there. But there was an old Bord Gáis attitude to the media of "fuck them",' said one former employee.

Mullins also knew how to work the system to get what he wanted. The number of customers being disconnected was rising due to the recession. Newly elected Fine Gael TD Leo Varadkar was coming across houses in darkness in his Dublin West constituency. 'Initially one thinks that nobody lives in it but while canvassing one realises that somebody who has been "de-energised" lives in the house,' he said back in 2010.[8]

Mullins knew that the best solution was to roll out pay-as-you-go meters to these households because they would always be able to scrape enough money each day to keep the lights on.

But first he had to beat the electricity and gas regulator, who would only allow a small number of these meters to be installed free of charge to customers. Mullins pointed out that it was pointless to ask people in financial trouble to pay almost €400 for a pay-as-you-go meter. He and his team in Bord Gáis deliberately started to publish the number of customers disconnected every month, which increased the pressure on the regulator. He briefed TDs about how people being disconnected were just as likely to come from middle-class neighbourhoods.

'This is a radically different scenario to the customer utility debt crisis of the late 1980s when the issue was predominantly associated with the less well off areas in our cities and towns,' he told an Oireachtas committee in 2010.[9]

The committee room was full to the rafters with TDs backing his pay-as-you-go plan. The regulator's resistance crumbled under the pressure. In the end almost 90,000 gas and electricity customers got free pay-as-you-go meters and the number of gas and electricity disconnections plummeted.[10]

Despite this win for Mullins, however, the prospects of Bord Gáis getting the contract to set up Irish Water looked poor in 2011. The government spent €180,000 on an expert report from PwC about how to set up Irish Water. The main recommendation was to set up Irish Water as a stand-alone company, rather than giving the job to an existing semi-state company like Bord Gáis or Bord na Móna. The big problem was management. The consultants believed that it would not be possible to have a 'fully focused management team' if there were two separate businesses under the one roof.

But the government was in a panic to bring in water charges. It would be impossible to set up a new company from scratch that would be ready to bill over one million households in less than two years' time. Minister for the Environment Phil Hogan told the cabinet sub-committee on economic infrastructure that the job of setting up Irish Water had to be given to either Bord Gáis or Bord na Móna, who were the only two semi-states interested. The need for speed trumped the advice from PwC to set up a stand-alone Irish Water company. 'You would have spent eighteen months putting together the core of a management team. You would lose a year,' said a government source.

The cabinet ultimately decided to give the job to Bord Gáis. After all, it was used to operating a network of pipes and collecting money from customers. Bord na Móna did not have the same level of experience.

Mullins and his team got down to work.

11

METERS, METERS EVERYWHERE

Environment Minister Phil Hogan was about to make the single biggest decision of his ministerial career. He had drafted a cabinet memo for a €450 million plan to put water meters in more than one million households. And he was going to set up Irish Water to take over water services from thirty-four councils. Hogan brought his memo to the cabinet room in the east wing of Government Buildings in December 2011.

The ministers were clustered around a cabinet table made out of dark Irish burr walnut and a lighter coloured European walnut. Each of them could see Hogan's memo on their own computer screen. This electronic e-cabinet system had gotten rid of the old paper cabinet memos that used to be sent out to ministers in departments all over Dublin city. Hogan told his fellow ministers that his plan represented 'a radical and complex transformation of water services provision in the State'.[1]

Then he moved on to the justification for setting up Irish Water. He said there were 'serious deficiencies' in how water services were being provided by the councils. The forty-nine per cent leakage rate in the water pipes was more than double the leakage rate in Britain. There were twenty-five per cent more staff in the water service here than in similar-sized British water companies. His memo clearly envisaged Irish Water bringing down this number, saying that 'efficiencies will allow for staff reductions'.

The Fine Gael ministers did not need the Troika to tell them to bring in water charges. The party as a whole was convinced that there had been too much reliance during the boom on once-off taxes like stamp duty on houses. It wanted to broaden the tax base with water charges and property tax. 'We saw the need for it,' said a Fine Gael source. The Labour ministers agreed, but there was far more reluctance in the party. One senior Labour source said the attitude was: 'If the Troika insist on it, we'll have to do it.'

But where was Hogan going to get the money to pay for the meters in the middle of the recession? Hogan's answer was to take €450 million from the fund set up after the privatisation of Telecom Éireann. This fund, named the National Pensions Reserve Fund, had already been tapped up for €10 billion to cover some of the cost of the bank bailout. But there was still around €7 billion left.

Hogan gave the ministers a secret, fifteen-page document, a cost–benefit analysis, to justify the introduction of water metering. It was not made available to the public or the opposition parties. It predicted that the ten per cent drop in water usage after metering would more than pay for the €450 million cost of installing the meters. This would mean Irish Water would have to produce less water and clean up less waste water. That would save a lot of money. All that pumping of water and treatment of sewage was costing over €60 million in electricity bills per year.

The installation of so many meters had never been done before. But the cost–benefit analysis presented confidently predicted that it would be all done in four years. Around two per cent of meters would be installed in 2012, thirty-four per cent in 2013, fifty-two per cent in 2014 and the final twelve per cent in 2015. There would be no water charges until one million homes were metered. The departmental study did call for a public awareness campaign in advance of the introduction of the water meters. 'As Irish households have not paid for water since 1996, there is likely to be opposition to the reintroduction of domestic water charges,' it said.[2]

But Hogan had to win over one Fine Gael minister who wanted to call a halt, and who had the reputation of being the wiliest of them all. Minister for Finance Michael Noonan had spent his career competing for votes in Limerick city, which has a mix of middle-class neighbourhoods and some of the poorest large-scale public housing estates in the country. He had a much better grasp than other Fine Gael ministers (who were representing better-off urban constituencies or rural ones) of the resistance that could develop once water meter installers rocked up in these deprived urban estates. 'He had a nose that the installers would be in the streets working away and it would be a very visible target,' said a government source.

Noonan believed that there was no point looking to collect water charges in working-class estates. According to a Leinster House source, he made this point directly to Kenny during a conversation about Irish Water with a group of people in the corridors of Leinster House. 'Why the fuck are Irish Water insisting on putting water meters there [in the working-class estates]? They are never going to pay,' he said. Kenny was standing beside Noonan. 'You know what, I think he's right, as usual,' he said.

Kenny was conscious of the potential backlash against water charges. It would have been impossible for him not to be, given that he had seen the successful protest campaigns against previous water charges in the 1980s and 1990s. He used to tell his advisers regularly: 'Keep the charges as low as possible. This is going to be difficult, families are going to find it hard to tolerate.'

However, both Kenny and Tánaiste Eamon Gilmore were convinced that water charges would not work without metering. They remembered the failure of the flat-rate water charges in the 1990s, when a Socialist Party councillor called Joe Higgins was heading up the protest campaign. 'They were very strongly of the view that unless you could tell people you could control the charge, it would be very difficult politically. That trumped Noonan's concern about the visible target on the streets,' a government source said.

There was one more hurdle to surmount. The Department of Public Expenditure did not like the plan to meter one million households at all. The main reason was the €450 million cost. They did their own examination of the cost–benefit analysis on water metering. It was highly critical. But it made no difference. The cabinet signed off on the decision. The ministers accepted that the metering project was justified based on the savings identified in Hogan's cost–benefit analysis. The Department of the Environment said there was a 'very strong political allegiance' to setting up Irish Water and using water meters for a 'fair charging regime'.[3]

Water charges were no longer just a plan. They were government policy. It was now up to the civil servants in the water division in the Department of the Environment's Custom House headquarters to implement it.

12

LABOUR'S BOGEYMAN

Joe Higgins had achieved fame for leading the campaign against water charges in Dublin in the 1990s. He delivered a fresh warning to the new Fine Gael–Labour government that he was getting ready for battle again on the first day of the new Dáil on 9 March 2011. He opposed the nomination of Enda Kenny for Taoiseach for proposing to introduce 'blatant new tax burdens on ordinary people, including a water tax and home tax'.[1]

Higgins was a relentless character. Asked once what he did in his free time, he said he had very little of it due to his commitment to politics. He would also favour the choosing of election candidates who were 'the most willing to make sacrifices in their personal lives for politics'.[2]

Higgins grew up on a small family farm in Ballineetig on the Dingle Peninsula in Kerry. He worked on the farm before and after school. And he walked to his classes barefoot during the summertime. Higgins was one of nine children in a house which had no running water and depended on a pump. 'When it dried up in hot weather, we walked a mile to a stream to get buckets of water. We understood the value of water,' he said.[3]

Higgins went to the US to study for the priesthood at St Mary's College in Minnesota. However, he left the seminary after becoming involved in civil rights and anti-Vietnam war protests. On his return home, he went to UCD and then became an English teacher in the vocational college sector. He joined the Labour Party in Dublin in 1974 and canvassed for the party in many elections. His belief was that a truly socialist Labour Party could take over from Fianna Fáil and Fine Gael. 'We wanted Labour to build a mass movement that would be capable of transforming society into a socialist democracy and never to go into coalition with a capitalist party,' he said.

Labour leader Dick Spring believed that Higgins and other members were trying to take over the party from within. They were part of a faction known as the 'Militant Tendency', which had its own magazine. Spring moved decisively against them by proposing to expel them. Labour members voted in favour at their annual conference in Tralee in 1989. One current Labour member who was there that day would later say it was the 'proudest day of his life' in the Labour Party.

The decision had to be formally implemented by Labour's 'administrative council' in September 1989. It held a special meeting in 88 Merrion Square, a publicly owned Georgian house that is now used by the National Gallery for its administrative offices. And one of the first people up for expulsion was Joe Higgins, for writing an article in the Militant Tendency's magazine. As part of his defence, he typed up a letter containing a heartfelt description of how he had never missed a single party meeting and had canvassed for Labour Party candidates in every election for the previous fifteen years. He also spoke at the meeting, saying it was obscene that the Labour Party would expel somebody for writing for a socialist newspaper. He eventually walked out of the meeting, calling it a charade. When invited to rejoin the meeting, he declined.

Ruairí Quinn, the Labour Party's deputy leader, then proposed the motion to expel Higgins but said he was doing it 'with great personal reluctance, because he had known Joe for so long'.[4] Joan Burton also said that she regretted this should happen to Higgins and she wished he had chosen the Labour Party rather than Militant. The motion to expel Higgins was carried by nineteen votes to five. 'The reason I was expelled is that they wanted to keep the Labour Party safe for the careerists at the top,' said Higgins.

In total, there were fourteen people expelled. They included Ruth Coppinger, Joan Collins, Clare Daly and Mick Barry. Mick Barry said Labour thought they would all be politically marginalised. 'I think they thought that when the expulsions were carried through, that we might stagger on for a few years and be in the wilderness,' he said.[5] In fact, Higgins and some of the others expelled at that time became founder members of the Socialist Party in 1996. They would go on to play a significant role in the anti-water charge movement two decades later – and help to seriously undermine the Labour Party which was in government.[6]

***

Opposing water charges was not what socialist parties around the world were known for. Indeed, there were water charges in socialist regimes in Cuba and Vietnam, and in Communist China. But Higgins and his Socialist Party were able to get a strong response to their anti-water charge campaigns. Some of that may be down to the fact that water has a special status. It is life giving. People can manage without electricity or gas, even though it is a great inconvenience, but they cannot survive without water.

Then water charges returned to Dublin in 1991, just as Higgins made his electoral breakthrough, becoming a councillor on Dublin County Council. That was the same year the council was split into four councils. Council managers saw it as a chance to get the citizens of Dublin to pay for water like their country cousins. There were three new councils – Fingal, South Dublin and Dún Laoghaire – which all started to bring in water charges of between IR£75 and £80 (€95 to €101) per household per year. The fourth council, Dublin Corporation, decided to wait and see.[7]

Higgins became the chairman of a new group called the Dublin Anti-Water Charges Campaign in 1994. He held public meetings and urged people to boycott the water charges. The campaign intensified when South Dublin County Council stared cutting off the water supply to households who had not paid their bills. It disconnected around 900 people. Higgins and the water charge protesters responded by following the water inspectors. They had Citizen Band (CB) radios and the early brick-like mobile phones to keep in touch, according to Socialist Party organiser Kevin McLoughlin. 'The moment they [the inspectors] went to do the dirty deed, they were followed by 14 campaign patrol cars which were centrally linked to a headquarters and therefore could be redirected to any location within minutes,' he wrote.[8] The water charge protesters would drum up a crowd by knocking on the doors of neighbours if water inspectors came into an area. If that did not stop the inspectors from cutting off a household's water supply, they had a list of plumbers who would reconnect the water supply within hours.

The councils soon had to change their tactics due to the arrival of a new party in government.

The Fianna Fáil–Labour government collapsed in December 1994 and Fine Gael leader John Bruton managed to cobble together a 'Rainbow Coalition' with the Labour Party to replace it. His government included a small left-wing party called Democratic Left, formed by ex-Workers' Party members like Proinsias De Rossa, Eamon Gilmore and Pat Rabbitte. They were all strongly opposed to water charges. They insisted on the water disconnections being halted.

South Dublin County Council then tried a carrot-and-stick approach. It offered households the chance of winning cars, holidays and shopping vouchers in a prize draw if they paid their water charges. And it started bringing people to court instead of cutting off their water supply. Rathfarnham courthouse, located in a former church, was the venue for the first fifty test cases for those who had not paid their bills. The tiny venue was surrounded by hundreds of noisy protesters. At one point, the sounds of Bobby Darin's song 'Jailer, Bring Me Water' being sung outside could be clearly heard in court. The whole court cracked up with laughter. The fifty cases were eventually thrown out.

The courts in Dublin were becoming clogged up with thousands of cases against people who had not paid their water charges. Higgins and his campaign raised IR£50,000 (€63,500) in voluntary donations to pay for legal teams. People were not afraid of being disconnected or being sentenced for refusing to pay their bills. That simply encouraged them to keep boycotting their water bills.

Then, in April 1996, there was a by-election in Dublin West. It was caused by the death of a former Fianna Fáil minister, Brian Lenihan Senior, from liver disease. His son, Brian Lenihan Junior, was expected to comfortably win the seat. But Higgins knew there was a golden opportunity to turn the by-election into a referendum on water charges. *The Irish Times* reported that anti-water charge groups from around the country had 'dispatched goodwill, money and canvassers to Dublin West for the cause'.[9]

Higgins' policy on how to pay for the water infrastructure would remain the same throughout his political career. His argument was always that water was already being paid for through general taxation. When his opponents told him there was not enough tax revenue to cover the costs, his follow-up was: 'Tax the millionaires and the billionaires.'[10]

The water charges were helping Higgins to get support from well-off middle-class voters in the constituency, who had no interest in his vision of a socialist republic. One Fine Gael minister, Hugh Coveney – the father of future cabinet minister Simon – met a lady who was unloading her shopping outside a large house in Castleknock when he called canvassing to the door during the by-election. She had no intention of voting for anyone but Higgins. 'It's the water charges,' she said, as she took bottles of water out of the boot of her car.

On the day of the count, Higgins, the ultimate political outsider, looked on the verge of a shock victory. The Fianna Fáil canvassers, drafted into Dublin West from all over the country, were fearing the worst. Fianna Fáil's Micheál Martin, then a backbench TD, decided it was time to go, thinking the race was lost. He was driving back to Cork when he got a phone call: 'Get back – we're winning this thing.'

Brian Lenihan Junior narrowly beat Higgins by 250 votes, thanks to Fine Gael transfers. Martin and the Fianna Fáil members who had canvassed had a 'great night' in Myos pub in Castleknock.[11]

The near miss sent Labour into a panic because it believed Higgins would take the seat of Joan Burton in Dublin West the next time out. As a result, Labour's Brendan Howlin, who was minister for the environment, announced in December 1996 that he was going to abolish water charges.[12] 'I abolished them because at that stage we had no meters and the simple logic to me was that if we were to spend many hundreds of millions of pounds at that stage, whether it would be better to spend the money to fix the leaks rather than to put in the meters,' he later recalled.[13]

Councils around the country had been getting around IR£50 million in water charges. The government decided that motor tax would be given to them to replace the shortfall. Stamp duty on the sale of houses was also increased.

Howlin got a round of applause at the Labour parliamentary party meeting in January 1997 for abolishing water charges. But when the general election was called in 1997, the issue failed to go away. Joe Higgins achieved a second victory over the party that had expelled him from its ranks. Having forced Labour to abolish water charges, which he saw as one of the biggest successes of his political career, he now took a seat in the Dáil in the Dublin West constituency at the expense of Labour's Joan Burton.

At the first Labour parliamentary party meeting after the 1997 general election, there was a post-mortem on how the party had gone from thirty-two seats to seventeen. Labour TD Róisín Shortall said the party had ignored the advice and contributions on water charges. 'Because of the water charges, we lost the seats of Sean Ryan, Eamonn Walsh, Joan Burton and Sean Kenny,' she said. There was an even more heated contribution from Labour TD Tommy Broughan, who said that 'the water charges issue was poison'.[14]

Higgins quickly built up a strong profile for himself in the Dáil. Despite his serious nature, he worked hard on coming up with quips and one-liners for Leaders' Questions with Taoiseach Bertie Ahern to get media attention for his causes. Humour was a weapon, he would say. Few politicians managed to come up with a better description of how good Bertie Ahern was at avoiding questions. Higgins compared it to playing handball against a haystack. 'You hear a dull thud but the ball does not come back to you. It goes all over the world, but it certainly does not come back to the person asking the question,' he once said.[15]

His ongoing political battle with Labour's Joan Burton in Dublin West continued. Both of them got elected in the 2002 general election. But in 2007, at the height of the Celtic Tiger, Higgins lost his seat to an up-and-coming Fine Gael politician called Leo Varadkar. He said that his battered 1992 Toyota Corolla car would just have to 'last a lot longer' as he prepared to begin his political comeback. He was back within two years, winning a seat in the European Parliament elections in Dublin in 2009.

Then he won back his Dáil seat in Dublin West in 2011. This time Joan Burton topped the poll, Leo Varadkar came second and Higgins took the third seat. The last seat went to Brian Lenihan, who cried with relief at having held onto his seat in the midst of a Fianna Fáil wipeout. He died just a few months later.

Higgins was back in the Dáil and he was able to pick a person to replace him in the European Parliament for the remaining three years of his term. He chose a young Socialist Party activist called Paul Murphy, who had previously been his parliamentary assistant. Higgins said that was due to Murphy's track record rather than designating him as his successor.

'I never see things in that kind of personalised way. Paul's a very intelligent, able activist. But it's fundamentally [about] policy and not personalities,' Higgins said.

With water charges once again coming to the fore, Higgins was ready for battle.

13

AWASH WITH WARNINGS

The cabinet decision to meter over one million households was going to set in motion one of the biggest construction projects in the state's history. Behind the scenes, though, Bord Gáis Chief Executive John Mullins was strongly opposed to the nationwide roll-out. Some of this was due to Mullins' own experience growing up in the working-class suburb of Knocknaheeny on the northside of Cork city.

'I remember protests on water charges and bin charges when I was growing up. In urban areas, I knew there were going to be flashpoints. When you actually start interfering with people's streets, right, people get quite upset. Particularly when what you are interfering with is going to create a charge. That's a problem,' he said.[1]

The main purpose of the water meters was to bill people for the amount of water they used.

However, Mullins had seen during his time working with water companies in England and Scotland that it was possible to bill people for water without installing meters. There were only 900 meters in the whole of Scotland, yet all their citizens were paying for water. And in England and Wales only forty per cent of households had water meters. Most customers got a fixed water bill every year, known as a flat charge. As a result, Mullins was very surprised that the government was so adamant about installing meters in every home to charge for water. 'You could have started with a flat charge, just like the British had done. And in many cases, a lot of the British companies hadn't even started metering programmes. They were private companies, if they saw a cost–benefit in that, why didn't they do that?'

The officials in the Department of the Environment had carried out a cost–benefit analysis which predicted that the installation of meters would reduce people's usage of water by ten per cent. It was a simple concept. If people were charged for how much water they used, they would use less of it. And there were international studies to back this up. Mullins got his Bord Gáis team to take a hard-headed look at the cost–benefit analysis. These were experienced utility workers, who were used to having to justify the case for investing in infrastructure. And they soon became very sceptical about the Department of the Environment's cost–benefit analysis.

There is a simple rule for cost–benefit analysis: the benefits have to outweigh the costs. Any cost–benefit analysis which has a cost of 1 and a benefit of more than 1 is a positive one. The cost–benefit ratio for water metering was 1:1.51. In other words, the state would gain €1.51 in savings on reduced water usage for every €1 it spent on installing water meters. That was a very good cost–benefit ratio.

But the Bord Gáis team raised questions about the predicted savings from people reducing their water usage once meters were installed. The department assumed that there would be no increases in the price of installing the meters, even though there were only a limited number of companies capable of putting in over one million meters. Bord Gáis said the assumption that there would be a 'zero' increase in prices in the construction sector was 'optimistic'. This was a polite way of saying it was 'unrealistic'.[2]

Bord Gáis had no issue with metering, in principle, but it needed the numbers to add up. It said, with notable understatement, that the department's business case 'requires more extensive work to reach an investment grade business case'. Mullins said the cost–benefit analysis of putting in meters from the start did not stack up. 'We had big debates at the time about that and clearly took a view that it might be better to start with a flat charge,' he said.

Bord Gáis laid out all its concerns in a confidential report to the department in June 2012.[3] It warned there was a risk of a 'public campaign of disruption' to a large-scale metering programme. Then there were the practical problems. Bord Gáis pointed out that there was no database 'with the location of each property or the name of each consumer'. Until all that information was gathered, no meters could be installed.

The department had also put forward a timeline that was madly ambitious. The government wanted to be able to say that it had metered almost every home by the time water charges were introduced in January 2014. The target was to have metered 924,000 homes by the end of 2014. Bord Gáis said it would be 'highly challenging' to install several hundred thousand water meters in time for the start of water charges in 2014. 'Experience from water utilities in other jurisdictions is that 100,000 installations per annum would be the limit of most ambition,' it said.

Despite these concerns, the government was already parroting the line that water meters were the 'fairest way' for people to pay for water. Bord Gáis pointed out there was a real risk of failing to install meters 'at a sufficient rate to meet public expectations'. If only a small percentage of the population had water meters by the time water charges were introduced, then the government's hard sell would be even harder.

Bord Gáis also pointed out that the decision to meter almost one million homes had been made by the government, and was not a Troika requirement. 'The EU/IMF programme of financial assistance includes a commitment that Ireland will introduce domestic water charges by January 2014. It does not make any commitment to introduce water meters,' it said. In fact, the Troika actually wanted to see flat charges for water introduced rather than waiting for meters to be installed. The reason was simple. They wanted to get their money back as fast as possible. 'There was pressure from the Troika – could we not just start off with a flat charge and then move on to meters?' said a Fine Gael source.

The ultimate fear for Bord Gáis was that metering would generate protests, which would in turn generate resistance to water charges in general. For all these reasons, Bord Gáis wanted to go with a flat charge and leave metering until a later date. 'While water meters are desirable, they are not essential; and they may not be affordable. If the water metering programme presents a risk to the billing programme, then the prudent approach is to break the link.'

The Bord Gáis report was a bombshell for the most senior civil servants in the Department of the Environment's water section. It was sent to Mark Griffin, the Galway-born assistant secretary for water, who was in charge of the 'water sector reform' programme. He was seen as one of the brightest of his generation and he would later be promoted to head of the Department of Communications. But he did not want word to spread around the department about Bord Gáis's opposition to water metering one million homes. Griffin made this clear to two senior colleagues – Ivan Grimes and Gerry Galvin – in an email.[4] 'Just received. I don't want this widely disseminated but would ask you to read it and discuss with me,' he wrote. The report had been marked 'commercially sensitive', so the usual practice was to share it only with the civil servants working on it.

There had been a unit in the Department of the Environment working on the issue of water metering even before the Fine Gael–Labour government took office. It dated back to the decision by the previous minister for the environment, John Gormley, to go for water metering. A metering procurement working group involving the councils had been running for eighteen months. 'When you create an entity like that, it takes on a life of its own. The concept of billing [with meters] was deeply embedded in the Department of Environment,' said one former Bord Gáis executive.

But it went deeper than that. The civil servants in the department had become convinced that it made no sense to have water services delivered by thirty-four different councils, most if not all of whom they felt were not up to scratch. Maria Graham had been working in the water policy division in the Custom House during the 'Big Freeze' in 2010. When the thaw came, nearly every pipe in the country seemed to burst. She found it very difficult to get information on the number of leaks from the staff in thirty-four different councils. 'Quite frankly, *The Irish Times* got there faster than me in trying to collate it. That said a lot about our capacity to have a national and regional perspective,' she said.[5]

Other civil servants in the department's water division had completely lost faith in the councils' ability to modernise the water service. 'The council service was crap,' said one civil servant. This civil servant was also relieved that there would now be one single body – Irish Water – to deliver a national service, and it would at last have the funding – through metered water charges – to improve it.

The government was also keen on water meters because they were needed to deliver on its pledge of a 'generous free allowance' of water for everyone. Enda Kenny was annoyed to find out that Bord Gáis was thinking differently. 'Kenny went mad about the Bord Gáis letter calling for no metering. His line was that the government had promised that people would be able to pay for their water through a meter,' said one source who was working with Irish Water in the period.

But Bord Gáis was not alone in its opposition to the metering plan. Dublin City Council was also completely opposed to a rapid metering programme. It said money would be better spent on fixing leaking water pipes first: 'Rolling out metering over a number of decades, as was done in the UK, will avoid using up valuable resources, which would be better spent on water mains rehabilitation.'[6]

The views of Dublin City Council were significant. It was headed by John Tierney, who was the most powerful county manager in the country because he had the most staff and the biggest budget. The council itself had a proud history of delivering water services due to the creation of the Vartry scheme back in the 1860s.[7] It was very unhappy with the notion of having to hand this over to a new entity called Irish Water.

Other submissions to the Department of the Environment's public consultation process on the water programme voiced their hostility to universal metering. Engineers Ireland and the Irish Academy of Engineering jointly called for a re-think. 'The plan to install over one million water meters by 2014 is highly ambitious, the total cost may be underestimated and we very much doubt if it can be completed in this timescale,' it said.[8]

But it all came to nothing. The Department of the Environment did mention the objections to metering when it assessed all the submissions. But it said the 'general thrust' of the contributions had reinforced the government view that metering was the way to go.[9]

Bord Gáis had found it frustrating dealing with some of the officials in the Department of the Environment as they tried to persuade them to abandon the headlong rush to water metering. 'You would have a meeting and they would nod their heads. Then when you walked away afterwards, it was like the meeting didn't happen,' said one Bord Gáis executive at the time.

Mullins himself was given an even clearer warning by one of the senior officials in the department. If he didn't go for metering, he would not get the job of setting up Irish Water. These were not just civil servants acting on a whim. The cabinet had decided on metering. Bord Gáis was going to have to implement the decision.

Mullins said afterwards that metering 'wasn't optional'. He added, 'The reality is that there was a policy decision to put in meters. Full stop.'

14

THE SECRET METER SURVEYS

Bord Gáis agreed to install over one million water meters. But it had no idea of where to put them. Almost every house in the country had its own stopcock. This was usually a tap-like device to turn the water off to a house, located under a metal lid marked 'Water' or 'Uisce' on the pavement outside the house. Any meter installer would need to have access to the stopcock to switch off the water supply. Then the installer would have to cut open the water pipe, put in a meter box and connect up the pipes on either side again.

The government decided that the councils were best placed to find and photograph the location of over 1.3 million stopcocks in the space of seven months. The surveyors were given a mobile phone to call for assistance, a sat nav to find their way around, a metal detector to find the metal lids which covered the stopcocks, and a shovel and pickaxe for any digging.

Around 125 council staff were trained to undertake the mammoth task between October 2012 and April 2013. They were given different targets depending on their council area. The surveyors in Dublin city were expected to photograph the stopcocks of 180 homes per day; in largely rural counties with dispersed housing like Donegal, the target was to photograph fifty-two homes per day. Then they had to upload the information on tablet computers to the metering survey database. That included the type of surface outside a person's home, such as concrete, dense bituminous macadam (aka tarmac), asphalt, brick or just grass. That was so the meter installers would have the right materials to reinstate the path after digging it up.

The Department of the Environment knew that even this first stage of the water metering programme was going to be a tricky task. The civil servants produced a policy for surveyors on how to minimise the risk of injury 'as a result of an encounter with a member of the public'.[1]

They were told to watch for signals that may be associated with impending violence: verbally expressed anger and frustration; body language such as threatening gestures; signs of drug or alcohol use; and the presence of a weapon. The surveyors were also advised to adopt a 'calm, caring attitude' in such situations and to avoid any behaviour that might be interpreted as aggressive, for example 'moving rapidly, getting too close, touching, or speaking loudly'.

The surveyors could explain to any curious householder that they were finding the locations for the installation of water meters. But they were told not to call to the house itself and not to talk about water charges. 'Surveyors should avoid engaging in more detailed discussions with regard to water charges and refer householders and members of the public to other sources of information such as public awareness material, free phone numbers or website,' the guidance document said.

It went on to say there was a 'medium' risk of a surveyor being injured by an attack from a member of the public. There was also a 'medium' risk of being injured by an attack from an 'aggressive dog'.

The surveyors had to mark the best spot to install a water meter before they took their photographs of the stopcock. The surveyors were warned to wear protective gloves while touching the stopcocks to avoid contracting Weil's disease, a potentially fatal infection caused by contact with the urine of infected rats.

Department officials were very keen for the meter boxes to be right on the boundary of the householder's property, which was usually at a front entrance, gate or wall. That meant that any leak in the pipe between the meter box and the house would be the householder's problem.[2]

Installing the meters was supposed to be a simple task at the hundreds of thousands of homes built during the Celtic Tiger era. It had been a condition of planning permission for years that homes have a meter box installed outside the property. A meter installer would only have to lift the lid and insert the meter in place. The councils had estimated that twenty per cent of homes had these meter boxes. But they had not been checking to see that the builders had actually put them in. This was another example of light-touch regulation. And the results were predictable. The builders had not bothered to follow the rules.

When the stopcock surveys started to roll in, Bord Gáis discovered to their horror that only six per cent of homes in Fingal had serviceable meter boxes. In Kerry, it was less than two per cent. The working assumption was now that the nationwide average would be around three per cent.

So, instead of having 233,000 homes out of 1.1 million which could be speedily metered, the actual figure was 'less than 35,000 properties', as Bord Gáis glumly noted.[3]

15

THE CRUSHING OF A PROTEST MOVEMENT

Phil Hogan got a warning shot of what lay ahead when he brought in the first version of the property tax on 1 January 2012. It was the €100 household charge and it applied to every home regardless of how big or small it was. It was laying the ground for the property tax, which was going to take much longer to implement. Small groups formed around the country, pledging to oppose both the household charge and water charges. Some of them were driven by what the government saw as the 'usual suspects' – Socialist Party TD Joe Higgins and his party members, the republican socialist party Éirígí, and a small number of anarchists.

However, the prospect of a household charge quickly managed to draw in people who had never been involved in political protests before. In Cobh, a young mother-of-three called Karen Doyle was asked for a lift to an anti-household charge meeting in the town by her mother. 'I didn't really want to go. It was a lousy night. But I said I'd drop my mother down and stay for a few minutes,' she said.[1]

There were around fifty people at the meeting in the Commodore Hotel in November 2011. There was a call for volunteers to distribute leaflets against the household charge. Doyle put her hand up. As a child in Cobh, she loved going to visit her grandfather Joey Cummins to listen to his stories. 'He was very passionate about social justice issues. He used to tell me: "Stand up when you see an injustice." He had a huge influence on me,' she said. When she was in first year in secondary school, she took part in protests in Cork in favour of the Dunnes Stores workers who were refusing to handle South African oranges. She followed the miners' strike in Britain. Then she got married, had three kids and settled into a 'comfortable life'. But that evening, in the Commodore Hotel, her interest in political action was reawakened.

Doyle became part of a group which eventually became known as 'Cobh

Says No to Austerity'. The name was taken from the 'Ballyhea Says No' group in the small village in north Cork, which was holding weekly marches to protest against the bank bailout. The Cobh Says No to Austerity group began regular 'white line' protests, where about ten of them marched along the road in the town with an anti-household charge banner. People watching from the footpath laughed at Doyle and her fellow protesters at times. 'I was doing it because it was the right thing to do. It was the only thing I could do because I didn't know what else to do. We did that week in, week out,' she said.

The group protested when Environment Minister Phil Hogan came to Cobh to announce the final stage of a €15 million project to stop landslides in the town. There was a little curtain set up in advance to cover the commemorative plaque. As Hogan was shown around, one of the protesters managed to stick an anti-household charge poster on top of the plaque and put the curtain back in place. Hogan pulled back the veil and revealed the poster. He complained afterwards about the ungrateful attitude of the protesters, having been forced to make a quick exit to chants of 'Won't Pay, Hogan Out.'[2]

The Cobh protesters were part of a loose national umbrella group set up called the Campaign against the Household and Water Taxes. And its main tactic was the boycott.[3] Socialist Party leader Joe Higgins had seen how mass non-payment had defeated the poll tax in Britain in the late 1980s. He had successfully called for a boycott of water charges as chair of an anti-water charge campaign in Dublin in the 1990s. And he had called for a boycott of bin charges in the early 2000s, although his opponents maintained that this had only resulted in the council-run bin service being starved of income and eventually privatised.

The Socialist Party had a strong influence in the Campaign against the Household and Water Taxes and it began to drum out the boycott message. The early signs were positive, even ahead of the household charge coming into force. And there were good-sized crowds turning up at the public meetings organised by the campaign. Around 200 people attended a 'Can't Pay Won't Pay' event in the community hall in Gweedore in the Donegal Gaeltacht in October 2011. Independent TD Thomas Pringle and Higgins both spoke.

The Socialist Party's Cork-city-based Mick Barry used to deliberately set out fewer chairs than was needed at the public meetings he helped organise in Cork. The councillor had picked up this tactic from John F. Kennedy's campaign to win the Democratic presidential nomination in 1960. 'The Kennedys used to go to villages in New England and they would set out thirty chairs for a meeting, even if they thought there would be fifty there,' said Barry.[4]

He laid out 150 chairs for one meeting in the Hibernian Hotel in Mallow towards the end of 2011. He was expecting more than that. 'So when the people would arrive, they'd have to unstack the chairs at the back of the room and they'd say, "Oh my God, it's bigger than they expected."' The extra stacks of chairs were soon gone because 400 people turned up. It was standing room only by the end. On the drive back to his home in Cork, Barry told some of his fellow socialists in the car: 'Lads, we've caught a big fish here.'

When the €100 household charge came into force in January 2012, there was even more interest. Local offshoots of the campaign 'sprang up like mushrooms in a field in the rainy season,' according to Barry. By April 2012 there were twenty branches of the Campaign against the Household and Water Taxes in Cork city and county alone.

***

One of the new groups was based in the working-class suburb of Ballyphehane on the southside of Cork city. The land was originally used by market gardeners to supply the vegetables for Cork. But from 1948 onwards, Cork Corporation started developing a 'model community' there for people who had been in crowded tenements in the city. Within two decades there were 10,000 people living in public housing in Ballyphehane. It was a tight-knit community that had higher than average levels of poverty but had started to see an increase in living standards during the Celtic Tiger era. Then the recession hit. Suddenly workers in the area were losing their jobs or having their hours cut – at the same time as the government announced a raft of tax hikes and new charges.

One of them was John Lonergan, who had started working at the age of thirteen. He had spent sixteen years in a gas manufacturing company, rising to the rank of assistant manager before he lost his job. Then he got work as a storeman in a forklift company. 'When I was working, I was happy, I was paying my bills. I had a nice job,' he said. Most of his spare time went into supporting his son John, who is a ten-time world champion Irish dancer and toured for years with *Riverdance*. 'That was what I was doing all my life, following him around to feises and world championships. I had no interest in politics in any shape or form,' he said.[5]

Lonergan had been mortgage free on his house in Ballyphehane but re-mortgaged in 2007. A year later, the crash came and Lonergan was let go from his job as a storeman. He suddenly had to try to find the money to pay off his €1,000-a-month mortgage and to meet the cost of the new property tax. 'That's what brought me into this. If they had never brought in a property tax, I don't think I would have been involved,' he said.

Lonergan went to the meetings in the Ballyphehane community centre organised by the Campaign against the Household and Water Taxes. Another person who attended was Keith O'Brien, a spray painter in the motor trade. He was put on a three-day week during the recession. He was 'sick of screaming at the telly' about the bank bailout and wanted to do something. He went to the anti-household charge meeting with his father. The Ballyphehane group marched in Cork city centre every Saturday for the best part of two years. Their prop was a 'gravy train' made out of plywood which had carriages with photos of politicians with their wages and salaries. It was so heavy that it took ten of them to carry it.

One of the prominent members of the group was Donal O'Sullivan, a tall, bearded, married father-of-three who had lived in Ballyphehane since he was four years old. He had worked for one of the quintessential Cork companies – Musgraves – doing forklift driving, order picking and stock control. This was his first involvement in a protest movement. 'I never belonged to any political party. My allegiance would have been to Labour,' he said. But he became politicised when he saw the €100 household charge being brought in after the bank bailout. 'This is what drives me, when I see the ordinary working man being screwed and I see this one per cent of people walking away with their big fat fucking pay cheques.'

His son, a self-employed plumber, had been doing okay during the construction boom. He had a mortgage on his home and then the payments for his work started to dry up. 'You have a bank bailout and money is tight for people. He is owed money here and owed money there. Next thing he's fucked,' said O'Sullivan. His son fell into mortgage trouble and received an eviction notice in 2013. He asked his father for help. O'Sullivan got on to the Ballyphehane/South Parish Says No group. By the time the sheriff arrived to enforce the eviction notice, there were fifty-five people outside his son's house. 'The sheriff never got out of the car,' said O'Sullivan. 'People came from Carlow, Dublin, Waterford, Wexford, Kerry. Absolutely incredible.' His son held on to his house.

***

During this time, the campaign against the €100 household charge was meeting with some success. Hundreds of thousands of people refused to pay it to their local council. Phil Hogan turned up at the call centre on the quays in Dublin to meet and greet the staff who were taking the payments. But his real purpose was to get more people to pay the charge.

Even at this stage, Hogan was the focus when the campaign organised a large protest outside the Fine Gael Ard Fheis in 2012. It was taking place in the Convention Centre, a €700 million building in the shape of a tilted glass barrel. Some of the 5,000 protesters outside spotted a man who looked like Phil Hogan. He was jostled and pushed to the ground by a small group of them. The man said repeatedly, 'I'm not Phil Hogan, they've got the wrong guy.' He was helped into a garda car, which was rocked by some protesters before it moved away, according to the *Irish Times* report.[6]

The introduction of the €100 household charge led to a backlash in his own county that embarrassed Hogan in the most public fashion. He was booed when he was introduced on stage at the homecoming celebration for the All-Ireland-winning Kilkenny hurling team in Nowlan Park in 2012.

But then the campaign against the household charge collapsed due to a single action. The government brought in the Revenue to take the money from people's bank accounts, both for the €100 household charge and the new property tax. For good measure, the Revenue was given unprecedented powers to take the money from social welfare payments and farmers' EU grants as well.

The Revenue's chairwoman, Josephine Feehily, had a private meeting with the four key figures in government – Taoiseach Enda Kenny, Tánaiste Eamon Gilmore, Finance Minister Michael Noonan and Public Expenditure Minister Brendan Howlin. She asked them if they were willing to back Revenue to the hilt in collecting the property tax. 'We needed everybody to hold their nerve when letters to 1.6 million people started flowing out of the organisation,' she said.[7]

She was assured that the government would stay the course. 'Easy to pay and hard to avoid' became the Revenue's slogan.

There was still some resistance. Protesters invaded lots of Revenue offices around the country. They chained themselves to radiators and jumped over the counters with banners and flags. Feehily herself got a death threat. But when the property tax kicked in during the middle of 2013, over ninety per cent of households paid it. The boycott tactic had failed.

'The arrival of the Revenue killed off the campaign against the household tax. People could protest all they liked, but the money was simply taken out of their bank account,' said one cabinet minister.

Socialist Party Councillor Mick Barry said attendances at the meetings of the anti-household charge campaigns started to drop off. 'It became increasingly clear that the broad mass of ordinary people saw this as a battle that couldn't be won,' he said.

The campaign against the household charge had been defeated. And it began to disintegrate, even though there was still a second battle left to fight against water charges. Many of the people who had joined the campaign were not keen on the Socialist Party's plan to run members of the campaign – who also often happened to be their own members – in the forthcoming local elections. The Socialist Party ran into stout Cork resistance. The Ballyphehane group contained many people who were intensely opposed to political parties. They did not want candidates running under their banner in the local elections. The Socialist Party members of their group kept pushing this.

John Lonergan and Keith O'Brien became even more suspicious when they found out that Socialist Party members in other branches of the Campaign against the Household and Water Taxes in Cork city were proposing identical motions about running candidates. O'Brien said some of these branches started to fold up because of the 'toxic' atmosphere that was developing between regular members and Socialist Party members. 'The Socialist Party liked to control political actions. And if they can't control it, they destroy it. It didn't take us that long to get rid of them,' he said.

Ballyphehane is only three generations old. In its early years, it had the social problems that often come with moving an entire community into a new area. But the area had since produced a very proud group of people who had done well for themselves after a hard upbringing. They were not going to be told what to do by the Socialist Party. The Ballyphehane group came up with a plan for a clear-out of the Socialist Party members in their ranks. They held a separate annual general meeting in 2012, at which John Lonergan was appointed as chairman. Six others joined him in various other key positions. They dubbed themselves the 'Magnificent Seven'.

The battle with the Socialist Party members was over. Lonergan said they got the hint. 'We never saw them no more. We stripped the politics out of it and we suddenly became an active working branch,' he said. But the internal row had taken its toll on some of the group's female members. They got fed up and drifted away, leaving a largely male core membership.

Mick Barry denied that his party had been trying to take over the Ballyphehane group. 'We didn't give people an ultimatum and say, "You have to row in behind the Socialist Party,"' he said. Barry had found that it was easy to have unity in a protest campaign when it was going well. But when it was failing, as the household charge campaign undoubtedly was, splits and tensions soon followed. 'The Socialist Party were honest and true builders of the anti-water charge movement at grassroots level. People can disagree with our politics, that's fine. But we're not going to stay silent if people try to traduce the genuine role we played everywhere,' he said.

The new group became known as Ballyphehane/South Parish Says No. It held meetings every Tuesday in the community centre in Ballyphehane, at the cost of €15 for the room hire. A core of around twenty-five people were in the group. And they were ready to focus on the issue that they believed would resonate with the public.

Water charges.

16

THE TROIKA TIME EXTENSION

Ever since the bailout in 2010, civil servants and politicians had feared the Troika.

There was a daily reminder for the civil servants in the Department of Finance just how much the Troika were watching over them. Their offices on Upper Merrion Street were across the road from the five-star Merrion Hotel that housed Patrick Guilbaud's two-star Michelin restaurant. The Merrion was the hotel of choice for the Troika. Even during the recession, the hotel was able to charge room rates of €485 per night and up €3,000 per night for its penthouse suites.[1] US President Barack Obama had stayed there with his wife, Michelle, during his morale-boosting visit to Ireland in 2011.

The Department of Finance's secretary general, John Moran, used to look out his office window late at night to see the lights on in the rooms of the Troika officials in the Merrion Hotel. 'I could kind of keep an eye on … when they were working late as well as … as when we were working late; they would see us,' he later said.[2] It was the street of the squinting windows.

The Troika were keen, too, on getting as many documents as possible. The officials in the Washington-based International Monetary Fund bought a photocopying machine as soon as they flew into Dublin.[3] They grabbed every single cabinet memo they could in the hunt for ways for the government to pay off its bailout loans.

The Troika had never insisted on water metering, but they had a strict timetable for water charges: 1 January 2014 was the agreed date. But reality was beginning to dawn towards the end of 2012. Bord Gáis would be able to install meters in only 162,000 homes by that date. That was way off Hogan's target of having one million homes metered by then. He needed the Troika to do him a favour.

The job of setting up a database of all households who would be getting water bills was still not complete. The software needed to generate bills from the water usage data provided by the meters was not ready either. The only way of bringing in water charges by 1 January 2014 was to issue households with a flat charge. Enda Kenny and Eamon Gilmore had already ruled that out. So Hogan needed to get the date pushed back. And he needed to get the Troika to agree to it.

He brought a memo to cabinet in October 2012, seeking to postpone the introduction of water charges by a full year to 1 January 2015. It stated: 'The minister believes that the compressed timetable for communication and building customer knowledge and understanding of the tariff regime and the fact that a relatively small proportion of households will be metered by end 2013 (162,000 households) creates a risk of non-payment of charges.'[4]

On the current timescale, households would be paying their first full year of property tax and water charges at the same time. Hogan and other ministers thought it would be harder to get people to pay both. His memo stated that bringing in water charges so quickly after the property tax 'will also have a considerable bearing on the acceptability of water charges'. He also had an eye on the local elections. Bringing in water charges in January 2014 would make it more difficult for Fine Gael and Labour councillors in the local elections in May that year. The cabinet approved his plan to delay the introduction of water charges and to open negotiations with the Troika about it.

The Troika agreed to the government's request. There was, however, one risk that had not been mentioned in Hogan's memo. The property tax had been introduced during the bailout programme. 'It was easier to do the property tax with the Troika around,' said a government source. But the Troika were due to pack their bags in the Merrion Hotel at the end of 2013, when the €85 billion bailout programme was due to finish up. Now water charges would be coming in a full year after that. The excuse of 'the Troika made us do it' would not work.

The government had just thrown away the best political cover it had.

17

IRISH WATER GETS ITS FIRST BOSS

John Mullins was the man who was going to set up Irish Water. Now there was a dispute about how much he would be paid for it. Mullins had been earning almost €400,000 in 2010 as the head of Bord Gáis. His salary was cut to €250,000 during the recession because the new government brought in a pay cap. He wanted to get his salary increased to €317,000 – the same salary as the head of the ESB – if he was to take charge of Irish Water as well. 'I took a particular view with ministers at the time that the combination of Bord Gáis and Irish Water was actually a bigger utility than the ESB and that the scale of the challenge that was involved at the time certainly needed to be recognised by government,' he said.[1]

The government department that was responsible for dealing with Bord Gáis and signing off on any big decisions it made was the Department of Communications. In April 2012 the officials there were still hoping that they could sort out the issue of Mullins' pay. They briefed their minister, Pat Rabbitte, about getting a bigger salary for Mullins from Public Expenditure Minister Brendan Howlin. And they even went to the trouble of coming up with the following draft speaking point for Rabbitte at the cabinet meeting: 'I believe that it is important that the CEO salary should be commensurate with the scale of the new responsibilities inherent in taking on the new water utility function and I hope that Minister Howlin and his department are positively disposed to consideration of this,' the suggested contribution said.[2]

But Howlin refused to breach the €250,000 public sector pay cap. The officials in the Department of Communications gave Rabbitte the bad news three months later in July 2012. 'The Minister for Public Expenditure and Reform has decided that no additional remuneration will be agreed,' their confidential memo stated.[3]

Then came the bombshell. Mullins was leaving his job as head of Bord

Gáis. The driving force of the Irish Water project was gone. 'The BGE CEO John Mullins has now formally advised that he will not be seeking a renewal of his contract,' the memo said. All of a sudden, Bord Gáis needed to find a new chief executive who would be able to sell off the retail arm, set up Irish Water and get the metering programme going.

Mullins said that a number of ministers may have underestimated essentially what was really involved. 'But then I can fully understand why they would, because how many of them would have had the experience of running utilities?' The key ministers involved largely came from a public service background. Taoiseach Enda Kenny, Minister for Finance Michael Noonan and Minister for Public Expenditure Brendan Howlin had all been teachers before they went into politics. Eamon Gilmore was a trade union organiser and Phil Hogan had been an auctioneer.

The Department of Communications' officials noted glumly that the government had decided that Mullins' successor at Bord Gáis should get an even lower salary of €191,000, unless a business case could be made for going up to a maximum of €238,000. They were concerned about whether a 'suitable candidate will be found at this salary level' with the necessary 'competence, experience and capacity'.[4]

***

Bord Gáis originally wanted to set up Irish Water as an extra division in the company – not a separate outfit. But the government was afraid that if Irish Water was a division of Bord Gáis, then it would have to give a chunk of the ownership to the existing Bord Gáis workers. It set up Irish Water as a subsidiary company of Bord Gáis. So Bord Gáis had a head of HR and Irish Water had a head of HR. The same went for other central services like asset management, communications, IT, billing and finance. It also meant hiring two chief executives. 'That imposed significant extra costs,' said one Bord Gáis manager. 'We didn't want to separate it out as an entity and duplicate everything.'

Mullins had intended to run Irish Water as a division of Bord Gáis and take personal responsibility for the whole lot. But instead of having one man in charge on a salary of €317,000, the government decided to hire two people on combined salaries of €450,000. There would now be a chief executive for

Bord Gáis and a managing director for Irish Water. They would have to figure out how to work together on the project.

The sequencing was important. The boss of Bord Gáis would be in charge of the boss of Irish Water. So, logically, the Bord Gáis position should be filled first to ensure that the Bord Gáis boss had a say in the appointment of who he or she would be working with. Instead, the Irish Water job was filled first.

Irish Water needed to have a leader who was able to communicate well with the public. One who understood all the technical workings of the water system would be even better. The country's foremost water engineer, Jerry Grant, ticked both boxes. He was born in 1953 on a farm in the mountainous parish of Upperchurch in Tipperary. When he was ten years old, his family got an offer of a better farm from the Land Commission. They moved to Fethard in south Tipperary. By the age of fifteen, Grant wanted to be a priest, which was relatively common at a time when the Catholic Church had immense influence and prestige. His enthusiasm started to wane, though, in the Redemptorist College in Limerick, where he was very good at maths and took part in an All-Ireland public speaking competition. At seventeen, he came home to his mother and told her that he wanted to be an engineer. That was a whole new world because he was the first in his family to go to university. She said to him: 'Would you not do teaching?'

Grant chose to study engineering in Dublin rather than Cork because of the tradition of Upperchurch men owning pubs in the capital. The owners of the first pubs had brought up men from the parish to work there. They then got enough money to buy their own pub, and on it went. Kennedy's in Drumcondra, The Lower Deck in Portobello, and Ryan's on Thomas Street in the Liberties. The last of these was owned by Grant's uncle. Grant was able to work there at night to earn his keep, and his fees for UCD were paid for through a scholarship.

After a brief spell in Birmingham, Grant came back to Ireland to join the company where he would spend the next thirty-three years – MC O'Sullivan in Cork. He led its water team for ten years. He was very proud to work on the Greater Dublin Strategic Drainage Study in the mid-1990s. That was where the idea of putting a pipeline to bring water from the River Shannon to Dublin came from.

Grant was someone who was respected by the water services sections in the councils for the knowledge he had of the water system. 'When he would come into the Dublin City Council's civic offices, you could sense the reverence. This guy knew what he was on about,' said one council official. His public debating skills made him one of a rare breed – an engineer who could communicate.

Grant rose up through the ranks of MC O'Sullivan to become its managing director in 2002. By then, it was the largest engineering and environmental consultancy firm in the country. A few months later, it was taken over by the London firm RPS in a €34 million deal. Grant stayed on as head of what was now called RPS-MCOS. He decided to set up a new communications division in the company, which was unusual at the time. He hired a young engineering graduate called Elizabeth Arnett to work there. She worked on the government contracts RPS won for the 'Race Against Waste Campaign'. Around €3 million was spent on TV and cinema ads urging people to recycle their waste instead of sending it to landfill.

Arnett worked for RPS on the communications for the controversial Corrib gas pipeline in Rossport in north Mayo. RPS designed the first pipeline route and then a revised second route. Arnett went around to visit families in their kitchens in Rossport to convince them that it was safe. But it was a hugely divisive project which took years to deliver. So too did another of the projects she worked on, the Poolbeg incinerator.

By 2012, Grant had spent ten tough years at the head of RPS. He had to cut staff salaries in the company to keep it going when government spending on infrastructure dried up during the recession. He was fifty-nine. There was a window to do one more big project before he reached retirement.

Grant contacted Bord Gáis to express an interest in working on its new Irish Water project. In August 2012 he was hired as Bord Gáis's chief technical adviser in its Irish Water Programme office. It was a dream job for him. He had grown up at a time when drinking water only had to pass a simple test. If it tasted, smelled and looked okay, then it was okay. Now it had to pass several hundred different tests to prove that it was free of bugs and pollutants.

Grant had been frustrated that little was being done to modernise the water system. He saw how council engineers had to switch from roads to water to waste to progress up the ranks to the top job of county engineer. He believed the country could produce brilliant water engineers if they were allowed to build up their skills in that area.

A Belfast engineer, William Mulholland, had built the aqueduct that supplied Los Angeles with its water. It took five years, 5,000 men and 6,000 mules. Michael Maurice O'Shaughnessy from Limerick was the chief city engineer in San Francisco who delivered the giant Hetch Hetchy Reservoir. It was controversial because it involved building a dam – named after him – to flood a valley in Yosemite National Park and piping the water for 241 kilometres to San Francisco. But to this day, it supplies eighty-five per cent of the city's drinking water.

The setting up of Irish Water potentially offered Grant the chance to implement some of the water studies he had written twenty years earlier. He would also be joined in the Irish Water office by another ex-RPS colleague in Elizabeth Arnett, whom he regarded highly. She was part of the team assigned to work on communications.

However, Grant was one of the sceptics about the government's plan to spend €500 million on metering, believing the money could be better spent on fixing leaking pipes first. He put his views on record at the Oireachtas environment committee when it was doing a report into the creation of Irish Water in 2011: 'the idea of taking €500 million and prioritising metering over other things that must be done seems unrealistic at the moment,' he said.[5]

There was no question that Grant, with his engineering background, understood the water system much better than anyone else did and he had an infectious enthusiasm for explaining how it worked. But the second key candidate for the Irish Water job had advantages of his own.

***

The Dublin city manager, John Tierney, had built up a reputation in the public sector, just as Grant had in the private sector. Born in Terryglass in north Tipperary, he knew how councils worked because he had worked in them all his life. He had got a summer job with North Tipperary County Council as a temporary clerical officer after finishing first year in Maynooth University. He liked it so much that he dropped out of his course. He went on to work with seven different councils and became county manager of three of them.

Tierney did not drink alcohol, which was obvious by his constant wearing of a Pioneer pin for much of his career. He eventually went back to college later in life and completed a PhD in ethics in Queen's University Belfast. He was a fanatical Tipperary hurling supporter, having been chairman of the Tipperary County Board for a year. He could be seen at all the Tipperary hurling matches in Croke Park wearing his county's blue and gold jersey. And he was the chairman of the Tipperary Supporters Club in Dublin, which raised money to keep the senior hurlers on the road.

Bord Gáis was looking for someone with Tierney's level of council experience. It believed that it needed someone who could persuade the county managers to hand over control of water services to Irish Water. They could not be forced to do it. County managers have such unconstrained power over their own councils that it is very difficult to make them do anything. 'They are a law unto themselves. They are as hard to sack as a judge,' said one Irish Water source. The legend was that if you ever wanted to meet a county manager, the place to go was the Ashling Hotel in Dublin 8 at a certain time every month. The county managers would come up on the train to Heuston Station and make the short three-minute walk to the hotel. They would have an evening meal there and stay overnight, before making the short trip in the morning to a meeting at their headquarters on Usher's Quay. This building is home to the Local Government Management Agency, which is little known to the public but has significant power.

Tierney was attractive to Bord Gáis because he was not just a county manager but the most powerful county manager in the country. The Dublin city manager has that status because he or she has the most money and the most influence.

Tierney ultimately got the job as managing director of Irish Water on a salary of €200,000, which was a slight increase on the €189,000 he was getting as Dublin city manager. 'Jerry Grant did go for the managing director job when John Tierney got it. But what Jerry hadn't got was the ability to get county managers onside,' said an Irish Water source.

When Tierney was appointed in January 2013, Bord Gáis went out of its way to send the message to the county managers that one of their own was taking charge. Bord Gáis mentioned how he had been county manager in Dublin city, Fingal and Galway city, and had a 'very impressive track record in local government'.[6]

A fateful choice had been made. Irish Water would be led by someone who was better at communicating with public servants than with the public. And it would be facing a new generation of protesters, who had smartphones and Facebook accounts instead of CB radios and pamphlets.

18

THE SMARTPHONE-WIELDING PROTESTERS

Derek Byrne had been a barman, a Dublin Airport worker and then a night-time security guard. He became involved in protests after the Universal Social Charge and other tax increases had cut down his wages from €47,000 in 2008 to €28,000 in 2011. 'I'm more or less better off … giving up working and going and signing on the dole, because it's not worth working in this country,' he said in one interview.[1] He started to go to marches with a group called 'Dublin Says No' in the city centre from 2013 onwards. At most, there were about twenty of them.

Byrne and some of the group were heading towards the Department of Finance on Merrion Street in July 2013 to submit a Freedom of Information request. They wanted to get hold of the Anglo Tapes, the recordings of conversations between Anglo Irish Bank executives which were running in the *Irish Independent*. These tapes were held by the Irish Bank Resolution Corporation (IBRC), the company formed out of the liquidated bank, and would never have been eligible for release.

Byrne and his group bumped into Public Expenditure Minister Brendan Howlin, who was walking back to the department. He started to video Howlin as he walked down the street. He got so close that Howlin pushed his camera away. Howlin told him: 'Will you please go away.' Byrne uploaded all the footage to YouTube. 'That was the first time we ever went after a politician. We said, "Fuck this, let's go after them and ask them a question,"' said Byrne.[2]

Byrne had been a Labour voter but had lost faith in the political system since the outbreak of the recession. He believed that none of the politicians had been affected by austerity. He came up with the idea of asking politicians: 'How has austerity affected you?' He ended up recording most of the cabinet as he asked them this question, uploading the footage to YouTube and Facebook.

Facebook in particular had given ordinary people a voice and an ability to organise. Byrne had a confrontational style. If a politician refused to answer his standard question about austerity, he kept following them and asking them again and again. He followed a Fine Gael minister, Richard Bruton, canvassing in the Dublin North East constituency. Bruton stayed silent while he went from door to door. Byrne went after Fine Gael's Simon Harris, who kept walking and talking into his phone. 'You can keep walking, you're just another parasite from Fine Gael,' said Byrne.

After a while the politicians would recognise him, standing outside with his digital camera hanging around his neck. It recorded high-definition footage. Byrne started to make a name for himself in protest circles. Later, he would introduce himself as the man doing videos of the politicians. The only politician that he didn't faze was Gerry Adams, who had no problem talking about austerity when Byrne doorstepped him. Adams responded to Byrne's queries, saying, 'All of us, including me, are a bit insulated from it, but if you're about your constituency … you can see … how all the wrong choices are putting huge pressures and hardship on working people,' said Adams.[3]

Byrne said that Adams 'knew how to play it'. Byrne added, 'I knew what way he was going to answer. But the rest of them couldn't answer.'

Byrne's approach was part of the breakdown of the old order, a decline of deference. Politicians had always been part of a group – the others being teachers, gardaí and clergymen – who had enjoyed a high social status. The notion of challenging them in the street, or calling them names, had been unthinkable prior to this. But that had changed during the recession. Minister for Health Mary Harney had red paint thrown at her. Minister for Transport Noel Dempsey had the word 'TRATIORS' daubed in red paint across his constituency office in Trim in Meath. He later joked that it could not have been any of his former students, as they would have spelt the word correctly.

What was also different was the ability of protesters to publicise their actions themselves on social media. Byrne was not only pursuing and questioning politicians on the streets, he was also recording it and showing it to the world. 'Now people will question them because they have seen people like me who are not afraid to go straight into their faces and tell them exactly what we think,' he said.

Other protesters were also using similar methods, as Minister for Communications Pat Rabbitte found out. He was drinking a pint outside

Doheny and Nesbitts – a famous political watering hole – one evening in July 2013 with his special adviser, Simon Nugent. A protester who was passing the pub recognised Rabbitte and turned back and tried to eavesdrop. Then he made a phone call.

Noticing the man, Rabbitte and Nugent guessed correctly that he was summoning reinforcements, so they went inside to seek sanctuary in the pub. But very soon afterwards, up to fifty protesters made their way in. They surrounded Rabbitte and Nugent, chanting, 'Traitor, traitor' and 'Rabbitte, Rabbitte, Rabbitte – run, run, run.'[4] Rabbitte stayed sitting on his bar stool, with his pint of Guinness half-empty on the counter beside him. He started checking his phone. One of the bar staff told the protesters to get out: 'You're on private property.' The protesters stayed where they were, waving flags and banners and shouting, 'Shame on you.' One female protester hit Rabbitte's pint of Guinness with her hand and sent it flying along the counter.

A tall young man came up to Rabbitte and whispered in his ear: 'Don't worry, we have it under control.' He was one of two garda special branch men who were in the pub – to look after not Rabbitte but Michael Noonan and Brendan Howlin, who were upstairs at a function with representatives of the Troika.

Uniformed gardaí arrived and got the protesters out of the pub. Rabbitte himself left shortly afterwards. It had reminded him of the treatment that politicians had received during the eighth amendment campaign in 1983. There had been threatening phone calls at home and obscene material put through their letter boxes. Their families were subjected to abuse and, often, young teenagers answering the phone were not spared.

The introduction of the household charge had only led to more incidents. Tánaiste Eamon Gilmore and Minister for Children Frances Fitzgerald were travelling together in a car to a youth centre in Ballyfermot in October 2012 when they were surrounded by protesters. The car was pelted with eggs. Fitzgerald said: 'There were fifteen or twenty people cracking the car with their placards.'[5] Their car had to turn back and the UNICEF event at the youth centre took place without them.

But the level of protest against politicians was to intensify as the plans to introduce water charges accelerated.

19

THE IRISH EXEMPTION FROM WATER CHARGES

Fianna Fáil, in opposition now, had stayed quiet on the €100 household charge. And it was also making very little noise about water charges. The party had, after all, signed up for them in the last government with the Green Party. It had also included them in the bailout deal. The Fianna Fáil environment spokesman, Barry Cowen TD, brother of former Taoiseach Brian Cowen, was maintaining a holding pattern on water charges. He was waiting to see how the public reacted to the setting up of Irish Water and for more information on the cost of it.

Fianna Fáil's most influential voice for many years on water policy was Noel Dempsey. He believed in the need for water charges due to his upbringing. His parents were very direct people who had to raise their twelve children on a very small farm near Longwood in Meath.

The family got their drinking water from a well in their front yard and they had a rainwater tank beside the house. 'Every drop of rainwater to this day goes into a tank, which is used for toilets and showers,' said Dempsey.[1] His mother used to bake all their bread and turned the leftover Odlums flour sack into pillow cases or sheets. 'I would put a lot of my interest in practical environmental matters down to seeing how we lived during the '50s and '60s. We had an acre of ground at that house and that was fully used for food,' he said.

One acre was not enough to feed the family, so Dempsey and his eleven brothers would sow potatoes for neighbouring farmers. 'We'd drop the spuds for them. We'd get two drills of spuds. We'd pick them. We'd pick all their spuds as well. We had our supply for the winter,' he said.

His childhood experiences in Longwood gave him a lifelong appreciation of having running water. 'People in cities, they don't know where it comes from. It just arrives in the tap. A fellow down the country has a well that dries up after three weeks of fine weather. He knows how precious the water is,' he said.

Dempsey had once studied for the priesthood but ended up becoming a teacher after doing his training in UCD. It was a time in Fianna Fáil when having a degree meant you were looked upon with suspicion in case you had any notions about yourself. He got elected as a Fianna Fáil councillor in Meath in 1977 and developed a reputation for being outspoken. When he made it into the Dáil in 1987, a friend told him: 'You know, you probably could have done this about ten years ago if you'd learned to keep your mouth shut.' Dempsey told him: 'Well I'm here now on my own terms. I owe nothing to anybody.'

Fianna Fáil's policy on water charges during the 1980s and early 1990s was fluid. When councils included them in their annual budgets, the party's councillors opposed them in some counties and supported them in others. When Fianna Fáil's Micheál Martin was lord mayor of Cork in 1992, he supported the inclusion of water charges in Cork City Council's budget. 'I was until 3 a.m. in the morning trying to get the estimates passed [for the annual council budget] and water charges was the issue,' he said.[2]

Dempsey was instinctively in favour of water charges when he became Fianna Fáil's environment spokesman in opposition in the mid-1990s. He condemned the abolition of water charges by the Fine Gael–Labour government in 1997 on the basis that it was unfair to people in rural Ireland who were paying for water. 'From a Fianna Fáil point of view, a good, strong position to adopt,' he said.

But as Fianna Fáil faced into the 1997 general election, Dempsey was told by his colleagues to come out and declare that it would not be re-introducing water charges. 'I tried to resist it as long as possible, but that was the party policy from then on,' he said. Fianna Fáil got back into government with the help of the Progressive Democrats and Dempsey was appointed as minister for the environment.

He was an unconventional politician. During his time as minister in various portfolios, he pushed for third-level fees, supported incinerators, abolished the right of TDs to be county councillors at the same time, brought in a requirement to give ten per cent of an estate's land or value for social housing, abolished the drift netting of salmon and lowered the drink driving limits. He pushed up airport charges in Dublin Airport by almost fifty per cent to pay for the building of Terminal Two. 'I would never have been content to just go with the flow. If I became convinced that something needed to be done, I would have just done it,' he said.

In a time when the Fianna Fáil-led governments of Bertie Ahern were afraid of any new policies that would unsettle the voters, Dempsey stuck out like a sore thumb. 'Some people put it all down to just being a thick Meath man. That's the stereotype,' he said.

As minister for the environment in the late 1990s, he had to deal with a proposed new EU rule to require all countries to have household water charges. Ireland argued that it was covering the cost of water from general taxation. But the European Commission was convinced that Ireland was not investing enough in its water system. The Irish civil servants in Brussels, known as the permanent representatives, warned Dempsey that he would have to bow to the European Commission's demands.

'They were saying we really couldn't stand out like this alone, and all sorts of reasons why we might need them in the future,' he said. But Dempsey threatened not to support the new rule, known as the Water Framework Directive, unless Ireland was allowed to avoid introducing household water charges. He had no veto, but the EU wanted to have a rule that every member state supported. So the other EU states reluctantly agreed to exempt Ireland from water charges in 2000. 'They put in what was called the Irish clause,' said Dempsey.

The 'Irish clause' was Article 9.4 of the Water Framework Directive on the requirement to introduce household water charges. It allowed Ireland to opt out of this obligation on the grounds that having no household water charges was 'in accordance with established practices' in the country.[3] Dempsey was often reminded of the water charge exemption he negotiated in the years afterwards. 'Europe never really accepted that we don't have water charges. It's totally anathema to them. And every available opportunity they got, they would remind us of that,' he said. The European Commission used to be told one of the old excuses in response: there was so much rain that Ireland could not charge for water. 'But there are plenty of other European countries that have more rainfall, particularly Norway and parts of western Scotland, but still charge for water,' said one European Commission official.

Given its belief in the need for water charges, the European Commission was very happy to see the Fianna Fáil–Green Party government agree in

December 2009 to bring them back in, and to include them in the bailout deal in 2010.

Dempsey's reputation took a severe hit during that time because he had been a key member of successive Fianna Fáil governments. He was frustrated that he had not spotted the economic danger signs and disheartened by having to impose cuts that were 'horrendous for people'.[4] Despite the hit to his reputation, some of his supporters were still amazed when he announced that he was not going to run in the 2011 general election. His thirty-four-year career in politics was over. 'He just lost the will to run again after the economic crash. He took it very hard,' said a Dempsey supporter.

The new Fine Gael–Labour government promised the Troika that it would bring in water charges, with the first bills to arrive in January 2015. Once that happened, it would no longer be 'established practice' in Ireland to have no household water charges. Noel Dempsey's 'Irish clause' would be gone.

20

THE METER CONTRACT CONTROVERSY

The collapse of the construction industry after the property crash had led to 160,000 building workers losing their jobs.[1] Tens of thousands emigrated to find work in Canada and Australia. The cement trucks went off the road. There were no more builders in yellow high-vis jackets queuing at garage forecourts to fuel up with diesel and jumbo breakfast rolls. There was simply no work at home. Some construction companies, which had been saddled with debts from unfinished developments and unpaid invoices, were hanging on grimly, desperate for whatever contract they could get. Now they could see the signs for an oasis in this desert. It was the €500 million water metering contract. There was enough work in this project to keep 1,400 construction workers going at full tilt for three-and-a-half years.

Bord Gáis could have offered the entire contract to one single firm. But it believed this was too risky because it would be left in the lurch if the contractor went bust or underperformed. The work was therefore divided into eight separate lots. Construction companies could bid for as many as they wanted, but four was the maximum they could win.

The big winner was J. Murphy & Sons. Its founder, John Murphy, left Caherciveen in Kerry as an 'illiterate, penniless teenager' in the 1930s and built up a construction empire in Britain.[2] His company's green vans became famous in Britain during the post-war era. J. Murphy & Sons won four of the eight regional water metering contracts. It would be installing 120,000 meters in Dublin County, 130,000 meters in the West of Ireland, 162,000 meters in the South West and 113,000 meters in the South East. The total fee for J. Murphy & Sons was €215 million.[3]

The next firm selected was a joint venture between GMC Utilities Group (sixty per cent ownership) and Sierra Support Services Group (forty per cent ownership), which won the contracts for 195,000 meters in Dublin

City, 100,000 meters in the North West region and 117,000 meters in the Midlands. This was worth €165 million.

The third and final consortium selected to install the water meters was made up of Irish building firm Coffeys and the English water company Northumbrian Water. It got the contract for 118,000 meters in the North East region, which was worth almost €60 million.

The cheapest cost of meter installation was in the South West region, where J. Murphy & Sons were getting €355 per meter, and Dublin City, where GMC/Sierra were getting €359 per meter. But the same companies were going to get paid a much higher price in other regions. For example, €491 per meter installed in the Midlands for GMC/Sierra and €490 per meter installed in Dublin County for J. Murphy & Sons. Bord Gáis said this was due to a different mix of bidders competing in each region and also due to the different surfaces in each region. It was easier to install water meters in grass verges outside houses than in concrete footpaths.

The board of Bord Gáis approved the awarding of the metering contracts at its meeting in June 2013. The budget was just shy of €500 million. However, the final decision had to be made by the government. After this, there would be no turning back.

The government asked its semi-state watchdog, NewERA, to carry out an independent assessment of the domestic metering project. The main justification for the water metering was the flawed cost–benefit analysis on water metering which had been criticised by Bord Gáis.

Now the Department of the Environment was having to revise the cost–benefit analysis because the price of the water metering contracts was going up from its original estimate of €464 million to €500 million. It still found that there was a favourable cost–benefit ratio. (The original cost–benefit analysis had put it at 1:1.51, so for every €1 spent on meters there would be benefits of €1.51. The revised cost–benefit analysis came out at 1:1.38.)

There had been another change that the department failed to account for in the new cost–benefit analysis. Value Added Tax (VAT) was being charged at 13.5 per cent on electricity and gas bills and the department had expected that it would be applied to water bills as well. But at some point in summer 2013, Minister for Finance Michael Noonan decided that there would be no VAT on water charges. No explanation was documented, but it is likely Noonan was moving to avoid an even bigger backlash against water charges. Households would not relish being taxed three times for water – through their income tax, their water charges and the VAT on those charges.

Noonan's decision to rule out VAT on water charges had a knock-on effect on the cost of the water metering contract. Under the VAT rules, you can only get VAT back from the Revenue if you are charging it on your own services. Now Irish Water would not be charging customers 13.5 per cent VAT on their water bills, a tax they already had to pay on electricity and gas bills. This meant it would not be able to claim back the €74 million in VAT on the fees it was paying to the water meter contractors and the project managers. As a result, the cost of water metering jumped from €500 million to €574 million.

Bord Gáis brought in accountancy firm KPMG to examine whether the metering tendering process had been carried out properly. It had been the auditor for AIB during the era of boom-time lending, earning almost €50 million in fees between 2002 and 2009.[4] Its report gave the all clear to the tendering process. 'We are able to confirm that all stages of the Metering Services and Works procurement process performed to date are considered compliant with no material issues outstanding,' it said.[5]

But then there was a big setback. J. Murphy & Sons pulled out of two of the four metering contracts it had won. An official briefing report said the company had 'advised Bord Gáis Éireann of concerns on the cost model used in their tenders and as a result withdrew their tenders for all but two of the contracts'. J. Murphy & Sons gave up the contracts it had won for Dublin County and the South East, which were worth a combined €110 million. It held onto its metering contracts for the South West and the West.[6]

An official in the Department of the Environment sent an email to another civil servant in the Department of Public Expenditure in July 2013 to explain that the metering contracts had been delayed. 'Just to let you know that there was a bit of a problem with contract awards which has delayed the consent process,' he wrote.[7]

There was now a big call to make due to the pull-out of J. Murphy & Sons from two of the metering contracts. Would the contracts have to be put out to tender again? That would delay the metering programme.

Bord Gáis and Irish Water – with the backing of the government – decided to give the contracts to the next highest-placed bidders in the tender process.

Therefore, the contract for the South East went to GMC/Sierra, which had already won water metering contracts in three other regions. The contract for Dublin County went to Farrans Construction. The two new metering contracts cost €39 million more because these bids had been more expensive than those previously submitted by J. Murphy & Sons. The metering project cost was now up from €574 million to €613 million. 'The total estimated aggregate value of the eight contracts has increased to €613 million including VAT, an increase of €39 million, primarily due to the prices tendered in the two new winning tenders [being] higher than the prices that had initially been tendered by Murphy,' said the official briefing report.[8]

The board of Bord Gáis approved the awarding of the revised metering contracts at its meeting on 23 July 2013. The Irish Water board was briefed about the situation at its first meeting a month later. Six of the contracts were about to be signed 'in order to avoid delays in the first meter installations' and the final two reallocated contracts would follow quickly. 'It was noted by the Board that the remaining two contracts are expected to be executed by 9 August 2013,' the minutes stated.[9]

The last thing the government would have wanted was to see newspaper headlines about a €39 million increase in the water metering project from the changeover of contractors and a further €74 million increase due to Noonan's VAT decision. But somehow, it never leaked out.

21

METER RUSH

There is something in the Irish psyche that loves to be able to boast about being 'better than the Brits'. Some would put it down to being under British rule for 800 years. This sentiment reared its head during the metering programme. The proud boast among Irish Water executives and government ministers was that their metering programme would be installing more meters per month than British water companies did in a year. It was described internally as an 'aggressive timeline'. Irish Water's managing director, John Tierney, said it was 'one of the most ambitious programmes ever seen internationally' with a target of installing 27,000 meters a month.[1]

Phil Hogan told his cabinet colleagues in October 2012 that only thirty-nine per cent of homes in England and Wales were metered. In Ireland, the plan was to meter every household in the country on a public water supply, even though the British water companies had never tried this. The government had promised that it would have meters in one million homes by December 2014, before later pushing back that target to December 2016.[2] The metering strategy was to hit the cities and towns first, due to the need for speed. 'In order to maximise the numbers of boundary boxes installed in the first years of the programme, installations countrywide will be focussed in the built-up areas, i.e. cities, towns and villages, where higher concentrations of houses served by public water supplies are found,' Hogan said in his cabinet memo.[3]

Normally, digging up public pavements would require a road opening licence from the local council. But to speed up the metering, the government gave Irish Water and its contractors an exemption from this in the new water services legislation. Irish Water decided to voluntarily apply for road opening licences in only one council, Dublin City Council, because there were so many underground pipes and traffic hazards in its area.

The metering plans were put together in Irish Water's temporary office on Foley Street in Dublin, which was previously used by Bord Gáis. There were ultimately 100 staff working on the metering programme, which was one in every seven people employed by Irish Water. By now, the data from the council surveyors was flooding in, with names and address of houses, and photos and GPS coordinates of the locations to meter outside their property boundary. There was a dedicated conference room in the Foley Street office for the meter project with posters on the wall showing phases one, two, three and four of the metering programme. Those who were brought in to see it described it as an extraordinary sight.

The metering staff were using programmes like Maximo and Small World to draw electronic polygons around the homes to be metered. The job lots would be sent to Irish Water's three appointed contractors, with 5,000 homes identified in each batch. The staff in Irish Water's regional teams would then work with the contractors on which locations to meter first. 'You'd always do a better-class area first. That was so the local authority estate wasn't being victimised. If you did the poorer area, they'd say you're picking on us and you're not doing them,' said an Irish Water source.

The plan was usually to do the council estates in the middle of the metering programme for a town or urban area. Irish Water was concerned that the residents there might have time to organise resistance if they were left till last. 'If it was the last part of a town, we thought they might put up a fight,' said the Irish Water source.

The Irish Water policy was to send a leaflet through the post to households to alert them of the meter installation two weeks in advance. The water supply had to be shut off while a meter was being installed. Households were promised that there would be minimal inconvenience because the meter would be installed under the footpath outside the property. Irish Water had its own engineers checking the quality of the work being done by contractors. This was due to some poor-quality work when water meters were being installed for businesses over the previous decade.[4]

***

The biggest force of meter installers in Irish history was about to fan out across the country. They had trucks, mini-diggers and consaws. The first batch of meters went into Kildare in August 2013 without incident. Irish Water bussed journalists to a mystery destination to mark the occasion. It turned out to be the Rockfield Grove estate in Maynooth. The *Irish Independent* said it had the 'dubious honour' of being the first place to have the meters installed.[5]

The meter installers wore yellow high-vis jackets and white helmets (often with the Irish Water logo on them). They would cut a square in the pavement with their consaw. Then they got the mini-digger to break it open. Then they cut the water pipe to a house and inserted a meter box with a meter inside. There was a white ring installed at the bottom, which allowed the water to flow through to the home. The meter had a radio transmitter installed, which allowed it to be read automatically by Irish Water staff driving by in a van. Irish Water had worked out that just nine people would be enough to read every single meter installed during each three-month billing period.

Once the meter was in, the contractors filled up the hole around it with stone chips. They had a plate compactor, which looked like a floating lawnmower, to push down the stone chips. Then the meter installers would finish off the job by going down on their hands and knees with trowels to plaster concrete on top of the compacted chips. They had to leave a smooth concrete finish around the meter box. And it had to be level with the footpath so that it would not become a trip hazard for people.

After the first meters went into Maynooth, the next roll-out was in Leixlip and Celbridge, followed by Tralee, Navan, Wexford town, Fingal, Castlebar and Limerick. The Irish Water metering staff were holding a meeting every week to assess if the metering was on target. They used traffic light updates: 'red, amber or green'.

Much of the initial media coverage focused on the 1,600 jobs that the metering programme was going to create for the 160,000 construction workers who had lost their jobs during the property crash. In Kerry, J. Murphy & Sons cleverly hired in local labour to install the meters. After all, it was hard to mount a protest against Johnny from down the road who had been out of work since the building crash. 'The jobs were huge in rural areas like that. They were well paid but it was hard manual work,' said an Irish Water staffer who was in the region.

In Dublin, there were no objections from the residents in the 'two-storey, over-basement' houses in affluent parts of Dublin. That did not mean that they liked it. One resident put it like this: 'It's a boring middle-class attitude –

obey the law.' Meters were also put into Finglas, which had a large number of working-class estates, without any protests either.

Socialist Party TD Joe Higgins turned up with Paul Murphy MEP and a local councillor, Ruth Coppinger, to block the installation of water meters in a private estate in Clonee in Dublin West in November 2013. Irish Water had one of its communications staff on the ground in the form of Pádraig Slyne, a fluent Irish speaker from Galway. He had worked as a special adviser in the Department of the Taoiseach during the Ahern and Cowen eras and was very familiar with Higgins. He told Joe in Irish that he did not want any *triblóid* (trouble). Higgins and his fellow Socialists eventually withdrew and the meters were put in. Socialist Party Councillor Mick Murphy said there had been 'no real spontaneous reaction' from the locals to the anti-meter protest. 'It was as if there was no real mood at that moment,' he said.[6]

In counties like Carlow, Kilkenny and Wexford, it was a 'doddle', according to an Irish Water staffer who worked on the programme. 'The meters were phenomenally successful. They were never done like that anywhere in the world,' he said.

John Tierney told the Irish Water board at the start of January 2014 that around 79,000 meters had been installed, a rate of around 16,000 meters per month. 'The expected output is anticipated to average 27,000 meters per month in 2014. Irish Water continues to install more meters in a week than UK utilities install in a month,' he said.[7]

Increasing signs of resistance were beginning to show, however. There were some problems with the surveying of the locations for water meters in the North West region. Tierney told the board that the number of surveys done there was 'well behind those in the rest of the country'. Up until the end of 2013, there had been 'zero refusals' that resulted in meters not being installed. But Tierney said there had now been an increase in the 'number of groups of organised resistance within each region' and 'the number of customer refusals has increased as a result'.

And there was the fact that Irish Water was already behind target. As Tierney mentioned to the board, Irish Water had managed to get in 79,000 meters by the start of 2014. But the government's wildly ambitious official target had been to get 160,000 meters installed by then. Fianna Fáil leader Micheál Martin was already being told by contacts in Bord Gáis that the targets they had been given were 'hopelessly unrealistic'. 'You always get this conflict when officials can't deliver in practical terms against the political commitments that are made,' he said.[8]

Even at this early stage, the metering programme was behind schedule. And Irish Water was starting to get an insight into just how bad the state of the water service was under thirty-four different councils.

22

A NEGLECTED WATER SERVICE

The councils running the water service had committed staff who had a great knowledge of the supply and a loyalty to their local area. For many years, the water caretakers were among the few public servants with their home numbers in the phone book, so they could be contacted about water outages day or night. But there were major problems. There was a good example of this on the border of Carlow and Laois.

Carlow town had its own public water supply for its population of 15,000 people. It also supplied water to the 4,000 people in the neighbouring town of Graiguecullen in Co. Laois, located on the other side of the River Barrow. But the Carlow town supply was hit by a cryptosporidium outbreak in 2005 because it did not have the necessary ultraviolet treatment to kill the bug. Around thirty people got the water-borne bug, which causes diarrhoea and can be fatal for some people.

After this incident, Laois County Council decided it needed to have its own supply of safe water for Graiguecullen, even though it was only separated from Carlow town by the river. It spent €2 million on its own water treatment plant, which opened in 2012. Irish Water engineer Sean Laffey said the water supply for the new plant was coming from a well. 'The pumps have to run 24/7 because the area is flat, so the water has to be pressurised the whole time. They didn't want to pay Carlow any more for the water,' he said.[1]

It was an astonishing waste of money, given that the Carlow water treatment plant was later upgraded to ensure that cryptosporidium could not happen. But this was the type of thing that happened when the water service was being managed by separate councils. To corroborate this point, a report carried out for the Commission for Energy Regulation found that it was costing twice as much to run the water service in Ireland as it was in similar-sized areas in England and Wales.

As well as putting the metering in place, one of Irish Water's first objectives was to close down the inefficient smaller water treatment plants. Many of them, like Graiguecullen, were getting their water from boreholes – holes drilled deep into the ground to access an underground spring or stream. These could often dry up or be polluted. One of the smallest water treatment plants in the country was located in Ballyverane, outside Macroom in Cork. It served just five people living in two houses beside the treatment plant. It was hugely expensive to have a council worker, known as a caretaker, looking after each of these small plants. Many of them did not even have the technology to produce safe water. Irish Water's plan was to reduce the 900 water treatment plants to around 300.

Another issue was that although there were lots of council water service workers who had a very good knowledge of the pipes and problems in their local area, many of them had been recruited as general operatives and did not have the technical skills to run modern water and wastewater treatment plants.

There were regular reports from the Environmental Protection Agency (EPA) about unsafe drinking water being produced from modern water treatment plants, even with all the required technology. Irish Water was appalled at the condition of some of them. 'We built water and wastewater treatment plants and handed them over to unskilled workers,' said an Irish Water source. The unions used to ask for the council workers to be trained up. But when one council tried this, the caretaker came back within a few days and asked to be moved to other duties. He found it too difficult. The councils responded by outsourcing the work to private firms. Eventually, they were paying over €100 million per year to private firms to design, build and operate the plants. Irish Water believed this scale of outsourcing would not be needed if there was more expertise available.

In England, Scotland and Wales, the old system of having councils provide the water services was being abandoned. The treatment plants were getting more complex and the European drinking water standards were going up. The British government set up big water companies to provide a more efficient service. In Ireland, it was left as the British had designed it a century earlier. 'The reason we did nothing is that the politicians liked going around giving out goodies,' said one water industry expert. 'Rather than an asset manager, you had a minister.'

Councils could only do so much because they had been starved of water infrastructure funding by central government for decades. Even when money was promised to repair pipes, the council had to endure what became known as the 'Thirty-Nine Steps'. This was the agonising process of getting approval from the civil servants in the water section of the Department of the Environment. The councils believed it was deliberately slow because the department did not really have the money. Councils could never be sure about when they were going to get any money again from the department to expand their wastewater treatment plants, so when they got a grant for a new one, the temptation was to build it as big as possible.

Wastewater treatment plants operate using bugs which digest the sewage. But if the plant is too big for a town and there is not enough sewage coming in, the bugs start to starve. They need to be fed extra molasses to survive, and the plant then needs extra electricity to operate. All of that wastes money that could be better spent elsewhere in the water service. Another aim of Irish Water was, therefore, to scale down many of the planned wastewater treatment plants to a smaller size. If they were being built too big, it was costing more money.

There were more than 800 wastewater treatment plants that had been built by developers to service the housing estates they were building in the Celtic Tiger boom. There were no specifications laid down for them to comply with. The natural temptation for developers was to build them at the lowest cost possible.

Irish Water executive Noel O'Keeffe did a tour of the country to see if these developer-provided wastewater treatment plants could be taken over by Irish Water. What he found was shocking. 'They were worse than useless. I came across one in Clare that was built in a bog by a developer. The first time he cleaned out the septic tanks, the water pressure popped the tanks out of the bog. It never worked after that,' he said.[2]

The Department of the Environment wanted Irish Water to take over the developers' wastewater treatment plants because they were becoming a major problem for the residents being served by them. O'Keeffe told them that Irish Water would do it only if it got the money to fix them. He was asked 'How much?'

'Somewhere between €200 million and €500 million,' he replied.[3]

***

The leakage of water from the aged pipe system was an even more urgent problem. Of the 1.7 billion litres of water being produced every day, around 600 million litres were being used by households and another 300 million litres by businesses, while around 765 million litres were leaking out of pipes.[4] Some councils had been better than others at tackling this forty-five per cent leakage rate. The four councils in Dublin had worked together to replace pipes out of necessity because the water supply for the capital was on a knife edge. But it would cost billions of euro to replace water pipes throughout the country, which were seventy-eight years old on average – twice the average age of water pipes in other European countries.

The councils had installed over 4,000 district meters at a cost of €130 million to track the leaks in local areas. Each covered a 'district' of around 1,500 people. But over the years, the water valves in the district meter areas had been opened up – for example, to get water for fighting a fire – and not been closed off again. As a result, it was now impossible to track the flow of water in the area; in other words, the district meters were effectively useless.

It transpired that around seventy-five per cent of the leaks were in Irish Water's own water distribution pipes, with the remaining twenty-five per cent in water pipes on people's property. It is relatively easy to find and fix leaks in the home. It is much harder to deal with leaks in the public pipes. There was little public understanding of this because the public had never been told.

Irish Water engineer Sean Laffey said there were four possible outcomes when leaks in the public pipes were fixed.[5] The first is that the increased pressure will cause a water burst further on down the line. 'Sometimes you crack pipes just by shutting them down, taking the water out of them and then refilling them and putting the pressure back up. They are so old and tired, they crack anyway,' said Laffey.

The second scenario is that fixing the leak increases the pressure in the rest of the pipe supplying a house. 'The result of that is when Mrs Murphy used to turn her tap on she gets eight litres a minute; now she's getting ten. So part of your saving is gone into better service for Mrs Murphy.' In other words, 'You don't see the saving back at the plant,' said Laffey.

The third scenario is that any saving in water from fixing the leak will be lost if there are other leaks further down the pipe. The higher water pressure will drive out more water there.

And the fourth scenario is the one that water engineers are hoping for. The leak is fixed, the use of water drops and money is saved.

The international experience is that a water company has to find three-to-four litres of leakage to save one litre back at the plant. Irish Water's target was to reduce leaks from the current forty-seven per cent level to twenty per cent. Beyond that level, it would cost more money to find leaks than they would save.

The councils were spending very little on fixing leaks. Their budget for repairs for their water and wastewater treatment plants was also tiny. The approach was to use it until it broke down. One Irish Water source estimated that the repairs budget for all the councils might have been as little as €10 million per year.

The councils had also slackened off on collecting water charges from businesses, who had always been paying for water. During the economic boom, the best the councils could manage was to get sixty-six per cent of businesses to pay their water bill. In response to this poor rate of paying, the councils installed 200,000 meters at business premises so they had to pay for what they used instead of getting a flat charge. That meant some business now had to pay more. By 2009, however, with the recession in full flow, only fifty-three per cent of businesses were paying their water bill. One county manager said councils were 'sympathetic and sensitive' to the plight of businesses in trouble during the recession. However, all this meant that before Irish Water even started collecting water charges from households, there was a non-payment culture in businesses.

Another issue facing Irish Water was that it had to take over responsibility not only for the water pipes, but also for the sewer network that transported people's urine and excrement to the wastewater treatment plants. However, due to poor record keeping, the councils did not know how long the sewers were. Irish Water eventually discovered that the sewer network was 32,000 kilometres long. Like the water pipes, the sewers, too, were old and leaking. Many sewers were part of combined systems that took in rainfall as well. So, when there was heavy rain, it mixed in with the sewage and often the wastewater treatment plants could not cope with the increased volume. As a result, the mix of sewage and rainfall had to be discharged straight into seas and rivers.

The councils were also pumping raw sewage from homes into rivers and seas. Under the Water Pollution Act introduced in 1977, factories could be prosecuted for releasing waste water into rivers and lakes. But councils were exempted from prosecution for the following thirty years. It was the European Commission that put a stop to this by taking Ireland to court for its failures to protect the water supply. That was how the EPA was finally given the power to inspect and licence council wastewater treatment plants in 2007.

Still, raw sewage was being pumped into the water in forty-four towns and villages as Irish Water was being set up in 2013. EPA Deputy Director Gerard O'Leary said one of them was the fishing village of Kilmore Quay in Wexford, where raw sewage was being pumped into the sea with a children's playground and beach beside it. 'You have a lot of kids swimming on one side of the pier and on the other side of the pier, the sewage is going out. We can't keep going this way,' he said.[6]

O'Leary pointed out that the state had been supposed to stop the discharge of raw sewage in large towns and villages under the EU's Urban Waste Water Treatment Directive in 1991. The deadline for sorting everything out was 2004. 'And we still have a considerable way to go,' he said.[7]

There were so many more problems. 180,000 homes were getting their drinking water from antiquated lead pipes, an issue which has been proven to reduce the IQ of children. Meter installers discovered four-foot lead pipes in Coolock and Clontarf in Dublin. These short pipes were connecting the public water main to the edge of a householder's property. They had to be cut in two to install the meter.

There were 600,000 people on public water supplies with potentially cancer-causing chemicals.[8] The councils had been putting chlorine in the water to kill off many of the water-borne bugs. But in rural areas, if chlorine mixes with peaty water, it forms trihalomethanes (THMs). Most people did not know about this because the councils had not told them.[9]

All over Europe, open reservoirs had been covered up to protect drinking water. But at the 150-year-old reservoir in Stillorgan in Dublin, council staff were using air guns and distressed bird calls to try to keep birds from fouling the water. It was supplying drinking water to 200,000 people in the capital.[10]

This was the system that Irish Water was inheriting. The estimated cost of bringing the water system up to international standards was a whopping €13 billion. At the current rate of spending on water infrastructure of €300 million per year, it would take forty years to fix.

Irish Water would have to work with the thirty-four councils who had been responsible for this water system. A key task was to get the cooperation of the 4,300 council water service workers who were represented by several strong trade unions. They were the people the government needed to keep the water system working while Irish Water was being set up. Ministers were terrified at the prospect of the workers going on strike, because they were the only ones who knew where the pipes were buried. The council workers were equally fearful of losing their jobs due to the establishment of Irish Water. It was going to make for difficult negotiations.

23

THE TWELVE-YEAR DEAL WITH THE UNIONS

Irish Water was a direct threat to the water service workers who were already running the system. They were protected against being fired by a series of public sector pay agreements. But the suggestion was that Irish Water would somehow reduce their numbers over time to cut costs. So the biggest fear for workers was 'Will I have a job?'

The council workers were heavily unionised and had experienced trade union negotiators to represent them. Trade union officials are often stereotyped as bearded fanatics wearing flat caps who shout and roar and thump the table during negotiations. But IMPACT trade union official Eamon Donnelly, originally from Finglas in Dublin, had no beard and during his fifteen years on the job he believed in what he termed 'nudge negotiations' – pushing gradually to get the desired outcome.[1] He had been drafted in at the last minute from the health sector because the regular negotiator had suffered a serious illness.

Donnelly worked according to the trade union playbook. He knew what he wanted and he knew the importance of telling management what his bottom line was. Donnelly said he was always prepared to strike if the council workers were not looked after. 'This wasn't the Boston Tea Party. This was difficult stuff,' he said. He also knew the importance of keeping the council workers onside. Before the talks even started, he went to meetings around the country telling his members: 'Yes you will have a job, and there will be no compulsory redundancies.' Under the Croke Park public sector agreement in 2010, the government guaranteed the security of public sector workers' jobs in return for a guarantee of industrial peace from their unions.

The unions were very wary about Bord Gáis being in charge of Irish Water. It had taken over the Dublin Gas Company when it collapsed in the 1980s. It had turned things around by shrinking down the number of Dublin Gas staff and outsourcing most of the work to private companies. By now, Bord

Gáis had around 900 staff of its own, but the majority of the work was done by 1,700 private contractors. The unions had members who had lived through the Bord Gáis takeover of Dublin Gas. The last thing they wanted was to see Bord Gáis use the same outsourcing tactic for Irish Water. 'It certainly wasn't going to be a model we would subscribe to,' said Donnelly.

The unions wasted no time in flexing their muscles. Phil Hogan said in a memo to cabinet that some of them had balloted for strike action 'if they are not adequately consulted on the transition of assets and workers' duties to Irish Water'. This would not only put the water supply in peril, it would also halt the surveying work being done by council staff to find the locations for the meters. 'If there are any delays on the surveying work, the meter installation programme will be delayed,' Hogan warned.[2]

Donnelly said he had to deal with loads of calls for strike action from the council workers he represented. 'Don't rule out the fact that those internal rows didn't take place because your biggest battle in any negotiation is keeping your own constituency onside. We had to do a lot of work in that regard,' he said.

Given the threat of disruption, unions were brought into the Department of the Environment in August 2012. The two most important were Donnelly's union, IMPACT, and SIPTU because they represented most of the 4,300 council water workers. But there were several others.

The decision was made to set up the 'Irish Water Consultative Group', so that the unions and the employers – the government, the councils and Irish Water – could thrash out an agreement about what to do. Kevin Foley, a noted industrial relations fixer, was the chair of the group.

It met in the headquarters of the Local Government Management Agency on Usher's Quay in Dublin. That location was chosen because it had a massive boardroom on the top floor which was big enough to fit all the union representatives, employers and civil servants at the same time. They would all sit around a square table with windows offering panoramic views of the Four Courts.

There were too many members in the group to negotiate with them all at the same time. So Foley set up sub-groups, who sorted out smaller issues in side rooms. They dealt with some of the main worries of the water workers. Will I still be driving my own van? Will I be based in the same depot or will they send me to the other end of the county?

Donnelly knew there was nothing that the unions could do to reverse the creation of Irish Water because that political decision had been 'nailed down'. 'We don't see ourselves as designing the political agenda in this country. We respond to it. We try to make sure that whatever changes come about [it's] in the way that's the least disadvantageous to the people we represent,' he said.

The government negotiated a series of deals so that council water workers would continue to provide services to Irish Water. These were known as 'service level agreements'. Critics later claimed that Irish Water should have been given the freedom to hire only the number of staff it actually needed. But Irish Water was installing meters, setting up billing systems and installing its own systems. It would not be able to cope with the complexity of having to hire thousands of council water service staff directly. 'We couldn't possibly have taken on the staff in 2014. We could not zap people across,' said an Irish Water source.

The service level agreements with the council workers took a year-and-a-half to thrash out. There were three key people in Irish Water who did the hard graft of negotiating with the county managers and the directors of water services in all thirty-four councils. They were Henry Smyth, Padraig Fleming and Noel O'Keeffe, a former Cork county engineer.

O'Keeffe had a reputation as a man who could get things done. Some of that was due to what he had achieved in the private sector. After graduating from UCC with a civil engineering degree, he worked with Imperial Chemical Industries, building a wastewater treatment plant in Tilbury in England in the early 1970s. He got a job in the Galway–Mayo Institute of Technology in 1993 and delivered a series of multi-million euro projects as the Cork county engineer from 2007 to 2012.

O'Keeffe had an understanding of how his job depended on keeping the politicians onside. He used to leave the door of his office open in Cork County Hall so that any councillor could drop in. And he attended every meeting of the council during his five-year term as county engineer. It was all about talking to the councillors and engaging with them. That was a lesson he learned from Cork County Manager Martin Riordan. Because he got on well with the councillors, he would always be tipped off by at least one of them if he was going to be ambushed at a council meeting. That gave him time to have his answers ready.

There was once a row in the village of Rathcormac in Cork about where a new pedestrian crossing should be located. One councillor wanted it near the school playground at one end of the village. Another councillor wanted it down at the community centre. Both were representing locals, who were split on the issue. O'Keeffe went to the village to mediate. He came up with a solution – he put it in the middle.

O'Keeffe and his team of Irish Water negotiators started holding meetings with county managers in June 2013 and kept going until the end of the year. The county managers agreed to keep providing water services for at least two years, under the direction of Irish Water. That was crucial because the water service would collapse without them. 'We met every local authority and outlined what the service level agreement was. They came back with a whole series of questions and we came back a second time and agreed it with them. There were a couple of round-up meetings with John Tierney,' said O'Keeffe.[3]

There were still problems to address, however. The government's original plan was to have Irish Water as a stand-alone company with all its own staff by 2017. Hogan told the cabinet in an October 2012 memo that the councils would work for Irish Water for a period with 'Irish Water taking over their operations on a phased basis from January 2015 with the full transfer of operations being completed by end 2017'.[4] Then Irish Water would directly employ whatever number of council water workers it actually needed. The idea was that this would lead to a cheaper water service – and potentially lower water bills for the public.

But the unions did not want their members going over to Irish Water by 2017. They feared a repeat of what had happened to maintenance workers in Aer Lingus. They had been transferred to a separate company called Team Aer Lingus, with 'letters of comfort' to declare that their jobs were safe. Team Aer Lingus was eventually privatised, however, and the jobs were ultimately lost. As a result, Eamon Donnelly and the other union negotiators for the council workers insisted on making the service level agreements with Irish Water last much longer than the government's 2017 target date. First they managed to get the agreement moved up to 2021. Then they looked to extend that again. The unions argued that the age profile of the council water service workers had to be taken into consideration. Up to half of them were aged over fifty. If they stayed working for another twelve years under the service level agreements with Irish Water, they would reach retirement age and the workforce would reduce naturally. 'We were doing our stuff and we were getting people as close to ten years as possible. The closer you get to an agreement, the more you have the opportunity to push it as far as you can. But nobody was being ripped off here,' said Donnelly.

To keep the unions onside, the government agreed to keep councils providing water services – under the supervision of Irish Water – for a whopping twelve years. That took them up to 2026. Donnelly said it was done gradually through 'nudge negotiations' rather than in one dramatic showdown. 'This is industrial relations, not Al Capone,' he said.

The government had already managed to pass the first Water Services Bill in March 2013 (it was such a complicated process that they needed two separate pieces of legislation, known as Water Services Bills One and Two). This first bill set up Irish Water on a temporary basis, gave it the power to install water meters and allowed it to start gathering the names and addresses of people for a customer database. But the unions wanted to ensure that the protection for council workers' jobs was rock solid. They lobbied hard to have the twelve-year service level agreements included in the second Water Services Bill, which would set up Irish Water on a full-time basis once passed. The government agreed to their demands.

Fianna Fáil's environment spokesman, Barry Cowen, said it had been easier for the unions to get what they wanted out of the negotiations than they expected. He had met privately with the unions before the talks. 'They were preparing for a battle on foot of what was coming down the tracks. They would have expected job losses. They put in what they wanted, and they couldn't believe it when it was accepted straight away,' he said.[5]

The twelve-year agreement between Irish Water and the councils provided industrial peace and a relatively smooth transition. The price was that people would have to pay water charges for a long time before they would get a more efficient water service.

John Mullins, a former Bord Gáis chief executive, believed that Irish Water's agreements with the councils should have been ended in 2017 rather than 2026. 'Regrettably, I never got to the position to make it stick to 2017. The intention here was to have a migration downwards in operating costs, that we would be using technology essentially to work smarter. That's the way all utilities work,' he said.[6]

Regardless of these concerns, the government had gotten the council workers onside. Now it needed to pass the legislation to bring in water charges.

24

THE DÁIL WALK OUT

Environment Minister Phil Hogan knew there would be media interest in the bill to pave the way for water charges. But he wanted to keep it quiet for now. A draft memo drawn up for Hogan in November 2013 on the second Water Services Bill explained his plan, under the heading 'Public Announcement': 'It is not the minister's intention to make a public announcement. However, it is proposed that the bill should be published immediately and that it should be initiated in Seanad Éireann at the earliest opportunity,' the memo said.[1]

Hogan had given the job of bringing the Irish Water legislation through the Seanad to Fergus O'Dowd, an experienced Fine Gael politician. His brother Niall had founded the *Irish Voice* newspaper in New York and was on good terms with former US President Bill Clinton.

Fergus O'Dowd grew up on a council estate in Drogheda and became a teacher. He joined the Labour Party, which had a strong base in what was a traditional industrial town, and ran unsuccessfully for the Dáil in the 1977 general election at the age of twenty-nine. But then O'Dowd became one of the few in his party to switch to Fine Gael. He made it into the Dáil in 2002. He was dogged in pursuing issues and had the ability to turn them into news stories, which is always a valuable skill for a politician. Enda Kenny sacked him from the Fine Gael front bench for backing Richard Bruton's failed heave against him in 2010. But Kenny decided to forget – if not forgive – O'Dowd by appointing him as a minister of state for NewERA. His key task was to set up Irish Water, which was in the NewERA plan that Fine Gael's chief economic adviser, Andrew McDowell, had come up with.

O'Dowd soon found that his influence on the actual set-up of Irish Water was very limited. He argued against the plan to meter one million households. He knew from growing up on a council estate that there would be 'war' over it. 'I was called to a meeting with Big Phil and his senior officials. At that meeting, it was me versus the lot. I said they should repair the network, fix the leaks. They said they were going ahead with the metering,' O'Dowd said.[2]

Despite his reservations, O'Dowd was given the job of bringing through the legislation to set up Irish Water.

The opposition was suspicious about why O'Dowd was becoming the frontman for an issue as important as water charges. Fianna Fáil leader Micheál Martin said it was the 'hapless minister of state, Deputy O'Dowd' who was always being sent out. 'Where is the [environment] minister, Deputy Hogan?' he asked during an early Leaders' Questions session.[3] Hogan had an excuse that time – he was in Denmark.

At this stage, Irish Water's office was crawling with private experts to make sure that a new state company was set up from scratch in just eighteen months. They were setting up the billing systems to start collecting water charges from 1.2 million households on the public water supply. And Irish Water wanted to take all the knowledge in the heads of the council water workers and store it in their new digital asset management systems. It hired hardware, software and programme management experts from all of the best-known international consultancy firms, including Accenture, IBM, KPMG and PwC. Their staff were paid an average of €600 per day, which would be equivalent to €3,000 for a five-day week.[4] John Mullins felt these hirings were necessary. He said the people hired were customising systems from an Irish point of view. 'They say, "Well, can you not just pull these out of a pack?" It doesn't work that way. Anyone who knows anything about the Garda Pulse system or other renowned systems in Ireland – you don't want things to have hiccups and failures.'[5]

The biggest beneficiary of the set-up spend was IBM, which got €44 million to establish Irish Water's household billing system, its asset management system and the IT system for the Irish Water customer contact centre that was to open in Cork. Next was Accenture, which got €17 million for programme management and developing Irish Water systems. Accounting firm Ernst & Young, the auditors who signed off on the accounts of Anglo Irish Bank before it was bailed out, were paid €4.6 million. One of the projects was on 'finance, governance and regulation'.[6] One Irish Water employee said that there were too many consultants who did not know what a water main or a sewer was. 'Irish Water was heavily weighted towards consultants and not enough people who knew how to dig up a street or fix a water main. You can't forget the guy on the ground. There were mountains of consultants there,' he said.

The opposition parties knew that Bord Gáis was racking up costs to establish Irish Water. Fianna Fáil's environment spokesman, Barry Cowen, put in a parliamentary question about the cost of the consultants who had been hired by Irish Water to date. Under the rules of the Dáil, the government is supposed to give full and complete replies to parliamentary questions. But the reply that came back was that the spending was 'an operational matter for Bord Gáis–Irish Water as these costs are not being funded from the Exchequer'.[7] The government was hiding the costs.

***

The passing of the second Water Services Bill was going to be difficult for the government. After all, it gave Irish Water the power to introduce water charges with a free allowance, and to cut the water supply of those who did not pay down to a trickle. To keep the unions happy, the twelve-year agreements between Irish Water and the councils were also made legally binding in the bill. But, most importantly, it would set up Irish Water on a permanent basis.

Phil Hogan told Fergus O'Dowd about the need for this bill 'to meet Troika target dates' during a meeting in the Custom House.[8] The Troika wanted the outline of the bill to be ready by June 2013. But the civil servants missed this deadline by a month. That worried Finance Minister Michael Noonan because the government needed to keep hitting its Troika targets to get out of the bailout deal by the end of the year. Noonan noted the 'slight delay' in producing the Water Services Bill in a memo to cabinet in July 2013: 'It is essential that such slippage is avoided, and that our strong programme performance is maintained,' he told fellow ministers.[9]

The next Troika deadline for O'Dowd to meet was to get the bill through the Dáil and Seanad by the end of 2013. The government was in a terrible rush, but it did not want to admit to the opposition that there was a second, bigger reason for meeting the end-of-year deadline. Irish Water was running out of cash. It was installing meters at a rate of 30,000 per month, but it also needed more money. Its €250 million loan from the National Pensions Reserve Fund was going to be all spent by January 2014.[10] No banks would loan Irish Water any money if it was not established in law. And Bord Gáis was not allowed to lend any more of its own money. So Irish Water had to be established on a legal basis by 1 January 2014 to be able to borrow money on its own behalf.

O'Dowd brought the second Water Services Bill into the Seanad in mid-December. He was annoyed to find that a section he had requested, which would rule out the privatisation of Irish Water, was missing from the bill. He complained to Hogan and it was later added back in. It was voted through the Seanad after a ten-hour debate.

Now the bill had to get through the Dáil with the Christmas deadline fast approaching. The government had a massive majority, so it could easily vote the bill through. But opposition TDs were determined to have a lengthy debate and to make it as difficult as possible for water charges to be brought in.

There was one weapon the government could use to get around this. It was the guillotine, the practice of halting all debate on a bill and voting the bill through immediately. The opposition hated it because it was the parliamentary equivalent of telling them to 'shut up'.

The bill arrived in the Dáil on 19 December 2013. Normally, it would take weeks for TDs to go through the four steps before passing a bill. There would be a second stage debate, votes on changes at committee stage and then more votes on last changes at the 'report and final stage'. The government wanted to get all these stages done and dusted in just five hours. Then it would bring down the guillotine. The opposition was outraged and walked out.[11]

Sinn Féin's environment spokesman, Brian Stanley, said it was a 'devastating day' because he had loads of questions to ask Hogan and O'Dowd about Irish Water. 'I was very clear that the stuff being given to ministers to read out was a load of bullshit. What they were getting from Irish Water and their own officials, a lot of it was half-cocked. Trying to justify the metering was bollocks,' he said.[12]

It was the first and only time that Fianna Fáil leader Micheál Martin, Sinn Féin president Gerry Adams, Socialist Party leader Joe Higgins, People Before Profit TD Richard Boyd Barrett and independent TDs walked out of the Dáil chamber in unison. Martin later recalled that the government TDs laughed at them as they made their way out in a 'quiet protest'. For him the use of the guillotine was a 'jackboot type of tactic'. 'I saw this as a political ruse by Fine Gael. They were concerned about the impact of this on their own backbenchers and Labour Party backbenchers. So they made the political calculation to ram this through,' he said.[13]

The government was storing up trouble for itself. It had denied the opposition TDs the opportunity to test the Water Services Bill for faults. There were lots of problems within the bill. Cutting people's water to a trickle was just one of them.

Martin said that the use of the guillotine ultimately backfired. 'In retrospect, the bill had a lot of holes in it and there wasn't proper scrutiny,' he said.

The government knew it had to get the Water Services Bill through to keep Irish Water afloat. In a sign of the urgency involved, President Michael D. Higgins signed it into law on 25 December 2013 – Christmas Day.

25

TURNING CITIZENS INTO CONSUMERS

The government knew that the third introduction of water charges was going to be difficult. They had generated resistance in the 1980s and 1990s, so communicating with the public was always going to be crucial.

Bord Gáis, the parent company overseeing the set-up of Irish Water, had flagged the need to get people to accept the principle of water charges before the installation of nearly one million meters. 'There can be no boots on the ground in advance of a comprehensive and honest communication and education exercise,' it said.[1]

There was also a warning from Siemens, the German firm who had built the Ardnacrusha hydro-electric dam for the newly established ESB in 1929. In its submission during the public consultation process on water charges, the company said there needed to be a clear communications plan. 'We suspect there will be continued resistance to water charges,' it said.[2] Even the Troika called for a communications campaign when they were briefed by Irish civil servants about the timeline for water charges.

A note of a meeting of senior officials in Government Buildings in September 2012 stated that the presentation to the Troika was very well received. 'They noted, in particular, the ambitious scale of the work involved and the critical need to communicate with the public and maximise public acceptance in the lead-in to the introduction of charges.'[3]

It was time to start talking to the public because the council surveyors were now outside their homes looking for locations for the water meters. Hogan had told the cabinet at a meeting in October 2012 that Bord Gáis would run a water reform communications campaign over the coming months. It would explain to people why the water reforms were being made and how important it was to have clean water and treated waste water 'for economy, jobs, environmental compliance and public health'.[4] This would be followed up by a more extensive communications campaign the following year to inform people about the introduction of water charges and the roll-out of water metering.

All of this was coming at a time when the government was slashing spending on repairing pipes and building new wastewater treatment plants. The government had a budget hole of €13.5 billion that year, which it was covering with borrowed money from the Troika. It decided to reduce the deficit by cutting spending on infrastructure because it was much less politically and socially painful than cutting social welfare rates or increasing income tax. The result was that the water services infrastructure budget went down from €371 million in 2012 to €296 million in 2014. That was far below the minimum figure of €600 million which Irish Water said was necessary.

By the time the cabinet met again in December 2012 to discuss the legislation needed to set up Irish Water, there was still no sign of a communications campaign by Bord Gáis about water metering or water charges. Minister for Agriculture Simon Coveney expressed concern about how the public would react to the prospect of paying water charges on top of the new property tax due for 2013. 'The Minister for Agriculture, Food and Marine … notes the complexities around communicating the introduction of water charges particularly in the context of the recent Budget and the introduction of the property tax,' the cabinet memo said. Hogan agreed that 'the communication surrounding the introduction of water charges will need to be carefully managed'.[5]

Bord Gáis carried out research around this time into what potential water 'customers' thought. It found that there was a 'lack of understanding' about water quality and the cost of producing clean water; that people supported water metering 'as it gives them an opportunity to control consumption and manage costs'; and that the public wanted 'clear, simple and honest communication'. 'Water charges are seen as inevitable and are likely to be more acceptable if perceived to be fair and equitable,' the research concluded.[6]

Bord Gáis sent out a seven-page booklet in Irish and English to two million homes in February 2013 to explain about the setting up of Irish Water, the installation of meters and the introduction of water charges. 'It is important to note that although meter installation to measure water usage will commence in 2013, no household on the public water system will be asked to pay water charges before 2014,' the leaflet said.[7]

For the first eight months of 2013, that was it. There were brainstorming meetings going on in Bord Gáis's offices at 1 Warrington Place, overlooking the Grand Canal in Dublin. They involved a mixture of communications staff from Bord Gáis. Irish Water had Elizabeth Arnett, its head of communications and corporate services, as well as staff from its 'customer experience' team. The campaign they settled on was one to promote the 'value of water' and then to follow up with another one in early 2014 about the need to pay water charges. Arnett later told the *Irish Examiner* that consumers were more likely to accept the concept of paying water bills once they had a better understanding of how water was sourced and delivered to their homes. 'Our core message is "value water",' she said.[8]

Irish Water believed that households would be able to cut back on their water use. The estimated use was 150 litres per person per day, which was high by international standards. Arnett said there were many opportunities for people 'to reduce water wastage'. The suggestions from Irish Water included reducing showers by one minute and turning off the tap when brushing your teeth.[9]

A beautifully filmed €600,000 television ad was developed showing water flowing down off the mountains to the swirling soundtrack of 'The Arrival of the Birds' by the British electronic group The Cinematic Orchestra.[10] The voiceover mentioned how the water system had been built up 'through our knowledge, hands and hard work'. That was a reference to council water service workers who were already running it, a tribute to keep them onside. 'There was a huge debate over that,' said an Irish Water source. The ad went on to show a water meter being installed. 'We need to change the way we pay for our water supply and wastewater treatment,' it said.

The TV ad was aired in September, October and November 2013 at a cost of €275,000. It was placed in the middle of programmes with the highest viewership like *Coronation Street* and *Emmerdale* on TV3, and RTÉ's *Six One* and *Nine O'Clock News* bulletins. The ad had to be taken off air for a few days in November 2013 when the water treatment plant featured in it – Ballymore Eustace in Kildare – had to suspend water production. That left Dublin city centre without water for three days, at a time when Paddy Cosgrave's Web Summit (a major international technology conference) was on. But one TV ad was not going to suddenly inform the public about the state of the water system or convince them to pay water charges.

Assistant Secretary Maria Graham, who by now had taken over as head of the water section in the Department of the Environment, said the insiders understood the need for Irish Water to be set up. But she acknowledged that the public did not. 'To some extent we set out to fix a problem that the general public didn't appreciate that we had,' she said.[11]

26

THE FATEFUL INTERVIEW

It was a very slow news day on 9 January 2014 until Irish Water Managing Director John Tierney agreed to go into the RTÉ studio in Donnybrook for an interview on the *Today with Seán O'Rourke* show on Radio 1. The programme's production team had been chasing this interview for some time. Water charges were due to be introduced later in the year. It was another part of the price of paying for the economic crash. Yet the public knew nothing about Irish Water and its plans.

O'Rourke knew that an interview with Tierney had the potential to set the news agenda because there was huge public interest in water charges. 'It was affecting every household in the country. He was the man in charge of making things happen. He was an important get,' he said.[1]

This was going to be a tricky encounter for Tierney. O'Rourke was both feared and respected by those who went into his studio because of his ability to latch onto an issue and pursue it until he got a straight answer. Having started with the *Connacht Tribune* newspaper in 1973, he went to *The Irish Press* and *The Sunday Press* before joining RTÉ in 1989. He had honed his interviewing techniques on all of the national station's flagship radio programmes – *Morning Ireland*, *This Week*, *The News at One* – as well as on TV – *Today Tonight*, *Prime Time* and *The Week in Politics*. He had clocked up well over 20,000 interviews during his journalism career and had set two basic principles for every interview. He did his research so that he had good questions to ask. And then he listened intently to what his subject was saying, so that he could come in with what he called the 'supplementary questions'.

'They can lead you in a more interesting direction than you were prepared to go. You think: "Am I being told something here?"' he said.

O'Rourke began his mid-morning show with a discussion on judges' pay before moving to an ad break. When the red light went on to show that the live broadcast had resumed, it was John Tierney's turn. He had officially taken control of the water system just six days earlier, on 1 January, when Irish Water legally came into existence.

O'Rourke began his introduction. 'With water charges due to be introduced later this year and the first bills issuing from January 2015, my next guest has to make palatable much more than the taste of the water being supplied,' he said.[2] Tierney was sitting on one side of a curved desk, which was just big enough to have one microphone pointing at him and another microphone pointing in the other direction at O'Rourke. There was one window to let in some natural light, but given that this was a studio within a studio, it was always slightly dark inside. For those who were not regular guests on the show, it could be a claustrophobic experience.

The interview began smoothly for Tierney. He was talking about things like service level agreements with the councils, which would have made no sense to the show's 300,000 listeners. He was using phrases like 'economy of scale' and 'asset management' and the 'regulated utility model'.

Then O'Rourke came in with his first tough question. He asked why some ex-county managers had been hired to manage Irish Water. Tierney, as a former county manager himself, was able to deal with that one. 'I've stood in the trenches with those people in very difficult times of water shortages, some very difficult times. There's some tremendous people working in this area. Of course you would start off with that experience,' he said.

There had been newspaper articles about the fact that two employees of the RPS company, the country's largest engineering and environmental consultancy firm, had been hired to work with Irish Water. O'Rourke described how the European Commission had criticised the €24 million in fees paid to RPS for its work on the Poolbeg incinerator in Dublin. He asked Tierney if it was 'a bit too insiderish' to be hiring two people from RPS. Tierney knew who he was referring to. One was Irish Water's head of asset management, Jerry Grant, who was known as one of the best water engineers in the country. The other was Irish Water's head of communications, Elizabeth Arnett, who had accompanied him to RTÉ for the interview. They got on well with Tierney and were loyal members of his team. Tierney batted off the question, saying that both of them had been hired through an 'open recruitment' process.

Then came the decisive moment, eight minutes into the interview. 'What kind of money are you spending on consultants or what have you spent so far?' asked O'Rourke. Tierney talked about how Irish Water had to set up from scratch in less than a year with no buildings, no people and no processes. O'Rourke was listening and knew he had not got an answer on the cost of the consultants. He came back at Tierney with his supplementary question. 'How much?'

'To date we have spent approximately €100 million on establishment, and over fifty per cent of that would be on consultancy,' Tierney said.

The word 'consultant' was used regularly in the local authority sector, where Tierney had spent all his career. Anybody who was not on the public payroll was a 'consultant', whether they were an engineer, IT expert, public relations person and so on. But when the public heard the word, it created an image of someone sitting in an office thinking of ideas and charging thousands of euro for it. It stood for wasteful spending.

The interview continued on for another fourteen minutes. O'Rourke asked Tierney about the potential cost of the water charges, the wages for Irish Water staff and what would happen to people who didn't pay. O'Rourke wrapped up the interview by thanking Tierney for coming into the studio. 'I hope you'll be back. I suspect we'll be inviting you at least,' he said.

O'Rourke did not anticipate much of a reaction to Tierney's comments. 'It didn't strike me at the time as being overly remarkable. But people were after taking the pain of tax impositions and pay cuts,' he said.[3] However, in the words of one Irish Water official, 'all hell broke loose' after the interview.

The media seized on the 'consultants' issue. Irish Water tried to explain that these were engineers, IT workers, metering experts and programme managers, all of whom were needed to set up the company in such a short space of time. But all the public could hear was 'consultants' and 'millions'. One minister who was in cabinet at the time said it was a 'disaster'. O'Rourke believed afterwards that if Tierney had explained what the consultants were doing, it might have been different. 'But it came across as money being spent on people coming in with sharp suits and well-polished shoes telling them what to do,' he said.

Fianna Fáil's environment spokesman, Barry Cowen, was one of the TDs who had repeatedly asked how much was being spent on consultants to set up Irish Water as fast as possible. He had been stonewalled. He was not happy when he heard Tierney's interview. 'For fuck's sake. Why couldn't they tell us that?' he said.[4] The government had been able to hide the details of the €180 million spend on the set-up costs of Irish Water on consultants because it came from the €450 million loan from the state's National Pensions Reserve Fund. Fianna Fáil leader Micheál Martin said it did not get the same scrutiny as money spent from a government department's budget. 'It's a pot of money. You had free reign to spend it,' he said.[5]

When Tierney did his interview, there were about 500 people working for Irish Water. Around half had come over from Bord Gáis or the councils, but there were also many college graduates. These were the chosen few of an astonishing 28,000 who had applied to work in Irish Water. 'We have some world experts. We got the cream of the crop because we were recruiting during the recession,' said one Irish Water manager.

The atmosphere at the start in Irish Water was great because most of the staff firmly believed in what they were doing. There was a real 'go-go attitude in the place' and people wanted to prove themselves, according to one Irish Water employee. The backlash after Tierney's interview did have an impact on staff morale. 'The sense of shock and disappointment was palpable,' said an Irish Water source.

There are two main conspiracy theories about Tierney's performance during that interview. The first is that O'Rourke had been tipped off in advance by a disgruntled Irish Water insider about the spend on consultants. Discussing that theory is territory that O'Rourke refused to enter into. Any journalists worth their salt do not talk about that kind of stuff. The other conspiracy theory is that Tierney deliberately talked about millions being spent on 'consultancy' to embarrass Bord Gáis. It was Bord Gáis who had planned and approved the use of consultants to set up Irish Water. But, at this stage, Tierney had been in charge for a full year and had overseen much of the spending himself. His supporters insist that he was not trying to shift the blame elsewhere. 'He would never say "this happened before I got here". He was not going to throw anybody else under the bus,' said one Irish Water staff member who worked with Tierney at the time.

A more experienced media performer might have dodged the bullet or explained it away more convincingly. But Tierney was a public servant rather than a politician. When he was later asked at a Dáil committee why he had answered in that way, his response was straightforward. 'The simple answer is that I was asked a question and provided the answer,' he said.[6]

Tierney's first in-depth media interview turned out to be his last. His future media appearances would be much more curtailed. 'John was wounded after Seán O'Rourke. He had lost the politicians at that stage. Irish Water didn't understand they were completely under the control of the politicians,' said an Irish Water source.

When Tierney appeared before a large number of TDs at the Oireachtas environment committee a few days after the Seán O'Rourke interview, the lack of relationship building was obvious. Barry Cowen and Sinn Féin's environment spokesman, Brian Stanley, complained that they had been asking questions about the set-up costs of Irish Water for two years but had not got answers. 'When things blew up, Irish Water had no friends politically,' said an Irish Water source.

Tierney performed relatively well at both committee sessions, which lasted for up to eight hours. At the next meeting of the Irish Water board, in February 2014, he told the directors that the company had come under 'intense media scrutiny' and 'intense political attention'. 'The focus for communications is now to rebuild confidence in Irish Water,' he said.[7]

It was clear that, even before water charges were introduced, Irish Water was already off to a bad start.

27

SON OF GARRET VERSUS BIG PHIL

Bord Gáis made a big mistake after John Tierney's interview with Seán O'Rourke. It decided to keep its head down. That might have worked thirty years earlier when there were only a handful of daily newspapers, much of the population were stuck in 'two channel land' and the Internet did not exist. Now Irish Water was dominating the news agenda, which was working on a twenty-four-hour basis, with the public able to voice their own opinions via Facebook, Twitter and YouTube. The story had an added potency because it was clear that water charges were going to be introduced before the end of the year.

The debate raged over January, February, March and April 2014. Bord Gáis, as the parent company of Irish Water, decided to stay out of it. This stance was deeply embedded in the company's culture. Until the arrival of John Mullins, the company rarely answered questions about anything. There was not a culture of engagement. The phrase being used internally at senior management level in Bord Gáis during these four months of public silence was 'get on a rock and stay on a rock'. There were people in the company who did not agree. 'We're not on a rock, we're on a pebble and the tide is coming in,' said one senior official at the time.

Even though Irish Water was fully set up, Bord Gáis still had ultimate control of communications, but it maintained the vow of silence. Requests to Irish Water for interviews with Tierney were turned down. Hundreds of media queries went unanswered. 'By the time Irish Water started talking, it was absolute carnage,' said an Irish Water source.

Irish Water and Bord Gáis had run the value of water ads at a time when few people were aware of water charges. Now the campaign had to convince people to pay them. This involved turning 'citizens' into 'customers'. The plan had been drawn up during those brainstorming sessions between the Irish

Water and Bord Gáis communications teams and marketing departments. Irish Water's head of communications, Elizabeth Arnett, gave a presentation to councillors about the company's plan to 'change how people think and act in relation to water'. Arnett described how people would start off thinking 'water is free', then would realise that 'water costs money'. 'Citizens need to understand that they are consumers' and 'Consumers need to appreciate that they are customers', she said in her presentation.[1] Irish Water needed to convince citizens to pay their water bills. It also had to convince them that Irish Water was not a new 'super quango' with no rationalisation of staff.

One of the country's most respected economists started asking awkward questions. John FitzGerald was the son of former Taoiseach Garret FitzGerald. Despite his family background, he was known for calling things as he saw them, regardless of the political parties involved. He had worked with the state's ESRI for more than thirty years. He fitted the image of a lifelong academic with his beard and spectacles and a solemn delivery. His concern was that Irish Water had agreed to keep employing 4,300 council water service workers for at least twelve years when he believed that the job could be done with just 1,700 workers. He warned that this could cost Irish Water an extra €2 billion over the twelve years. It would be families who would have to pay for it through higher water charges. The *Irish Independent* did the maths – it would add around €90 a year to water bills.[2]

FitzGerald's intervention was doubly damaging for Irish Water and the government. It infuriated the unions that they had worked so hard to pacify. And it alarmed the public, who were already starting to have doubts about the notion of paying for water. Comparisons were drawn between Irish Water and the creation of the Health Service Executive (HSE). When it was set up, the aim was to draw together eleven local health boards into one national health service. But every health board worker was guaranteed they could stay working where they were, as part of a deal between the government and the public sector unions.

FitzGerald said that he believed Irish Water should have been allowed to hire the number of council water service staff it actually needed. 'Then the government didn't allow them to do it. They just put all the costs in there and said, "We're going to hand you over a major problem and allow you to deal with it." A hospital pass doesn't describe it,' he said.[3]

FitzGerald had kicked off a debate about the cost of Irish Water at a very sensitive time. The unions wanted Irish Water to maintain their members' public sector jobs. FitzGerald was instead suggesting that Irish Water slim down its staff numbers and outsource much of the work to the private sector to save money. 'Irish Water should have been set up as a clean, lean organisation, which could have contracted with the local authorities, which said, "We'll pay you if you can dig holes cheaper than the private sector can,"' he said.

His comments were informed by his experience doing a review of Northern Ireland Water. It had also been 'dumped' with lots of excess staff from the councils in Northern Ireland. FitzGerald and other members of the independent review team recommended using private contractors instead to provide much of the water service at a cheaper price. But the politicians in the Northern Ireland Assembly rejected this. FitzGerald said that had left 'costs in the system'.

Phil Hogan let fly when he was questioned about FitzGerald's comments regarding the set-up of Irish Water. He told the *Irish Independent* that Fitz-Gerald had failed to back up his claim that 4,300 local authority staff working in water services could be reduced to 1,700 in a few years. 'Making wild assertions of this nature is irresponsible, in particular by an economist,' he said.[4]

FitzGerald was used to dealing with flak from ministers in his career with the ESRI. He and his colleagues had been branded 'left-wing pinkos' by a previous finance minister, Charlie McCreevy, for warning that the Irish economy was overheating in the early 2000s. In his experience, ministers and civil servants would listen to ESRI research one-third of the time and about two-thirds not. He was not surprised by the criticism. He believed that the Department of the Environment had chosen to lump Irish Water with all the council water service staff for twelve years to avoid the hassle of having to redeploy them elsewhere. 'The Department of Environment had made a bad mistake. The department were looking over their shoulder at the local authorities rather than at what would deliver efficiency. Phil Hogan was looking at political issues,' he said.

Hogan now had the big unions and the county managers onside for the establishment of Irish Water. But he was about to find out that Fine Gael's coalition partner, Labour, had lost faith in water charges – and wanted to stop them.

28

LABOUR PAINS

Tánaiste Eamon Gilmore was a reserved individual who normally kept his emotions in check. But he could not contain his delight at the exit of the country from the bailout in mid-December 2013. He gave a speech at the Institute of International and European Affairs think tank on North Georges Street in north inner city Dublin about how it was 'a moment that many believed would never happen'. 'As we exit the bailout, and set out on the next stage of recovery and renewal, we can do so with confidence,' he said.[1] Gilmore told reporters afterwards that his only regret at the moment was that Ireland had narrowly failed to beat the All Blacks for the first time at the Aviva Stadium a few weeks earlier.

But Gilmore was worried about the Irish Water project after the briefing he had gotten at Irish Water's headquarters in Talbot Street. Gilmore had expected to be told that the metering would be largely done by the time water charges were introduced. That was what Hogan had promised in the Dáil in 2012. 'There will be no up-front charges for meters and their installation, no charge for water until metering is rolled out nationally, and no earlier than 2014,' he had said.[2]

But Gilmore was now being told that only forty per cent of households would be metered by the end of 2014 when charges were due to come in. 'I was taken aback at how little metering had been done. I asked them to speed it up,' he said.[3]

From the very beginning the government had put pressure on Bord Gáis to do metering at a pace that no one had ever managed before. Bord Gáis's interim chief executive, John Barry, called a senior official in the Department of Communications to express his concerns about the 'renewed pressure' to speed up the metering programme. 'He is rightly adamant that they can't sign up to a contract or a programme which it is not possible to deliver and I think they need to know that this department is strongly in their corner on this,' wrote the civil servant in an email.[4] Communications Minister

Pat Rabbitte subsequently supported Bord Gáis's position at a cabinet sub-committee meeting in April 2013, in advance of the start of metering, due to the company's expertise. 'We should not lightly set aside their advice,' he said.[5]

To keep the government happy, Bord Gáis gave a commitment to beat its average installation rate of 27,000 meters per month through the 'incentivisation of contractors'.[6] In other words, it was going to pay them more.

But as Gilmore faced into the prospect of introducing water charges at the end of 2014, he believed he needed more meters installed to justify the charging system as fair. He told Irish Water that seventy per cent of homes had to be metered by the end of the year.[7] To achieve this, Irish Water would have had to go from 107,000 meters in January 2014 to 700,000 meters by December 2014. That would be an increase in the rate of installations from 27,000 meters per month to 50,000 meters per month. It was an impossible target.

Gilmore may not have wanted a two-tier system, with some people on metered charges and others on a flat charge, but that was precisely what was going to happen if only forty per cent of households had meters by the time the bills arrived. So Gilmore decided that water charges would have to be postponed.

That decision led to a showdown at the Economic Management Council (EMC). It was a mini-version of the cabinet and was attended by only four ministers – Gilmore, Taoiseach Enda Kenny, Finance Minister Michael Noonan and Public Expenditure Minister Brendan Howlin. It was set up that way at Labour's insistence, because the party feared a loss of influence after failing to get the minister for finance job from Fine Gael. All key decisions were run through the EMC in advance of cabinet. There were two Fine Gael ministers and two Labour ministers, so Labour had an equal say before decisions went to cabinet, where it was ten Fine Gael and five Labour ministers. 'The EMC gave us fifty per cent of the action,' said one Labour minister. It met once a week before every cabinet meeting – and sometimes twice a week.

'All the big decisions on Irish Water ended up being made at the Economic Management Council,' said a government source.

The EMC meetings were usually held in the Sycamore Room in Government Buildings, which gets its name from its oval-shaped sycamore table. Senior civil servants and senior advisers would join Kenny, Gilmore, Howlin and Noonan.

In February 2014 there was an even more private EMC meeting held in Taoiseach Enda Kenny's ante-room. Only the four ministers were present. The discussion on water charges was too sensitive to allow anyone else in.

Brendan Howlin said that he and Gilmore called for the postponement of water charges, which were due to start in October that year. 'Both Eamon Gilmore and I had certainly come to the conclusion that this had to be delayed, that it was a project that wasn't ready, that we needed to have full metering done and full demonstration charges available to people well in advance of normal charging,' he said.[8]

It led to a serious row between Kenny and Gilmore. At one point, Kenny thumped the table with his fist and said, 'I gave my word to the Dáil.'[9] He had indeed promised Fianna Fáil leader Micheál Martin in the Dáil that he would reveal the size of the water charge bills before the local elections in May. He also made an insulting remark to Gilmore.

'I haven't repeated what was said, but it's not what would normally be the exchange between partners in coalition,' said Howlin. He characterised that EMC meeting as the 'tetchiest' during his time in government with 'very, very strong words exchanged'.

Gilmore would not reveal what Kenny said to him either. 'There was a lot of tough talk done on water charges,' he said.[10]

Kenny was convinced that people would be prepared to pay their water charges as long as the price was right. Labour suspected that this was based on private Fine Gael opinion polls. A senior Fine Gael source confirmed this to be the case. 'We polled all the way through this. The principle of water charges was rarely challenged by the public,' he said. The research was commissioned by Fine Gael's Washington-based consultants, Greenberg Quinlan Rosner, and carried out in Ireland by Amárach consulting. It helped to reinforce Kenny's belief that people would be happy to pay water charges if the price was reasonable.

Howlin said the Taoiseach wanted to put out an average figure for the bills as soon as possible. 'Because there were all sorts of ludicrous sums being suggested, people would start off at €1,000 or €2,000. And he thought that needed to be debunked and the way to do that was to actually set a charge and go ahead,' he said.

Gilmore's opposition to bringing in water charges was a serious setback given there was so little time left to organise the billing. Irish Water Managing Director John Tierney had been told by the government in February that they would be making decisions 'within the next few weeks'.

'The timelines are very tight and any delay would have significant knock-on effects to the publication of the water charges plan in June,' he told the Irish Water board.[11]

Kenny had already been promising in the Dáil that he would reveal the average water charge bill for families before the local and European elections in May. But now he had seriously damaged his relationship with Gilmore.

Kenny had to find someone to act as a peacemaker. He turned to Labour's minister for communications, Pat Rabbitte. He was a fellow Mayoman who shared Kenny's obsession with the Mayo senior football team winning a long-awaited All-Ireland title. Both of them were also working on a plan to bring high-speed broadband to businesses in Claremorris in Co. Mayo. The town had a high-speed, state-owned broadband network, but it had not been switched on.

Even though Rabbitte had built up his political career as a TD for Dublin South West, he was still happy to help out the town where he had attended St Coleman's College as a student.

Rabbitte and Kenny both turned up in Claremorris to announce that €500,000 of state money was being invested to open up the high-speed broadband network to every business in the town. There was a big crowd for the event in April 2014 in the McWilliam Park Hotel. It was a four-star, 122-bedroom hotel, built at the height of the Celtic Tiger with the aid of generous tax breaks.

According to a source, Kenny asked Rabbitte to have a quiet word with him after the broadband launch. They went over into a corner of the hotel and Kenny put his arm around Rabbitte's shoulder. 'Eamon is very difficult,' he said. 'It's this fucking water. Gilmore wants us to leave the charges till later. But we'll be destroyed in the local elections.' Kenny had not changed in his desire to keep his promise of getting out a water charges bill before the local elections. 'If we don't put out a figure, Fianna Fáil and Sinn Féin will put out a figure for us. We'd better fix it,' he said.

Rabbitte told Kenny: 'You know that water is a different issue for us than for Fine Gael.'

Gilmore and Rabbitte had spent the earlier part of their political careers opposing water charges tooth-and-nail. They knew the reaction that water charges might have in the working-class estates in Dublin where they had got votes. Fine Gael had a more middle-class and rural voting base. Water charges appealed to the Fine Gael philosophy of making everybody pay something. Its TDs and senators were 'rock solid' on bringing in water charges, according to one party source.

Rabbitte left the McWilliam Park Hotel with the clear impression that Kenny thought that a modest water charge would be acceptable to voters. Phil Hogan was certain too.

Rabbitte got in touch with Gilmore, who felt it was going to be very damaging for Labour.

'It coincided with the first full year of property tax. We were in a colossal economic mess. There was no easy way of doing it,' said Gilmore.[12]

The talks on water charges resumed between the two parties at the EMC. Even though there had been a major row, it never leaked out. That was another reason why so much business was done at the EMC. Gilmore suspected one of his ministers of leaking stories from cabinet to the media to undermine him. Kenny suspected that one of his was leaking too.

They both hoped that they could resolve the issue of water charges behind the scenes.

29

THE WATER METER REBELS

The Ballyphehane/South Parish Says No group had spent a year leafleting houses and knocking on doors to raise awareness about the forthcoming water charges. They picked the Ashbrook estate in Togher as the location to make a stand against water meters. It is located halfway up one of Cork city's steep hills. The residents were all buying bottled water because the water coming from their taps was dirty. The group knew that meter installers were coming because of Irish Water's policy of giving two weeks' advance notice of metering.

When the Irish Water leaflets arrived in Ashbrook estate in early April 2014, a friend of one of the residents tipped off the Ballyphehane/South Parish Says No group. The group headed up with their anti-water charge leaflets and went door-to-door to each of the sixty-five houses in the estate over the course of a weekend. The householders at the front of the estate were against the metering, while people at the back were 'humming and hawing'. John Lonergan, the former storeman turned protester, was unsure how residents would react to the arrival of the meter installers. 'Even up to the day Irish Water came into Ballyphehane, we still didn't know if people were going to come out or not,' he said.[1]

The group got ready on the Monday morning at 6.30 a.m. at the main entrance to the Ashbrook estate. They had stools and banners. Long before the *gilets jaunes* in France, they wore yellow high-vis jackets. It let local residents know who they were and gave them a group identity. Day after day, the Ballyphehane/South Parish Says No group waited for the meter installers, but there was no sign of them.

The contractors arrived a week later, on Tuesday 22 April 2014. 'When they tried to get in, we stopped them. We stood in front of them,' said Lonergan. The members of the group had deliberately parked their cars along the narrow entrance in a staggered fashion, which meant that the contractors could not drive into the estate. Gardaí warned the group to move the cars, but they argued that they were allowed to park there. Some of the meter installers had managed to dig holes at the back of the estate. But protesters jumped into the holes and stopped them from digging further.

The meter installers were unable to get into the estate for the next three weeks. Residents parked their cars directly over water stopcocks to prevent the meters from being installed there. At one point, a crew from Murphys did manage to get in at 5.30 a.m., knowing that the protesters were only starting at 6.30 a.m. They got their barriers set up and started work at 6.30 a.m. But Lonergan said the early morning racket annoyed the residents at the back of the estate who had not been actively supporting the protest. The meter installers were outside the entrances to their houses. 'They woke the kids up and they blocked people getting their kids to school. Suddenly, in the part of the estate where it was fifty-fifty, we had all of them out,' he said.

Eddie O'Sullivan, a former Telecom Éireann worker and Cork City supporter, had got involved with the campaign against the household charge. He pulled away a consaw which was lying on the ground. 'Another lad [a contractor] came along and took it back again,' he said. The TV3 cameras were there and the footage was endlessly replayed. He was nicknamed 'Consaw Eddie' after that.

One of the protesters fell down after an incident with a contractor. There was a furore and an ambulance was called.

Lonergan said that they told the contractors to take out the three water meters they had installed. They were removed a few days later. Irish Water told reporters that the meters were being taken out for repairs. They never put them back in. It was a big victory for the Ballyphehane/South Parish Says No group. 'Nobody else had done this in Ireland. This was the first time anyone had said "No, you can't come in,"' said Lonergan.

The poster they designed – 'No meters, no contract, no consent' – started to appear on the windows of houses across Ballyphehane and Togher. It had their phone number on it, with an appeal to make contact if Irish Water's vans were spotted. It became a visible sign of how opposition to water charges was growing.

Much of the media focus was on an eloquent local resident, mother-of-two Suzanne O'Flynn, who had taken part in the protests against the meters. A myth developed that the meter installers had been stopped because of this one brave woman. It was a colourful story. But it was not true.

Keith O'Brien, a member of the Ballyphehane/South Parish Says No group, said a year's worth of work had gone into different places: 'We had leaflet drops, all that kind of carry on. So by the time they came around Ballyphehane/Togher/South Parish, people were aware of what was going on.'

Their televised protest victory had been seen across the nation. Now people knew that it was possible to stop water meter installations. And within one week, their tactics would be taken on in Dublin.

30

WATER LEAKS

Taoiseach Enda Kenny had hoped that his hotel meeting with Pat Rabbitte would help to achieve a breakthrough on water charges. Instead there was another breakdown a week later.

There had been no agreement reached between Fine Gael and Labour at the EMC. Kenny took the unusual step of deciding to bring the issue to cabinet on Tuesday 15 April 2014. He had promised to reveal the average water charge before May's local elections. However, Fine Gael feared that Labour was going to hold off on any decision on water charges until after the local elections. If a large number of Labour councillors lost their seats, Gilmore could argue that the public was against water charges and that Labour would no longer support bringing them in.

Kenny decided to increase the pressure on Labour. He told the fourteen other ministers at cabinet that the memo containing the average water charge would be circulated among the cabinet members after RTÉ's *Nine O'Clock News*, so that no one could leak it. Then they could discuss it at the following morning's cabinet meeting. Minister for Social Protection Joan Burton protested that there was not enough time for ministers to analyse it properly. But Kenny insisted. He put the water charges issue on the cabinet agenda for the next day without Gilmore's agreement, which was the first time that had ever happened.

The water charges memo was circulated after RTÉ's *Nine O'Clock News*. This level of paranoia about cabinet leaks was not new. A month earlier, Kenny had asked all the ministers to put their phones on the table when he announced that Garda Commissioner Martin Callinan had resigned. It showed an unhealthy level of distrust at cabinet level.

But the next morning it became clear that his precautions had not gone far enough. There had still been a huge leak from cabinet. After all Kenny's concern about keeping the average charge watertight, the *Irish Independent* had it all over their front page. The headline was: 'Revealed: average family will pay €248 water bills'.[1] The story also had the full details of the free allowance and the different prices for metered and unmetered homes. This was not an off-the-cuff cabinet leak, where a journalist had managed to get a quick word with a minister. The level of detail showed it was completely deliberate.

It did not help Labour's mood to see that one of the authors of the story was the *Irish Independent*'s political editor, Fionnán Sheahan. He had been in Young Fine Gael while at UCC but soon turned his attention to journalism. He was a relentless worker who had a good nose for political stories.

The details of the water charging plan had leaked elsewhere too. *The Irish Times* also had a story about the water charges.

There is a rule of thumb in journalism about leaks. The source of the leak can be predicted by examining who benefits the most from it. The answer here was clearly Fine Gael. The Labour ministers were furious with the coordinated leak because they all knew what Fine Gael was up to. Howlin said the leak aimed to push Labour into supporting water charges before the local elections. 'It was to ensure this was out there and this couldn't be stopped,' he said.[2]

Gilmore was boiling over about the leak as he went into the cabinet meeting that morning. He clashed with Kenny. 'It was the worst row ever,' said one Labour minister. 'It was unbelievably raw. Fine Gael didn't understand, after all we'd been through, how water charges – at the price of two pints a week – could become such a big issue for us.'

During the meeting, Kenny threatened to put the issue to a vote. It was the first time he had done that.[3] Calling a vote in cabinet in a coalition government is always a last resort. It is a sign that you cannot win the argument and are going to force your partners to go along with you. Fine Gael was going to win because it had ten ministers and Labour had five. But Kenny did not go through with his threat to call a vote on water charges. As Gilmore later said, that would have meant the end of the government. Labour could not accept staying in power after being humiliated in that way.

The argument went on for an hour and a half. It ended just as Joan Burton was returning from doing ministerial question time in the Dáil. She said Gilmore was incredibly angry about being ambushed by Fine Gael on the water charges issue. 'I can't remember Eamon Gilmore being as angry about anything else as he was about that. He did indicate to Labour ministers that he was considering his position,' she said.[4]

Fine Gael and Labour had maintained a united front publicly during most of their time in office. They had worked hard to rebuild relations with the Troika after the financial crash. 'Each party knew that if there was a chink, the Troika would have lost confidence in us. The government had to show it was serious and stay the course,' said one minister. Fine Gael and Labour were more afraid of the Troika than the opposition.

Kenny had to go into Leaders' Questions almost immediately after his cabinet row with Gilmore. Fianna Fáil leader Micheál Martin tackled him immediately over the newspaper leaks about the water charges memo. 'The Taoiseach also said that the Government has not signed off, but what does that mean in real terms? Is it because Labour angrily raised the leaks to the newspapers this morning and the Taoiseach has deferred it from today?' he asked.[5]

Some of the Dáil's best hecklers could not resist making water puns. 'Wikileaks,' shouted Fianna Fáil TD Barry Cowen. Independent TD Finian McGrath chipped in: 'It is like the water-pipe, leaking all over the place,' he said.

Kenny had just been involved in an epic cabinet row. At that very moment, Labour had told all its advisers and staff to start preparing ideas for a general election manifesto, so it would be ready for a snap election. But one of the skills of politics is to be able to pretend that there is 'nothing to see' here. Kenny said the government was 'united' on making Hogan's proposed water charges as fair, affordable and as equitable as possible. 'We have not signed off on the Minister's proposition for the very good reason that we want to get this as right as possible,' he said.[6]

It was the worst row between Fine Gael and Labour during their time in government. That night Gilmore seriously discussed pulling out of government with his ministers and advisers. 'The feeling was that we had to stay the course or else we would torpedo the economic recovery,' said one Labour minister. All of this took place behind closed doors. The public never realised how close the government came to collapsing. The next day, word went around the Labour corridors that the row was over, for now. Joan Burton told her staff that there would be no election. Discussions over the water charges continued between Fine Gael and Labour.

Gilmore said these were very tense times. 'There was a standoff that lasted for several months,' he said.[7] Labour's poll ratings had gone from nineteen per cent in the general election to around eleven per cent during the first three years in government in the regular *Sunday Business Post*/Red C opinion polls. Then Labour's support plunged to seven per cent once the water charges were announced.

Fine Gael had never believed that Labour was going to pull out of government because the party risked losing so many seats. 'Where would they go? Labour was never going to pull down the shutters,' said a Fine Gael source.

There was an interesting postscript to the leak of the cabinet memo. In the *Irish Independent*'s office on Talbot Street, which coincidentally was right beside Irish Water's Colville House headquarters, Fionnán Sheahan decided to write further stories based on the memo. He wrote about how some households would get higher fixed water charges if there was no meter installed: 'Miss out on water meter and you're stuck on fixed charge.'[8] The Department of the Environment contacted the newspaper to insist that the story was wrong. Sheahan took a photo of the relevant section of the cabinet memo and sent it to the department. That was the end of the complaints.

Irish Water was always conscious of how physically close it was to the *Irish Independent*. At one stage, the water company had to evacuate all its staff onto the street. Within minutes a reporter from the *Irish Independent* was ringing to ask what was going on. The Irish Water press office was able to answer quickly. It was a fire drill.

Meanwhile the frantic metering was continuing.

Within the space of a week, a young woman was going to make an appeal for help on Facebook that would bring the anti-water meter protests from Cork to Dublin. It was on a street called, ironically enough, Watermill Drive.

31

BLUE RISING

The Ballyphehane/South Parish Says No group had become the first to stop meter installations in the country. Now a group of protesters in Dublin were going to follow their example.

Resistance to water charges in Dublin went back a long way. During the reign of King Henry III, his governor in Ireland, the Justiciar Maurice Fitzgerald, told the sheriff of Dublin to take a hardline approach to anyone who resisted the new water taxes. 'Any who oppose are to be suppressed by force and to be attached to appear before the Jcr [Justiciar] at the next assizes [courts].'[1] Basically, those who resist are to be arrested and held until further order.

Then the first Duke of Ormonde, James Butler, brought in new water regulations for the city in 1663. The author Michael Corcoran in his history of Dublin's public water system described how people who did not pay their charges 'could expect to have their supplies cut off'.[2]

Fast forward to 1775 when Arthur Guinness was paying nothing for the water from the city supply he used to make his famous stout. The city authorities tried to bill him for the water from the two illegal pipes supplying what is now St James's Gate brewery. Arthur Guinness told them 'the water was his, and he would defend it by force of arms'. Workers from Dublin Corporation arrived to disconnect supplies. An infuriated Arthur Guinness snatched a pickaxe from a member of the work gang and used 'very much improper language' towards them.[3] The dispute was only settled ten years later when Arthur Guinness signed an agreement for an 8,795-year lease on the St James's Gate site. He agreed to pay an extra £10 annually on his lease for using the city water.[4]

There had been no water charges in Dublin city since 1977, except for two brief interludes. An attempt to bring them in during the 1980s was quickly abandoned and another attempt in the early 1990s also failed. As a result, an entire generation grew up in the capital getting water for free. Now Irish Water had 1,300 contractors on the ground installing meters all around the country.

The first significant resistance in the city to the government's forthcoming water charges kicked off when contractors turned up on a quiet street in Raheny on the northside of Dublin. Watermill Drive was known as a middle-class area with civil servants and retired gardaí living there. There were no objections when the contractors started erecting barriers and installing meters. But there was one person on the street who certainly did not want a meter.

Donna Thompson-Griffin, a childminder with stand-out pink hair, put up a Facebook post on the 'Dublin Says No' page to appeal for help. Derek Byrne, who was still working nights as a security guard, arrived the next morning at 7 a.m. outside her house. 'Most of the meters were installed on Donna's road, except for hers. People were determined to stop them. It was Ground Zero to us. This is it,' he said.[5]

Byrne was joined shortly afterwards by Ciaran O'Moore, an Aer Lingus shop steward who was also a member of Sinn Féin. Ciarán Heaphy, a milkman who was a member of the republican socialist party Éirígí, turned up after doing his milk run, along with Bernie Hughes, a prominent member of Dublin Says No. Carole and Ken Purcell came all the way from Jobstown.

Donna Thompson-Griffin needed the back-up when the contractors arrived at 8 a.m. because she did not get much support from her neighbours in stopping the meter. 'The people of Raheny, there was only a few that stood with me. And they were all just, you know, looking down their nose, "Just pay your bill, pay this, pay that,"' she said later.[6]

The contractors could not install a meter outside her house due to the presence of ten or so protesters. They kept trying for two days before eventually moving off.

It was the start of the 'proxy protest' – people who moved from area to area to protest against water meters as self-appointed representatives of the community. Some left-wing politicians disagreed strongly with this. But Byrne and his band of protesters had been emboldened by their first successful stoppage of a meter installation.

They followed the contractors to their next work site, the nearby Station Road. They stood on the road with placards: 'Honk if you are Against Irish Water.' Byrne said it did not stop the contractors from putting in meters. 'We hadn't a clue what we were doing. We were in areas where the residents didn't support us. And no one knew what a protest was,' he said.

The next day the meter installers moved into the Edenmore estate, on the outskirts of Raheny village. It was built for Dublin Corporation by the well-regarded building firm G. & T. Crampton between 1963 and 1965. The workers drove their trucks into a cul-de-sac in the estate. The protesters parked their cars at the end of the cul-de-sac. 'That was the biggest mistake they made. They couldn't get their machinery back out,' said Byrne. He stood up on the digger holding a sign 'No to Irish Water' and refused to get off it.

The estate was busy because it was a school holiday. Rather than being isolated like the day before, Byrne and his fellow protesters had a crowd of over 100 schoolchildren and adults. 'The workers were actually terrified because there were kids climbing on top of the trucks. It was like the Wild West,' he said.

One of the new protesters was pensioner Michael Batty, a chronic asthmatic who lived in the Edenmore estate. He had been working in England in the 1980s when there were clashes between striking coal miners and police officers. 'When I moved to Ireland, it was so peaceful, I couldn't understand it. Nelson Mandela was violent. Michael Collins was violent,' he said. He was later nicknamed 'Meter Mick' by the Irish Water contractors because he kept jumping into holes to stop the meters going in. 'I was totally determined not to let them install a meter in my house. I was going to prevent them physically. I've always been totally honest about that, never denied it,' he said.[7]

By now the Dublin Says No Facebook page had become an information-sharing centre as well as a propaganda outlet. 'When people spotted vehicles in estates, the message went onto the page. The administrators would alert other people to where they were. It was the eyes and ears of the city,' said Byrne.

However, there were bogus tip-offs on the page on a daily basis. Byrne said he believed this was from the contractors who were trying to send them to the wrong locations. 'What they didn't understand is that we live in the area. We just had to ring or text someone to see "Are they down there?" It was always a cat and mouse game,' he said.

Later on, the Dublin Says No group got a call about a man in a wheelchair who was stopping an Irish Water digger in the Ard na Gréine estate, two kilometres from Edenmore. Austin Dwyer of Elton Park was not alone. His mother, Bridie (eighty-nine), was out blocking the meter installers as well. He did not know any of the protesters who arrived on the scene. 'That was me first time meeting this lot,' he said. Dwyer went out again when the installers came back to his estate the next week. 'I got the wheelchair and sat in behind the digger all day.' He had no toilet break and he was 'freezing' in the shade all day. On the next day's protest, he made sure that he was in a sunny spot when he was blocking the digger with his wheelchair.[8]

In June the meter installers moved on to homes near Blunden Drive in Ayrfield. Dwyer went up there to keep blocking the diggers. 'I got in front of the digger. The digger started working with me underneath it and it knocked me flying,' he said. Dwyer was in a wheelchair because he suffered from severe epilepsy. He had a seizure.

At the same time Derek Byrne was down in a hole dug by the contractors, trying to stop them. 'They got the shovel down on me. I collapsed into the hole and I refused to leave the hole,' he said.

The weather in the summer of 2014 was very hot, which helped the protesters. Ironically, Byrne needed water. 'I was lying in the hole and screaming out for people to get me water, something to drink, because I was dying,' he said. He had to abandon his protest in the hole to go to the aid of fellow protester Dwyer, who was in the midst of an epileptic seizure.

The father-of-four was secured to a spinal board and taken to hospital in an ambulance. Dublin Says No later put up a picture of him in his hospital bed in Beaumont holding up two placards opposing Irish Water. The contractors had to abandon their attempts to meter homes around Blunden Drive. The protesters shut down both ends of the road. Byrne said they stopped the contractors from moving their machines. 'People came from everywhere. There was a lot of anger,' he said.

Byrne used to bring his son Josh (nine) with him to the protests. At one point, the contractors installed a water meter outside the house where Josh lived with Byrne's ex-partner. She was pregnant at the time. She couldn't even bring the children to school because the driveway was blocked with rubble.[9] 'Me and her hadn't talked in years. And she rang me,' Byrne said. He turned up with a shovel and filled in the hole. Then the workers came back. He blocked them in with his car and they called the gardaí.

The workers thought they had managed to meter the home of one of the most prominent water charge protesters. They went to a local shop and bought a bag of lemons to wave at Byrne. 'Are you bitter?' they asked Byrne, who told them he did not live there because it was his ex-fiancée's house. 'We haven't spoken in years. We've actually started speaking to each other because of you,' he said.

The contractors were now encountering protests in estate after estate in the north-east Dublin region. They all had one thing in common. They were largely working-class estates where lower income residents had got waivers from water charges in the 1990s.

All eyes were now on the government to see if it would announce exemptions, which could take the heat out of some of the protests.

32

CAN'T PAY, WON'T PAY

Fine Gael was determined that everybody would have to pay water charges. It disliked the idea of granting exemptions to people on low incomes, which had happened before with water charges in the 1990s and with bin charges in the 2000s.

Phil Hogan had made the argument during the 2011 general election campaign that the only alternative to water charges was to increase tax on working people. 'If you don't adopt a position of charging customers for a service that is provided, then the only other option is to go for higher income tax, which is unacceptable to Fine Gael,' he said.[1]

Former Fine Gael minister of state Lucinda Creighton said there was definitely a view in Fine Gael that the middle classes had paid the price of the economic crash. 'People who paid their taxes, who had bank shares and maybe lost them all. The feeling was that the people most insulated were those in receipt of benefits,' she said.[2]

The previous Fianna Fáil–Green government had imposed a ten per cent cut to all social welfare payments, including the state pension, in its final budget in 2010. When it came into government, Labour insisted there would be no repeat of this. Creighton said that helped to preserve political stability. 'But if you exempted a whole cohort of people from water charges, the middle classes would have felt they are paying for everything,' she said.

One Labour adviser in government said Fine Gael did not want anyone to be exempt from water charges. 'Their attitude was "Those people get everything for free and pay for nothing. We'll get them at last."'

Labour on the other hand traditionally had won votes in working-class areas in the cities and towns. These same working-class communities expected Labour to protect them against any plans by Fine Gael to bring in water charges. But there were many Labour ministers and TDs who believed that there were good environmental reasons for bringing in water charges. They bought into the argument that getting people to pay for water would encourage them to be more careful using it. 'It was the principle of the usage charge: "Everybody should pay something",' said a senior Labour source.

Labour had already got complaints about how around 130,000 council tenants had escaped the property tax. The councils had paid their €90 property tax bills and had not passed it on through higher rents. Anyone who had bought their council house in the same estate had to pay up.[3] The same senior Labour source said there was a 'lot of kickback' from the property tax. 'People were living beside council house tenants who did not have to pay the property tax. But because they owned their house, they did.'

However, the issue of waivers for people on low incomes when it came to the water charges was discussed by Phil Hogan, his minister of state Fergus O'Dowd and Labour's minister of state for housing Jan O'Sullivan at a meeting in the Custom House in April 2012. The notes of the meeting said that 'discussions were taking place with Department of Social Protection on the complex issues involved'.[4] The Department of the Environment looked to the state's think tank, the ESRI for some help.

One of the researchers on the ESRI water affordability study was Edgar Morgenroth. He was born in the city of Wuppertal in Germany. The river there was polluted by local industries and he was warned as a child, 'If you fell in, you would be dead.'[5] But the Germans cleaned it up and the salmon and trout came back. Morgenroth came to Ireland as a teenager with his family on a fishing holiday. He came back to work and met his wife, who is from Longford. For a time, he was a sheep farmer in Monaghan and he sat on the Irish Farmers' Association national sheep committee with its one-time president Tom Parlon. Most of his career, though, was as an economist with the ESRI. He had made a detailed submission with his ESRI colleague, Professor John FitzGerald, during the public consultation on water.

Morgenroth suggested that the government could save money by installing water meters inside houses: 'Normally the mains supply goes straight into the kitchen sink, and under the kitchen sink is where you would have put the meter. It's as simple as that.' He said this would be up to €300 cheaper than digging up the pavement to put a meter outside the house. But the kitchen meter would not identify any leaks in the pipes under the driveway and under the house. The civil servants in the Department of the Environment wanted water meters located outside houses to find those leaks. These meters could be read automatically by a passing car – whereas kitchen meters would have required a more expensive wireless smart meter. That was the end of the debate as to the location of the meter.

Now Morgenroth and his colleagues had to do the affordability study quickly because the government was in a 'wild panic' about it.[6] Morgenroth quickly came to the conclusion that the government's promise to provide everyone with a 'generous free allowance' of water would not solve water poverty. 'This wasn't really fair when the billionaire got the same allowance as the unemployed. That doesn't make much sense,' he said. Another problem with the free allowance of water was that it did not encourage water conservation, which was the government's main 'selling point' for water charges.

Morgenroth and his two colleagues, Sean Lyons and Paul Gorecki, advised the government to get rid of the 'generous free allowance' because it was a 'crude and blunt instrument'.[7] They said the state would be better served targeting those who were in water poverty with a special €5 per week welfare payment. How many people would have to be helped? The ESRI study found that around four per cent of the population – roughly 180,000 people – would be in water poverty if the government decided to bring in water charges of around €450 or €500.[8]

The ESRI was not alone in thinking that the free allowance was a bad idea. Engineers Ireland had sent in a submission to the government which opposed the introduction of a free allowance for water and suggested instead that a welfare payment should be devised. One of the people who drew up that submission was Jerry Grant, later to become head of asset management for Irish Water.

Morgenroth and his colleague handed over the water affordability report to the Department of the Environment in March 2013. The minister in charge, Phil Hogan, had paid the ESRI over €57,000 for the report.[9] He now had enough information to act. The clear recommendation was to drop the free allowance and develop a new welfare 'water' payment. Instead he decided to set up an interdepartmental 'working group' to look at the whole issue again. This was often the way ministers and civil servants killed off plans they did not like. And, sure enough, nothing of substance came out of the working group.

The Department of Social Protection was represented on the interdepartmental working group. It should have been the department to design a 'water' welfare payment, but it hated the idea of getting involved with water charges. There were a few different reasons. It was afraid that a new welfare payment to reduce the cost of water charges would permanently come out of its €20 billion budget. And it was going to consume a lot of time and be highly controversial. 'The department were quite unhelpful. They didn't want to engage. They didn't want to take on a fresh piece of challenging work,' said one former civil servant.

The minister for social protection, Joan Burton, insisted that she never heard any suggestion of a waiver for people on low incomes. 'There was a whole meme in Fine Gael that there were people who got everything for nothing,' she said.[10]

The interdepartmental group completely failed to come up with any practical solution. Its excuse was that it could not make any firm recommendations on tackling water poverty without knowing what the size of the free allowance would be.

Phil Hogan now had a problem. He was about to bring in water charges based on the programme for government commitment for a free allowance. But his department had a report in its possession from the ESRI, since March 2013, which effectively said the free allowance was daft and would not solve water poverty.

What happened next was a classic attempt to bury bad news. The Department of the Environment released the inconclusive report from the interdepartmental working group in May 2014.[11] It published the ESRI report 'as Appendix Five' of this report. Any journalist examining the report would have had to read through fifty pages first to get to the ESRI's sixty-six-page study.

It worked. The ESRI's damning report into water affordability was completely missed by the media. Morgenroth said the government probably felt it could not go back on its promise to have a generous free allowance of water. He said that the government had already decided on a free allowance before it asked the ESRI to report on it. 'So there clearly wasn't a big enthusiasm amongst some of the decision makers for the analysis, for the evidence that was provided. I don't know who stopped it from coming out but it was stopped from coming out. And it wasn't really talked about,' he said.[12]

The free water allowance was retained. But there would be no exemptions from water charges for people on low incomes, as had happened during the 1980s. Socialist Party Councillor Mick Murphy was amazed at the government's approach. 'They made a fundamental mistake by taking on the whole country with no waivers. There was guaranteed to be trouble,' he said.[13]

All that remained was for the water charges plan to be announced by Phil Hogan. It would make things even worse.

Part Three

WATER FLOWS

33

HOGAN'S TRICKLE-DOWN THREAT

Phil Hogan was preparing to pack his bag for Brussels. It was the worst-kept secret in Irish politics that he was going to be nominated as Ireland's next European commissioner by Taoiseach Enda Kenny. First, though, he had to get the water charges launch out of the way.

He had ticked several boxes. Irish Water was up and running. The unionised council water workers had been brought on board with the twelve-year-long service level agreements. And most importantly, after three months of arguing, Labour had reluctantly decided to go along with Hogan's plan of announcing the average charge before the local elections at the end of the month. They knew it was likely to cost them, however. Brendan Howlin said he had met Labour councillors who believed very strongly that the water charges issue would be a huge liability for them. 'The idea would be that we'd announce it to people so they'd have clarity about it and they could go to the polls for the local elections at least with clarity about what was coming,' he said.[1]

Labour leader Eamon Gilmore got assurances from Hogan that there would be extra free water allowances for the most vulnerable groups – families with children, people with medical needs and single people with low incomes. He later said it was 'not a bad deal' and a 'far cry' from the €500 water charge planned by Fianna Fáil in the last government.[2]

Hogan asked the new water regulator, the Commission for Energy Regulation, to calculate the free allowances to address the issue of water poverty. The commission was full of clever technical staff, but assessing people's ability to pay water charges was not their natural skillset, to put it mildly. That should have been a political decision. However, it suited Hogan. The water regulator would have to take its share of any public backlash that arose. A Fine Gael minister who worked with Hogan in government said he had tried to satisfy the big stakeholders in the unions, Labour and the county managers but had forgotten about the general public. 'Phil was too cute by half in many regards. He failed to understand that this was not a parliamentary party heave.'

Hogan turned up to make the water charges announcement in the Government Press Centre in early May 2014. He confirmed that the average charge per household would be around €240, very close to what had been leaked to the *Irish Independent* a few weeks beforehand. Then he was asked about what would happen to people who did not pay their water charges. 'Water will be turned down to a trickle for basic human health reasons.' He started to twiddle his right thumb. 'And, ah, obviously that won't be too attractive for them.'[3]

Hogan had always expected there would be resistance to setting up Irish Water and bringing in water charges. 'You can't make an omelette without breaking eggs,' he once said.[4] But those on the Labour side of government winced when they saw how Hogan delivered his trickle-down threat. 'He was heading out the gap. He almost took pleasure in it. That didn't help,' a senior Labour source said.

The Department of the Environment had discussions with group water schemes about how they had managed to collect water charges for decades. Non-payment was never a big problem because everyone depended on each other. If someone did not pay, they endangered not only their own water supply but their neighbours' as well. There were some people disconnected, but it was extremely rare.

Irish Water did not have this local connection and indeed, as a new national utility, it had no track record of trust like the ESB or Bord Gáis had. So Hogan and certain civil servants believed they needed the threat of reducing the water supply to get people to pay their bills. This attitude was evident in one of the emails sent to his department during the set-up period.

'What about right of Irish Water to turn down or cut off water supplies for non payment? There will be a lot of bad debts otherwise which would be detrimental to ability to become self-funding,' the civil servant wrote.[5]

The water meters had been deliberately manufactured to allow a household's water supply to be reduced to a trickle. Each one had a white ring installed at the bottom, which allowed the water to flow through to a home. But these white rings could be easily replaced with narrower yellow rings to restrict the flow of a water to a home.

The photographers in the Government Press Centre had their lenses trained on Hogan's glass of water throughout the news conference. He kept them waiting for a while. Then he stretched out his hand, lifted up the glass and had a sip. The room exploded with the sound of every photographer snapping Hogan drinking his water. Hogan was grinning. He knew that was the picture the photographers had been waiting for. He had his next job as European commissioner in the bag and now Irish Water would be somebody else's problem. That was indeed Hogan's last public involvement with water charges.

It was now up to the water regulator to work out the precise details of the charges and the free allowances. It puzzled many commentators why the government had directed that the average water bill be at least €240. A much lower bill would have been easier to get over the line, especially as the country was still in recession. The reason for this figure lay in the headquarters of the EU's statistics agency, Eurostat, in Luxembourg. The government was desperate for Irish Water to pass what became known as the 'Eurostat test'.

Imagine Irish Water as a young twenty-something looking to move out of home. The government is the anxious parent and Eurostat is the hard-to-please bank manager. The parent is desperate to get the grown-up child out because he is costing a lot of money to feed and house. But the grown-up child needs to convince the bank manager that he is financially independent. He has to show that he is earning enough from his job to pay the mortgage all on his own. He cannot be relying on top-ups every month from 'the bank of mum and dad'.

In real life, the government had to be able to convince Eurostat that Irish Water was financially independent. To do that, Irish Water needed to be bringing in at least fifty per cent of its cash from water charges on households and businesses and the rest from the government. If Eurostat could be convinced, it would declare that Irish Water deserved to be classified as being off the government's books. The government had calculated that the average water charge needed to be at least €240 for Irish Water to pass the Eurostat test.

If Irish Water succeeded, it would be able to borrow money on its own to pay for new water treatment plants and water pipes. It would no longer be dependent on its government parent. And there was a huge prize for the government too: it would now have extra money to spend. It could build more schools and houses instead of having to spend its money on the water treatment plants and the pipes.

The theory was apparently so complex, however, that the government proved incapable of explaining it to the public. The best ministers could do was say that Irish Water would become 'like the ESB'. The ESB had always been off the government's books because it was earning its own money from electricity charges. When the government slashed spending on infrastructure to balance the books, it did not matter to the ESB. It kept spending on the electricity network right through the recession in the 1980s and 1990s.

Minister of state Paudie Coffey had worked on this 'network renewal programme' during his twenty years with the ESB. He had been an electrician and then a project planner there. 'The ESB never got the credit they deserved for it. Because when the economy started to boom then, in the early 2000s, we would never have been able to add new houses and new businesses without that network renewal,' he said.[6]

Communications Minister Pat Rabbitte saw how easy it was for the ESB to get a loan of €235 million from the EU's European Investment Bank in the middle of the bailout.[7] He told people privately after the launch in ESB headquarters that the state could not borrow a euro because it was broke. But the ESB was getting a huge loan to upgrade the electricity network because the bankers knew it had the money – from electricity bills – to pay it back.

It was this dream of getting Irish Water off the state's balance sheet that had convinced Eamon Gilmore to reluctantly agree to water charges ahead of the local elections. He knew the strict borrowing limits that were on the state during the bailout. And he knew from his time as Labour's environment spokesman how bad the country's water pipes were. 'We were conscious there had been an underinvestment in water. And the capital programme had been cut. We wanted to restart it. We couldn't borrow. The idea of getting Irish Water off balance sheet was very attractive,' he said.[8]

Public Expenditure Minister Brendan Howlin knew that if Irish Water was able to borrow its own money, he would have more money to spend on schools, housing and hospitals. 'So we had to ensure that we at least made a sterling effort to keep it off the balance sheet. That was a legitimate requirement. Otherwise it would be a big chunk of money taken out of the spend on infrastructure and make health and education worse,' he said.

Water was a service only noticed when it stopped coming out of the tap. Fianna Fáil Senator Gerry Horkan noted during his time as a councillor in Dún Laoghaire that there were few votes in water for this very reason. 'Will we spend the money on water pipes, or on a new all-weather pitch or more books for the library? All of these things are very visible and very tangible. All of these things [i.e. the pitch and books] are vote winners. Repairing pipes is not,' he said.[9]

Dealing with raw sewage was even less of a vote winner. There was a lack of public outrage in some of the forty-four towns where raw sewage was being pumped out. It was almost accepted as just one of those things. Politicians would get invited to the launch of a new wastewater treatment plant, but they were always more enthusiastic going to the opening of a new road or school. Sewage treatment was yucky stuff.

Minister for Social Protection Joan Burton said water and waste water were invisible to householders. 'It's underground when it comes into the house in a tap and it's underground when it leaves the house in a sewerage pipe. Unlike anything else, all you care about is when you see the tap and when your toilet works,' she said.[10]

Irish Water had ambitious plans to spend billions on the water network. But a power struggle developing within the company threatened all that.

34

THE IRISH WATER POWER STRUGGLE

There was a problem at the very top of Irish Water. John Tierney had been appointed in January 2013 as the managing director of the company. But the man who would be in charge of him was appointed four months later.

Michael McNicholas had been on a salary of €1 million with National Toll Roads – the company which had made a fortune on the Westlink Toll Bridge on the M50 and then used the money to expand into other areas. But he accepted the much reduced salary of €250,000 to take up the job as head of Bord Gáis. There were additional benefits in the form of holiday pay and health insurance, which brought the total package up to €334,000 in 2014.

Given the timing of his appointment, he had no role in Tierney getting his job. That would have been fine if the two men got along. 'But they didn't get on,' said an Irish Water source.

McNicholas was from Swinford in Mayo. A civil engineer, he had joined the ESB in 1982 and risen up through the ranks over the following twenty-eight years. He spent three years as head of ESB International, where he had 1,000 people to manage across thirty countries. ESB Chief Executive Padraig McManus said he had been 'highly respected there' when he left in 2010 to take over as chief executive of National Toll Roads.[1]

Due to the structure of Irish Water as a subsidiary of Bord Gáis, Tierney and McNicholas had separate offices on either side of the River Liffey. Tierney's office was in Colville House, which had formerly been a Bank of Ireland branch on Talbot Street in Dublin. When the Irish Water staff arrived, there were discarded phones lying all around the building. The office itself had cheap carpets and standard issue desks and chairs. The back of the building faced onto an area once called 'Monto', one of the biggest centres of prostitution in Europe in the nineteenth century. The location of the headquarters here was a deliberate decision so that Irish Water could not be accused of wanting to collect water charges to pay for an expensive office.

Meanwhile, McNicholas was working out of Bord Gáis's Dublin base – a magnificent building on Warrington Place with enormous windows looking onto the Grand Canal. That was where Tierney went to deliver his first Irish Water board report to McNicholas at 8 a.m. on 24 July 2013.

Tierney suggested having difficult-to-resolve disputes dealt with by senior managers in the company. The Bord Gáis directors signed off on this 'escalation' policy. But Tierney was reminded that he was required 'to keep the chairman of Irish Water [Rose Hynes] and the chief executive of Bord Gáis [Michael McNicholas] promptly informed on issues that may arise between scheduled board meetings which are of a significant nature'.[2]

It was standard corporate governance to outline the reporting relationship. But from that first Irish Water board meeting in Bord Gáis's headquarters, Tierney was left in no doubt about who was in charge.

By the start of 2014, as the tension mounted between the two men, McNicholas had to change the name of Bord Gáis. This was one of the conditions of the sale of the retail arm of the company to a private company under a government plan known as 'Project Sapphire'. The Troika wanted state assets sold off to reduce the national debt. After the sale, Bord Gáis was left with the gas network – and Irish Water. Its new name was a made-up one: 'Ervia'.

Some of the tension between McNicholas and Tierney was likely down to the fact that both men were used to being the top dog. Tierney was an experienced county manager. McNicholas was an ESB man who had been chief executive of National Toll Roads. They were prisoners of an unwieldy structure that had divided responsibility. 'The managing director of Irish Water has a statutory post. He is accountable to the minister. How can he be accountable to the head of Ervia as well? That is a dilemma that John shouldn't have been faced with,' said one Irish Water source.

The coverage of Irish Water was ramping up as the prospect of water charges drew closer. It was under immense pressure to complete a hugely ambitious metering programme, to start unifying the operations of the water divisions in thirty-four councils and to create a billing system for 1.3 million households from scratch. The power struggle between Tierney and McNicholas made it worse. 'It was a fractious time internally,' said an Irish Water source.

People who worked with both men said they had different visions for Irish

Water. McNicholas, with his significant private sector expertise, was tuned in to the culture of Bord Gáis. It had a history of outsourcing work on its gas network to the private sector, which was a proven way of reducing costs. This was the approach that Fine Gael liked. Tierney had a different approach, and one which was closer to Labour's vision. He was a public servant through and through. He wanted to keep using councils' water services staff. He had found those in Dublin City Council to be 'excellent' and said he would not swap them for anyone. And even before he was in charge of Irish Water, he was saying publicly that it had to be publicly owned. 'We do not support privatisation in any form. We would see any new model, if there were to be one, remaining in State hands,' he told the Oireachtas environment committee in 2011.[3]

Tierney had given the unions for the council workers a personal commitment that he was not going to outsource work on a large scale, as Bord Gáis had done for its gas network. That was part of the price of keeping the unions on board. An Irish Water executive said Tierney had been the perfect person to reassure the unions and the council workers during the set-up of Irish Water. 'It was very fortuitous that John was there in that respect. There wasn't a single day lost to industrial action. That was some achievement,' he said.

There was recrimination over the decision to send 300 Irish Water staff to a laughing yoga class in Croke Park. Tierney had needed a venue to speak about the company's plans to staff because the Colville House HQ did not have a big enough room. But his supporters insisted that it was Bord Gáis who booked a laughing yoga instructor at a cost of €200. Yet when the *Irish Mail on Sunday* revealed the story, it was Irish Water rather than Bord Gáis that was ridiculed.[4]

'Tierney was a man of integrity and he never lost that. No matter how much pressure, he would never shout at anyone,' said one Irish Water staffer. Tierney had at least one thing in common with Phil Hogan: he was good at remembering who staff were and where they were from. He would stop to talk to the Irish Water workers in the narrow corridors of the Colville House office. 'He would know your name and have a chat,' said another Irish Water employee.

But the power struggle between Tierney and McNicholas was creating divisions at a time when Irish Water needed to be united. Government ministers were aware of it. Environment Minister Alan Kelly said it was a problem: 'There was an additional complication which wasn't helpful. Irish

Water was a subset of Ervia. There was a gentleman who was chief executive of Ervia on top of it. It would be wrong to say that there weren't tensions there,' he said.[5]

35

WATER WOMEN

The bankers, politicians and developers who wrecked the economy and drove it into a Troika bailout programme were mostly male. But in north Dublin, it was mainly women who were the driving force against the water charges that were now a commitment in the Troika programme. When the men in working-class estates went out to work, it was the women who ensured that the protest continued throughout the day.

Metered charges also meant there was potential for family rows over teenagers staying too long in the shower. And there would be no free water allowance for adult children still living at home. All of these things resonated with women.

A typical 'water woman' was in her fifties. She was a housewife looking after others, be it children or elderly parents. She was conscious of the impact that water charges would have on the family finances.

One of the water women involved in the protests was Denise Mitchell, a Sinn Féin activist. She had grown up in Darndale in the 1980s at a time of high unemployment. Many of her friends were dropping out of school to get jobs. Her mother did not want her to do this and told her that she had to stay in school until she found a job. 'That was the worst thing she could have said because I walked right into a job in the local knitwear factory,' she said.[1]

Shamrock Apparel in Coolock employed hundreds of people in the 1980s. Mitchell was there for six years. She went on to work in Motorola, then the Gateway 2000 computer-manufacturing factory and in the accounts department of the Brinks Ireland cash-in-transit business. She moved into the Ayrfield estate with her husband and their three children in the early 2000s. It was known locally as a 'good estate', located between Edenmore and Darndale on the northside of the city. 'I was living there for thirteen years, but I didn't know everyone. People were juggling kids, going in and out of work,' she said.

In the summer of 2014 Irish Water sent out a notice that meters would be installed in the estate. A few local residents sent around their own home-printed leaflets in response. 'It was nothing fancy, just a white piece of paper, saying they were going to have a meeting on an open green. All residents came out and we were getting consensus that the people were opposed,' said Mitchell. She noticed that there were many other local women at the street meeting on the green in Ayrfield. 'I think any time when it comes to family life, it's women who do the household budgets. These were women who would have seen that their household money was already cut. Here was something else. They were finding they were struggling,' she said.

When the meter installers arrived into the Ayrfield estate, the residents knew that the workers needed to access their stopcocks. That was the spot which the contractors needed to reach to turn off the water and start installing the meter. In Dublin, they were often called 'shores' rather than stopcocks. Mitchell stood on her 'shore' outside her house and told the contractors that she did not want a meter installed. 'It was very courteous at the start. There was no bad feeling,' she said. The contractor sprayed the words 'No meter' on the pavement outside her house.

Mitchell went to protests against meter installations in neighbouring areas. She encouraged the water women to take part in the protests at a street meeting in Kilmore West.

'I appeal now to the women who are here today, that while the menfolk are off at work, we can play our part. All we need to do is stand on your shore. That's all we need to do,' she told residents.[2]

The street meetings were being called by political and community activists. It was not driven by any one party. And it was clear that no party would be allowed to take over either. Mitchell said that when public meetings were held in the Ayrfield community centre, any politicians were invited to speak from the floor rather than getting a spot on the stage.

'You weren't given a platform, which was very fair. If you did try and muscle in, it wasn't long before you were told, "This isn't the Sinn Féin show, this isn't the People Before Profit show,"' she said.

The government had been aware of the risk of the metering programme provoking public unrest. But it had not foreseen women becoming a driving force in the protests. There was certainly an absence of women's voices at the very top level. All the key decisions on Irish Water had been made in the EMC, the 'mini-cabinet' set up by the Fine Gael–Labour government. It had four male members – Taoiseach Enda Kenny, Tánaiste Eamon Gilmore, Finance Minister Michael Noonan and Public Expenditure Minister Brendan Howlin.

Irish Water's struggles could not be attributed to a group of largely male engineers. Surprisingly, it had one of the best gender balances of any public or private sector organisation. A tot-up was done at one point when it had two-thirds of its staff recruited. Almost forty per cent – 230 out of 587 – were women.[3]

The ESB had already shown just how influential women could be in determining the success of a new national project. When it started to bring electricity to rural Ireland in 1946, there was a lot of resistance among farmers. Some thought it was too dangerous and others thought it would be too expensive. The ESB knew that if it could convince the farmer's wife, she could change her husband's attitude. Farmers' wives were the ones doing the hard labour of cooking on open fires and washing clothes by hand.

The ESB got the Irish Countrywomen's Association to do cookery demonstrations for housewives using electric cookers. And it had over 700 rural organisers who helped women to use their new appliances. The ESB also had teams of rural organisers going into local communities, canvassing neighbours and getting the local parish priest on board. All of this was hugely important in getting the women of Ireland to back rural electrification.[4]

The group water scheme movement was also aware of the decisive influence of women. Over the past two decades, the National Federation of Group Water Schemes had been quietly working to amalgamate smaller schemes. It is easier to ensure there is safe drinking water in one large group water scheme than trying to look after six smaller ones. The decision to amalgamate, though, had to be made by a democratic vote of the members of each group water scheme. The national federation's policy adviser, Sean Clerkin, spent many late nights in rural community centres trying to dissolve these small schemes. The older members – usually men – would be reluctant to dissolve the scheme because they had set it up and laid the pipes and thought the water was okay. But Clerkin said the key was to get young mothers in the audience.

'The mood would change once one of the young mothers got up and said: "All I want is a drop of clean water twenty-four hours a day for my children." That was the turning point,' he said.[5]

Now the involvement of women in the water charge protests was becoming a turning point for Irish Water.

Damien Farrell, a Dublin taxi driver and long-time member of the republican socialist party Éirígí, said the women were instrumental in the 'all-day protest'. He said they would balance the protest with all their other daily tasks. 'Most of the women were also mothers. They wouldn't be available till after breakfast and school morning runs. Then they had to collect children from school and settle them in with a bit of lunch. If everything was calm, and weather permitting, they would bring the children back out again,' he said.[6]

Many of the women were doing more than making up the numbers. Bernie Hughes from Finglas and Audrey Clancy from Edenmore were leaders in the water charge protests in north Dublin.

In Bluebell, in west Dublin, women came out to stop the water meter installers from accessing the stopcocks outside their houses. They would put their plastic chairs on top of the stopcocks and start doing their knitting. The women used to tell the meter installers: 'Jaysus, you're gorgeous love. Do you want to sit on me lap?' Veteran female protester Bríd Smith said these women were brilliant for lightening the atmosphere during the protests. 'They knew full well they were embarrassing the young fellows, but they were getting a good laugh out of it. They did it with guards and everything, they'd tell the guards they were gorgeous,' she said.[7]

Smith, from Rathfarnham in Dublin, came from a republican family which had sheltered IRA men on the run during the Troubles. One of them, Martin Forsyth (nineteen), was shot dead in Belfast city centre by Royal Ulster Constabulary detectives as he attempted to plant a bomb in 1971. He had stayed with Smith's family the night before he died. 'It was shockingly real to have met a lovely young guy and then he goes home and he's killed by the RUC,' she later said.[8]

Smith had been involved in the Hunger Strike campaign's national committee with Gerry Adams in 1981 when Bobby Sands died. She organised collections for the Dunnes Stores workers who refused to handle oranges from South Africa during apartheid in the mid-1980s and had protested against water charges in the 1990s. She had been jailed along with Socialist Party TD Joe Higgins in Mountjoy prison for refusing to pay bin charges in 2003. The same year, she helped organise the march of 100,000 people on O'Connell Street in Dublin against the invasion of Iraq. She was elected as a People Before Profit councillor in the local elections in 2009.

Now Smith decided to organise a significant anti-water charge conference in the Gresham Hotel in April 2014 while she was running in the European Parliament elections in Dublin. It was based on the international battles against water privatisation.

Smith invited Marcela Olivera to the conference, whose brother was the leader of the successful resistance campaign against the privatisation of water in Bolivia. Water charges had gone up 200 per cent in that country after the state water company was sold off. A mass boycott of bills and public street protests led to the sell-off being reversed and water charges dropping back to their previous levels. Smith needed money to pay for Olivera's flights. She went to the Unite trade union, where she was working as a tutor. 'I asked them would they back me on this because it was quite an expensive operation,' she said. With Unite on board, Smith also invited representatives of an EU-wide movement called Right2Water, which actually was about keeping European water supplies in public control rather than necessarily getting free water.

The decision to set up an Irish Right2Water campaign came out of this Gresham Hotel conference. Smith asked People Before Profit TD Richard Boyd Barrett – whose birth mother was actress Sinéad Cusack – to organise a cross-party meeting in Leinster House to get it up and running.

'We were looking at water as a global commodity – the new oil,' she said.

Smith went on to contest the European elections for People Before Profit in May against sitting socialist MEP Paul Murphy. Both of them lost out to Sinn Féin's candidate Lynn Boylan and Nessa Childers, an independent candidate and the daughter of a former president, Erskine Childers. Smith was the one accused of splitting the left-wing vote and denying Murphy the momentum he needed to retain his seat. 'It's bollocks. I am a member of a party. I'm not being nasty. I was trying to build up our profile,' she said.

By now the government realised that the anti-meter protesters were more than just the usual suspects like Bríd Smith and Paul Murphy. They could see that ordinary people were being drawn in. 'The protesters were going to extraordinary lengths. They weren't just a rabble,' said a Labour source.

Fine Gael and Labour councillors had been tripping over water meters on their way to canvass voters in both the European and the local elections in May 2014. But it was Labour that was going to pay the heaviest price.

36

GILMORE OUT, BURTON IN

In the run-up to the local elections, Eamon Gilmore had to endure a series of political humiliations. There was the release of Pat Leahy's *The Price of Power*, which detailed the tension between Gilmore and Joan Burton. There were colourful stories about how Burton had left the 'Gilmore for Taoiseach' posters for the 2011 general election campaign in her shed. Burton did little to lessen the impression that she was waiting in the wings if Gilmore's leadership became a live issue after the local elections. Then there was the declaration by Labour Party MEP Phil Prendergast that she had 'no confidence' in Gilmore's leadership. It was too late to find a loyal candidate to replace her, so Gilmore had to turn up stoically for Prendergast's official campaign launch for the European elections and bat off questions from journalists about it. He knew that the controversy over water charges was going to hurt Labour in the local and European elections. 'It didn't come as a surprise that we were going to get a kicking electorally. All governments get a mid-term kicking,' he said.[1]

Working-class communities felt they had been deserted by Labour, the party they expected to protect them from water charges. In parts of Dublin, Labour was rotating canvassers every couple of hours to give them a break from the negativity on the doorsteps. Martina Genocky, a young, first-time candidate, was branded a 'traitor' while out canvassing in Jobstown in Tallaght. She gave as good as she got. 'This is a democracy. This is a democracy. This is a democracy. I want to run for the Labour Party. ... I'm entitled to do that,' she said.[2] The two water charge protesters who were following and filming her were Ken and Carole Purcell, the husband and wife team who had taken part in the first successful anti-meter installation protest on Watermill Drive in Raheny.

'You deserve electoral humiliation,' said Carole Purcell.

'You'll be slaughtered in the elections anyway,' said Ken Purcell.

Genocky was accompanied by her mother, Anne, who worked in the An Cosán education centre in Jobstown. The video also features a woman walking by with a child in a buggy. 'Just let her do her own thing for fuck's sake. Just let her alone. She's only a young woman,' she said.

The film footage of the incident attracted over 10,000 views on YouTube during the local election campaign. Gilmore and Burton rang Genocky to sympathise, and she got a round of applause from fellow candidates at Labour's election launch in the Smock Alley Theatre in Temple Bar.

Then the results came in. Labour lost its three MEP seats, including Prendergast's. The losses were even more shocking in the local elections. Labour lost eighty-one of its 132 councillors. One of its few new councillors was Martina Genocky in the Tallaght South electoral area.

Fine Gael did very badly, too, with 105 of its 340 councillors losing their seats.

The Labour Party went into panic mode. A group of seven Labour back-benchers signed a motion declaring they no longer had confidence in Gilmore as Labour leader. He had a crisis meeting with close allies like Pat Rabbitte and Ruairí Quinn. Rabbitte had defended Gilmore to the end. 'If John the Baptist was leading Labour, we wouldn't have done any better,' he said at the time.[3]

Gilmore, however, decided that it was time to go. He announced his resignation on Monday 26 May 2014 – two days after the local election results. 'The hope was that if we got out of the bailout, there would be two years to the general election. That did happen. But ultimately, I didn't survive long enough to see it,' he said.

Labour TD Aodhán Ó Ríordáin, who had signed the motion of no confidence in Gilmore, had a tearful one-on-one meeting with him before he left. He said afterwards that Gilmore could not have been more decent or more honest. Gilmore told him: 'It's a great country, it's a great party and when you have a responsibility it's more than about me and you.'[4]

Joan Burton won the subsequent Labour leadership contest. She decided to take a different approach to water charges. 'I took a harder line with Fine Gael than Eamon ever did. I don't think he was ever mates with Enda, but I think my attitude to him was a lot tougher. I just had red lines,' she said.[5]

Gilmore had grown up without knowing his father, who had died when he was just fourteen months old. Burton never got to meet either of her parents. She was born on a farm in Carlow in 1949 to an unmarried mother before being adopted by Bridie and John Burton in Stoneybatter in Dublin. When she was a Labour councillor in the 1990s in Dublin, there were developers and lobbyists openly offering bribes in brown envelopes in return for planning re-zonings. Burton was one of the few politicians who had the courage to stand up and make allegations of corruption in Dublin County Council, according to the *Irish Times* journalist Frank McDonald.

As the first ever female leader of the Labour Party, Burton's declared intention was for Labour to govern 'more with the heart than the head'. Her plan for water charges was to reduce the costs and impose a price cap so that families would no longer be afraid of receiving huge water bills. She said Fine Gael had allowed the public to believe that water charges could potentially be very high. 'If you met a family of five, mother and father and three children, particularly people coming into the teenage years, they felt they'll be in there showering every day and doing their hair. Quickly the idea developed that it was possible that families would end up with water charges which could be very significant,' she said.

Burton considered appointing Labour TD Alex White as environment minister during her post-win reshuffle. But she decided the former barrister was more suited to the 'legally orientated portfolio' of work as communications minister. Pat Rabbitte, who was one of Gilmore's most loyal supporters, had known that he was for the chop. He later said that his conversation with Burton about his departure lasted 'about twenty seconds'. That was little surprise to anyone, given how poor relations were between them. Burton picked the combative Tipperary TD Alan Kelly for the Custom House. His nickname in Leinster House was AK-47, after the Russian assault rifle. He had been voted in as Labour deputy leader by the party membership. When Kelly was given his ministerial seal of office, he thought that property tax would be the big issue. But he realised within weeks that it was going to be water charges. The water charges plan was due to be announced at the end of the month by the economic regulator.

Kelly said his predecessor in the department, Phil Hogan, had 'designed the ditches' and he now had to 'drive the tractor through'. 'I didn't get to make the ditches and I would not have tolerated those lines if I had been there from the beginning,' he said.[6] He blamed Hogan for agreeing to the rushed establishment of Irish Water. The tight timeline for introducing water charges.

And those threats. 'The set-up was too quick. The timeline was too short. And threats were not the way to be treating people in a recession, where you have austerity,' he said. Kelly thought it was easy for Hogan to threaten to cut people's water down to a trickle just before he headed off to Brussels to take up the job of European commissioner. 'That was the one thing that really, really annoyed me. He just pushed it out there and somebody else was going to have to clean up the mess. As it turned out, that was me.'

One of the first things Kelly did was to drop the policy of cutting people's water to a trickle. 'I thought it was totally wrong. If you were trying to bring in a charging regime, you don't treat people like that,' he said.

Kelly had a new minister of state in his department. Taoiseach Enda Kenny had sacked Fergus O'Dowd, who had been responsible for bringing through all the legislation to set up Irish Water. He did not give O'Dowd a reason for his decision, but it was widely viewed as a punishment for the growing public backlash against Irish Water. Fine Gael TD Paudie Coffey from Waterford had been appointed to work alongside Kelly instead. To the surprise of many, Kelly got along well with him. 'Paudie was excellent, a brilliant colleague,' he said.

Kelly knew that the two of them would have to overhaul the first water charges plan announced by the Commission for Energy Regulation. The average bill was to be €176 for a single adult and €278 for households of two people or more. But households with more than four adults were facing bills of around €470 per year. There were charges for people who had a meter and people who did not have a meter. There was a cap on charges, but only for nine months. Kelly said the charges were too complicated: 'They were like a matrix.' Furthermore, there were no waivers for people on a low income.

The government was sticking to the notion that this problem would be solved by providing free water allowances for everyone. But it looked like it was already going to be forced to reduce the size of the free allowance for each child from 38,000 litres per year to 21,000 litres. It was all down to the work of the German-born ESRI Professor Edgar Morgenroth. His findings on people's actual water use had stunned both the government and Irish Water.

37

THE WATER WASTERS

For years, officials had believed that people in Ireland were water wasters. It was one of the key justifications for water charges. The Commission on Taxation in 2009 had noted that households had free water and no incentive to conserve, which had led to people using '30% more in Ireland than in jurisdictions that charge based on use'.[1] The Department of the Environment's cost–benefit analysis had leaned heavily on the notion that there would be huge cost savings if people could just reduce their water consumption by ten per cent. It estimated that people were using 150 litres per person per day.[2] As is often the case with civil service documents, the authors were not identified.

Environment Minister Phil Hogan insisted publicly that there would be a ten per cent reduction in water usage because 'metering changes habits'. 'We have taken a conservative estimate of a ten per cent potential reduction in consumption that could be achieved following the introduction of water meters in households,' he told TDs in the Dáil.[3] And the information leaflet that Bord Gáis had sent out to two million homes in 2013 said the same: 'International experience suggests the introduction of water meters can achieve a reduction in consumption of at least 10 per cent.'[4]

But nobody knew for sure because there were no household meters. Now Irish Water had installed 335,000 of them. It handed over the early data from 1,650 of the homes metered to get a definitive answer.

The man chosen to carry out the analysis was Professor Edgar Morgenroth of the ESRI. His report a year earlier on making water charges more affordable for families on lower incomes had been buried by the government.

Within a short period of time, Morgenroth had a 'Eureka' moment in the ESRI's headquarters on Sir John Rogerson's Quay in the Dublin docklands. The meter data was showing that the water usage per person was around 109 litres per day, which was way below the official estimate of 150 litres per day. He had discovered for the first time that the Irish people were not in fact water wasters. 'It was "wow". It was a surprise,' he said.[5] He went straight into the office of his ESRI colleague Sean Lyons to tell him about it: 'We're looking at actual consumption being thirty per cent less than what at that point had been estimated. That makes an enormous difference in a cost–benefit analysis.'

The cabinet had been told in 2011 that the cost–benefit analysis on water metering was 'robust' and based on 'realistic and achievable assumptions regarding the benefits'. Now it had fallen apart. Around eighty-five per cent of the savings it had promised meters could deliver were from people dropping their supposed water consumption from 150 to 135 litres per day. Morgenroth's study had shown these figures to be pie in the sky.[6]

This finding came as a shock to Irish Water because it had also bought into the notion that people were wasting water. Its managing director, John Tierney, had said that water meters would reduce people's usage because 'Irish people use twenty-four per cent more per capita than our Danish counterparts'.[7] The high usage of water instead turned out to be down to leaks in Irish Water's own pipes, which were responsible for seventy-five per cent of all water lost.[8]

The government was spending €500 million on water meters based on a faulty cost–benefit analysis. Morgenroth said it should have used a pilot project before it committed to metering: 'You could have found that out with less money spent. You could have just sampled. If you had installed 10,000 meters, you would have got the same information you did from 800,000 meters.'

Morgenroth's report on the real level of water consumption was released in August 2014. There were just two months to go until water charges kicked in. There was now another problem for the government.

Hogan had announced a free water allowance for children, thinking that they were using more water than they actually were. Now Irish Water believed that the child allowance had to be reduced from 38,000 free litres of water per year to 21,000 litres. The economic regulator approved this, but it went down badly with the public. Morgenroth said his study had found that a child used twenty-three litres less per day than an adult did. 'Your water intake is proportionate to your body. Seventy per cent of your body is water, so when you are smaller, you drink a lower volume,' he said.

Later, the government would try to justify the meters by arguing that they were very effective in detecting household leaks. This was true because all the meters were fitted with night flow alarms. If there was a leak beyond the meter, the water would be running all night even while people were asleep. However, just twenty-five per cent of water lost was due to leaks in the pipes in people's gardens, under their homes or in the internal plumbing. The much bigger issue with leakage was clearly in Irish Water's own pipes.

The meters were supposed to be the 'fairest' way to charge for water. But water is different to gas and electricity. Rainwater arrives for free via rivers, lakes or groundwater, unlike gas, which has to be bought, or electricity, which has to be generated. Around eighty-five per cent of the cost of water is fixed. It is operating and maintaining the water pipe network, the sewers, the water treatment plants and the wastewater treatment plants.[9]

Some senior Bord Gáis officials could not understand the hurry to meter when water usage was driving just fifteen per cent of the cost. 'Even if one family uses six times as much water as another, the actual cost is very similar. Even if a family uses no water at all, Irish Water still has to pay for the cost of the infrastructure,' said one staffer.

The Department of the Environment had been warned not to rely on its metering cost–benefit analysis study two years earlier, when Bord Gáis had raised some very serious questions about it. It could have re-examined the study. But in the rush to get things going, it did not.

The department could also have commissioned a small metering programme to gather the data before spending a full €500 million on meters. Bord Gáis had wanted the Commission for Energy Regulation to carry out a cost–benefit analysis on the metering programme 'given the scale of investment associated with deployment of water meters'.[10] The Commission for Energy Regulation confirmed it was never asked by the government to do this.[11]

It appeared the government was in a huge rush to meter households to justify bringing in water charges. The government was telling voters that they needed water meters to conserve water. But this was simply wrong: the best way to save water was to repair the leaks in the main distribution networks.

One Bord Gáis staffer at the time said the notion that all the leaks were in people's homes was a joke. 'That was a flaw. It didn't gel with people. The public are not stupid. They have a means of identifying something which doesn't sit right,' he said.

It was no surprise that the protests continued to intensify.

38

THE PROTESTERS' FLYING COLUMN

Irish Water contractors were facing a new challenge in parts of Dublin after the announcement of the water charges in May 2014. It was called 'the flying column'. A band of water charge protesters were travelling around in cars to wherever the meter installers were going. The group had a core of around thirty to forty members from areas like Rialto, Crumlin, Inchicore, Tallaght and Coolock.

One of its members was Damien Farrell from Rialto, who was a local election candidate for the republican socialist party Éirígí. He had occupied the headquarters of Anglo Irish Bank on St Stephen's Green in 2010 with other Éirígí members. Then he occupied the constituency office of Fine Gael TD Catherine Byrne in Inchicore in 2013 with members of the Campaign against the Household and Water Taxes.[1] Now his focus was all on water charges. He worked as a taxi driver through the night. 'Then I'd get home for a couple of hours' sleep and go back out again [protesting] in the afternoon,' he said.[2]

The protesters were well aware of the IRA 'flying columns' in the War of Independence which had attacked British forces. They first started calling themselves 'the flying column' as a joke as they roved around Crumlin, Drimnagh and Bluebell. 'We supported each other. The flying column was to keep things fresh, to keep us all together, to keep supporting areas where they were a bit weaker on the ground or maybe struggling,' said Farrell.

The protesters' regular meeting point in the mornings was the petrol station in Dolphin's Barn. One day they came across the military replica truck from the '1916 Freedom Tour' refuelling there. Farrell and the other fourteen flying column members who were present went over to get a photograph. They stood in front of the truck, with a tour guide in British uniform with a replica .303 rifle standing behind them. They had been offered the chance to hold replica rifles as well, but the members turned that offer down, knowing full well what the media reaction might be if such a photo went out.

The flying column's tactic was to get out at 6 a.m. to stand on the stopcocks, so that water meters could not be installed. It would link up with local groups, such as the Crumlin Says No group, an area where there was a strong resistance to water meters.

They were 'extremely keen to stress their use of "peaceful non-violent tactics" in resisting water meter installations', according to a sociology researcher, Criostoir MacCionnath, who was embedded in the group for his master's thesis at NUI Maynooth.[3]

Farrell said he was the first person to stop a water meter being installed in Crumlin. 'They put the jackhammer of the mini-digger right beside me foot. They had to stop then,' he said.

Afterwards, the protesters warned the contractors in Crumlin not to force through the installation of meters. The message was: 'If you do that again, it will be very easy to change the whole atmosphere of how this campaign is going around here.'

Farrell was one of the administrators of the flying column's Facebook page: 'D8 and D12 Say No To Water Tax'. He used it to make appeals for back-up for fellow protesters from other areas and to upload the latest footage from the scene of the latest protest. 'It was video, it was going up instantaneous. It was like a live feed,' said Farrell.

Numbers were crucial to stopping meter installations. The flying column members would knock on doors when they got to an area, trying to get local residents to join the protests. They got a big response in Maryland, an area made up of terraced red-brick houses just off Cork Street in Dublin 8. There were up to 300 people protesting against contractors trying to install meters outside their homes. The contractors were not even able to take down their safety barriers from their lorry to set up workstations. Farrell said there were two people up on the contractors' lorry. 'We had a guy up on it and they had a guy up on it. Their guy was handing the barriers down for their people. We were taking them before they could get them, passing them around to the other side of the lorry and stacking them back up on the lorry,' he said. Farrell said this type of protest was not violent or aggressive 'but it breaks them down'. 'After a day and a half, they just stopped,' he said.

If the weather was bad, it might have been harder to get numbers out on the streets to protest. Talk to any garda on duty at night and they will tell you they love to see the rain coming. It means that troublemakers stay off the streets and that gives them a quieter night's work. But the summer of 2014 in Dublin was very dry. Farrell said it made it easier to protest. 'The weather was on our side as well. It was a fantastic Indian summer,' he said.

Farrell used to stand on stopcocks for up to seven hours at a time without a toilet break. He got used to drinking as little as possible. 'You had minimal water and you had to watch what your food intake was going to be. You needed to get enough fluid in that you didn't dehydrate,' he said.

Some pubs in the Dublin 8 area allowed them to use their toilets. The Pimlico Tavern in the Liberties was one. Kavanaghs on Clanbrassil Street was another. The protesters would arrange for someone to come and stand on the stopcocks while they went to the pub for their toilet break. Farrell said they did have a 'bit of fun' on the protests. 'It was the camaraderie. But everyone knew what they were doing and there were risks involved,' he said.

There were protesters who got burnt-out from the early morning starts and long days – particularly if they were holding down a job as well. They would be told to 'Take the afternoon off' or 'Don't come out in the morning.'

Some of the local politicians wanted the Dublin 8 group to allow house-holders to get water meters if they wanted. But Farrell said the group decided it would not allow water meters in any circumstances. 'Our position was clear. It's a national campaign. No meters are going in. If Mary Byrne wants a water meter, well she can wait until the campaign is over.'

That led to some rows on the streets. During one protest, Farrell was standing on the stopcock outside a house on Rialto Street in Dublin 8 even though the woman living there was telling him to move. 'I don't want you outside my house,' she said. Farrell stayed put. He told her that it was the installers who should go. 'These are the people who have come into the community to install water meters and to drive through a water tax that most people can't afford in that community. I suggest you direct your demand to leave to them. I live here in this community.'

But while he was arguing with the woman who didn't want him there, a crew was preparing to install a water meter outside his own house down the road. He got another protester to stand in for him and went up to stand on his own stopcock. No water meter was installed in either house.

The protest on Rialto Street lasted a week. They had a barbecue on the street. 'It was all about lifting people's spirits to try and break theirs,' said Farrell. The contractors managed to dig some holes, but the protesters were not bothered. At this stage of the campaign, they knew that breaking the ground meant nothing. It was always possible to jump into the hole and stop the meter box going in. 'That was the focus of the resistance,' said Farrell.

As part of its activities, Farrell said the flying column photographed the names of plant hire firms that were supplying machinery and equipment to the contractors. 'We'd message the hire-all company, saying, "Remember when this campaign is over, you still have to keep your business going and anyone around here won't hire from you."'

That was another use of the boycott tactic, but it was controversial because the law of the land allowed for water metering. It was perfectly legitimate for businesses to supply equipment to the contractors. But that was not how the protesters saw it.

Farrell said there was an informal code of conduct in operation during the campaign against the water meters. 'You couldn't be a bollocks, pardon the expression. No effing and blinding, there was none of that. We're weren't getting into personal insults with people. And we weren't going to get into fisticuffs with guards or the workers,' he said.

At one stage, one of the men who took part in the protest made a threatening remark to an Irish Water worker. 'It was something along the lines of "What's underneath your van?"' said Farrell. The protesters told him afterwards that he was not welcome anymore. And they kicked out some other protesters too. 'We had a few people we didn't want in Dublin 8 and Dublin 12. We didn't trust them. It didn't fit the strategy,' said Farrell.

The protesters believed that keeping the 'idiots' on board would have damaged their support in the community. Farrell said they needed numbers on the streets and they would only get them if the protests were 'non-aggressive and non-violent'. He added, 'We were all about building a movement that a big guy, six foot tall, can be part of and so can the frail old woman who goes out shopping and to get her pension. All walks and all classes of people, that's what we were trying to build.'

However, there were clashes between some of the protesters about how long the Irish Water workers should be kept in an estate. 'We had a few people come along at the end of the protest and think they could keep Irish Water (contractors) there till nine o'clock at night. We insisted that the will of the people in the communities we were in didn't want that,' said Farrell. The women from the estates who were out protesting had no desire to stay on the picket lines all night. They wanted the contractors out as fast as possible so they could get back to their daily routines.

Farrell said the usual practice was to walk out the contractors with a slow march by 4.30 or 5 p.m. 'so they could get away'. 'We kind of had an understanding with them – if you behave yourself, you'll get out at half four or five o'clock, but only if you go straight home or back to the depot,' he said.

Farrell said there were some protesters in other parts of Dublin who kept workers in till all hours of the night to punish them and to put them off from coming again the next day. 'Of course they came the next day. That was dodgy ground,' he said.

By the summer of 2014 there were 300,000 water meters installed in nineteen counties, despite the growing protests from the likes of the flying column protesters. Irish Water Managing Director John Tierney told the Irish Water board that they were hoping to increase the speed of the metering to 27,000 meters per month, 'despite the level and intensity of protests'. He was satisfied that media coverage of the 'fragmented' anti-meter protests had been relatively sparse. The main national papers carried only occasional stories and there was very little coverage on RTÉ. That was good from Tierney's point of view because more coverage might encourage more copycat protests. 'We are working hard to ensure there is not sustained national coverage which can act as a flash point for activities on the ground,' he told the board.[4]

However, there was wall-to-wall coverage of the protests on Facebook and YouTube. Derek Byrne was churning out videos of clashes between protesters and guards. He was providing a running commentary too. In the Clare Hall estate in north-east Dublin, he shouted, 'Go back to Pearse Street, ya scumbag' at gardaí who were pushing and pulling protesters off the road to allow the meter installers' vans and diggers to pass. He called another guard a 'lanky prick' and called a senior garda a 'thug'.[5] Byrne said he was reacting after gardaí were clearing protesters out of the way of the meter installers' vans. 'I've used the vernacular of the working class to educate the working class and get them to stand up,' he said.

This protest footage was not making the television news bulletins. But it was being widely viewed and shared on Facebook and YouTube. The growing resistance prompted the country's most senior civil servant to sound the alarm.

39

THE CIVIL SERVANT
WHO SHOUTED STOP

From early 2014 the country's most senior civil servant was openly sceptical about the government's plan to bring in water charges. Martin Fraser was a no-nonsense operator from Malahide in Dublin who had been appointed as secretary general to the government in 2011. He was a big Dublin GAA fan who preferred to watch his team from Hill 16 rather than the corporate boxes in Croke Park. And he once told a Dáil committee that it was healthy to have a 'row every now and then' over government policies. It amused his fellow civil servants no end when they read about it in the papers. One civil servant came dancing up to him with his two fists in the air, challenging him to a fight.

Fraser had seen how senior civil servants had been savagely criticised at the banking inquiry for not warning successive Fianna Fáil-led governments about the dangers of overheating the property bubble. It may have influenced his own decision to speak up about water charges. Fraser foresaw how water charges would threaten the stability of the government. In the months leading up to the launch of the charges, he made his reservations known in typically blunt fashion to Taoiseach Enda Kenny, according to a Fine Gael source. 'You're not seriously thinking of going on with this?' he asked him.

Fraser did not have the authority to overrule Kenny or to act against a government's wishes. But as the secretary general to the government and to the Department of the Taoiseach, his words carried weight.

His concerns appear to have increased further when the introduction of water charges became a key issue in the local elections in May that year.

Fraser made his reservations known to the Labour Party's political director, David Leach. 'This is madness. This is all for €300 million. Why are we doing it?' he asked him. This was something that Leach himself had been saying internally in Labour but to little effect. But Fraser's attitude motivated him to have another go at stopping the water charges. 'It's not going to fly,' Fraser told a government official, after a meeting of the EMC.

Joan Burton, newly appointed Labour leader and Tánaiste, confirmed that Fraser wanted to halt the water charges. 'Martin was of that view. The first item on the agenda, was how he put it,' she said.[1]

Financially, it was possible to kill off water charges. The income from domestic water charges was less than €300 million. The government had managed to find hundreds of millions every year to cover the overruns in the health budget. 'There was no financial need for this to happen. We found €300 million one year in receipts from the Central Bank,' said a government source.

There was a fear, though, at the highest level of government, about the international impact of scrapping water charges. Kenny's government had spent three years getting out of the bailout and trying to show international lenders that the country could be trusted again. The fear then was that the international lenders might take fright if water charges were dropped. For this reason, Kenny was convinced that there was a need for the government to stick to the plan to introduce water charges, even after the Troika had left. 'We were still very nervous about the signal it would send internationally if we dropped a key element of our structural reforms. In 2014, things were very fragile,' said a government source. The government did not want to be cut off from the international lenders again, having spent years trying to re-establish the country's economic reputation.

Then there was Kenny's natural stubbornness, which had served him well in his long journey to become Taoiseach. He had been told that he would never revive Fine Gael after its drubbing in the 2002 general election. Political commentators then dismissed him as a lightweight who had not a hope of becoming Taoiseach. His enemies in Fine Gael had tried to topple him at the last moment in 2010. But he had persevered. And his government had managed to get the property tax implemented, despite all the predictions of doom. He believed he could do the same with water charges. No protester was going to put him off, no matter how much they chanted at him or tried to disrupt his public appearances. Kenny made a big point of saying that he had not requested any extra garda protection despite the growing protests at every event he went to. He even used to give a 'thumbs-up' to the protesters sometimes, which infuriated them even more.

One government source said there was a certain element of 'gung-ho-ism' in government about water charges. He said the attitude was: 'We just have to plough ahead, to hell with the naysayers, this will come good in the end.' There was no dissent from the Fine Gael parliamentary party. But there was still a recognition in government that the first water charges plan was a failure even before it was put into effect.

Joan Burton was of the view that water charges needed to be made more affordable and predictable, rather than be scrapped altogether. 'Phil Hogan didn't serve the argument very well. Fine Gael was prepared to allow the idea to develop that potentially the water charges could be very, very high,' she said. She knew that was a big worry for parents with teenage and adult children.

Independent Galway West TD Noel Grealish told the story of how parents were telling their children to have their showers in the clubhouse after training because it would cost too much to shower at home.

Fianna Fáil leader Micheál Martin was picking this up too, during his regular canvassing outings. 'The original regime would have meant massive charges on families with teenagers. You have three kids and they come home for showers. This is what the mothers were saying to us. They were right,' he said.[2]

The newspapers were full of examples of just how quickly someone could use up their free allowance of water each day by using the dishwasher, the shower and the washing machine. People were urged to change their toilet flushing habits to save water: 'If it's yellow, let it mellow. If it's brown, flush it down.'

Burton said that she had sought to cap the water charges to deal with people's fears about high water bills. The main work on the revised water charges plan was done by Minister for Finance Michael Noonan and Minister for Public Expenditure Brendan Howlin and their respective secretaries general, Robert Watt and John Moran. Noonan had been a lone voice in opposing the plan to install one million meters. Now, after the loss of so many Fine Gael and Labour council seats in the local elections, he was arguing for a flat charge and for more people to be made exempt. 'Himself and Brendan Howlin formed an alliance to overhaul the water charges themselves, with Robert Watt and John Moran.

'It was a make or break moment,' said a government source.

40

THE RIGHT2WATER
MOVEMENT BEGINS

The anti-meter protests were slowing down Irish Water contractors in Dublin city, Cork city and a number of other locations. But the anti-water charge campaigners knew that it would take a display of 'people power' to get the government to back down on water charges. The strategic plan behind what became the Right2Water campaign was to broaden the water charges movement beyond the active protesters who were stopping meter installers in north Dublin and the southside of Cork city.

There was no chance of the main trade unions, SIPTU and IMPACT, taking part in the campaign because their focus was on protecting the jobs of the 4,300 council water workers they represented. However, a Tesco worker ensured that a smaller union was brought on board. He put forward an anti-water charge motion at the annual conference of the Mandate trade union for retail workers in April. Some Mandate officials thought it was pointless wasting money opposing water charges when it was clear government policy. After all, every other budget measure, such as the property tax, had been implemented without any significant protests. However, the motion was passed by the majority of Mandate members.

Mandate representatives were at the anti-water charge conference at the Gresham Hotel organised by People Before Profit Councillor Bríd Smith. When People Before Profit TD Richard Boyd Barrett followed up with a cross-party meeting in Leinster House, he invited Mandate to that too. There was also another union there, Unite, and its new political organiser, Brendan Ogle. Ogle's job was to work with politicians and the public to help Unite achieve its objectives. It represented only a small number of council water service workers, but it had a history of challenging the social partnership pay deals which were agreed to by the big unions like SIPTU and IMPACT.

Brendan Ogle had grown up in Drogheda in Louth and was one of the country's most strong-willed trade unionists. He had described how his approach made him 'public enemy number one' when he led a train drivers' strike in the 2000s.[1] He gave a fiery speech to the republican socialist party Éirígí in 2011 about resisting the Troika's demands to sell off state assets.[2] In it, he said, 'It's going to require more than good marches, burning cars and smashing up buildings. It's going to require militant industrial action, no holds barred.'[3]

As head of the powerful ESB unions, Ogle had threatened a strike in the run-up to Christmas 2013 over cuts to pensions. It was averted at the last minute. He left his position in February 2014 and decided to take some time out after the death of his father. He went on holiday to a tobacco farm in Cuba.[4]

Ogle started his a new job as political organiser for the Unite trade union when he came back from Cuba. He turned up for the first cross-party meeting in Leinster House in June 2014 with the aim of organising a movement against water charges. There was a mixture of left-wing TDs at the meeting, which was usually a recipe for chaos. Sure enough, Sinn Féin, the Socialist Party and left-wing independents disagreed on what type of protest movement to set up.

Ogle described that first meeting as a 'disaster' in his subsequent book about the anti-water charge movement. Socialist Party TD Ruth Coppinger, who had just won a by-election in Dublin West, said that it was great to see the unions standing up for workers for once. Ogle told her that Unite was always defending workers and did not need to answer to her. 'It was a sour note to a dreadful and almost hopeless meeting. Oh, take me back to that tobacco farm!' he wrote.[5]

Dave Gibney of the Mandate trade union was also there, and he had some practical ideas. Gibney had completed a post-grad course in public relations and worked for the PR guru Pat Montague – a well-known Labour Party activist – for several years. He had just come back from a two-year stint in Melbourne, where he worked with several campaigning Australian labour unions. The unions there had often been founded by Irish-Australians. That meant that anyone with an Irish accent and the right experience could walk into an interview and get hired on the spot. While he was working there, Gibney noticed how they used social media constantly to get their message out.

At the Leinster House meeting, Gibney said that the campaign should be about water as a human right. It had to be 'for something' rather than just against water charges.

'The idea we had was to appeal to the middle ground and not have a protest movement based on the usual suspects who were on every protest. We had to appeal to a different cohort of people,' said Gibney.[6]

Ogle had never met Gibney before. But to break the stalemate, he proposed to the meeting that the two of them would come back in three weeks' time with a plan. Finally, there was agreement at the Leinster House meeting.

Ogle and Gibney met up a week later for a chat. They came up with a plan for three big 'mobilisations'. The first protest march in October would be in one location and as big as possible to give people confidence. The second round of protest marches would be held in local communities. And that would then feed into a third mid-week march to Leinster House in December, to 'frighten the establishment there,' according to Gibney.

After the squabbling at the first meeting in Leinster House, Ogle made it clear that the unions would be in control of the Right2Water messaging – and would pay for it. 'Not being overly aggressive' and 'trying to educate people' had to be two key goals of the Right2Water campaign. Ogle said later that it was about uniting three pillars – the community, the trade unions and the political parties. 'Right2Water was an umbrella campaign. It sought to bring these disparate elements under one heading.'[7]

His fellow organiser, Dave Gibney, knew that relying on the traditional media would not work. Right2Water held several press conferences which got minimal coverage. That in itself was not unusual. 'Protesters announce date of protest' is not the most exciting story. Gibney instead created an event page on Facebook to ensure that social media was used to get the word out about the Right2Water protest on the anti-water charge pages. It in turn was shared by all the left-wing political parties on their Facebook pages.

There is a common perception that having a good Facebook page is enough to draw a crowd to a protest. That is a myth. So Gibney and the Right2Water campaign used other tactics to generate some interest ahead of the first big march.

They had the advantage of having two strong unions, Unite and Mandate, behind them. That meant money to print a huge number of leaflets to publicise the marches. Due to long-standing bulk deals with union printers, the €7,000 supplied by Unite and Mandate was enough to pay for 500,000 leaflets for the major protest marches. Mandate staff member Moira Murphy designed the Right2Water protest march fliers, while Gibney wrote the messages. An oversight committee with members from all the different left-wing parties organised the distribution of the fliers. It was a very valuable network of unpaid couriers.

Gibney said each party should distribute in the areas where they were strongest. 'Sinn Féin would say, "We'll take 60,000 fliers," People Before Profit said, "We'll take 20,000 and distribute them in Dún Laoghaire." It was door-to-door stuff,' said Gibney. Any remaining leaflets were posted out by Mandate and Unite to their shop stewards and to regular union members.

The second awareness-raising tactic was a series of local Right2Water meetings around the country to get people interested. Each of them was arranged by local political parties in their strongholds. At a public meeting in the Newgrange Hotel in Navan, a woman stood up to tell the others how she was getting ready for water charges. She had a skin condition and had been told to have a bath once a day. But she was getting herself used to a bath once a week. 'I've been preparing for this for a couple of weeks now,' she said.

Nobody was clear about how much the bill would cost, or how the system of household allowances would work. 'It was that arrogance that really got to people. Just go away. We're bringing this in whether you like it or not,' said Gibney.

Water charges were due to begin on 1 October. The rate of installation of meters in parts of Dublin suddenly started to drop off, as protests started to intensify. Irish Water turned to the gardaí for help.

41

THE THIN BLUE LINE

The gardaí had never seen anything like the water protests before. At the start, there had been no significant garda presence during the meter installations. But Irish Water Managing Director John Tierney held a meeting with Garda Commissioner Nóirín O'Sullivan in June 2014 to appeal for garda protection for the meter installers. After that meeting the gardaí became a very visible presence, in the estates on the northside of Dublin in particular.

The planning by gardaí in the Dublin Metropolitan Region's Northern Division was shambolic at the start. Around twelve gardaí would be sent into estates in Edenmore and Ayrfield for continuous twelve-hour shifts. They had no meal breaks and no toilets. 'We were pissed off. You were stuck in one spot with gougers shouting at you and no break,' said one garda who was there at the time.

When the water meter installers tried to dig a hole, the protesters jumped into it, preventing them from working. Gardaí pulled protesters out of the holes. There was an angry reaction. 'The crowd were nearly hissing at you, with cameras in your face. It was gone nearly to the riot stage,' said the garda. Some of the protesters called gardaí 'scumbags' and 'gobshites'. Other protesters taunted gardaí that they were the 'Black and Tans'. 'Is your mother proud of you, guard?' was another popular jibe. Gardaí were finding their authority being undermined on a daily basis. They were telling protesters to get out from behind barriers, to stop interfering with meter installations and to get off the road. The protesters refused.

Damien Farrell said a lot of the gardaí could not come to terms with this. 'You're not getting off the road, you're not doing what I'm telling you to do. Even the younger ones couldn't comprehend that. We weren't scumbags, we weren't drug dealers. We weren't the usual person they were used to dealing with. And they were really frustrated by it,' he said.[1]

The official garda policy had three objectives: to allow the meter installers to do their work, to allow peaceful protest and to protect the safety of the public.

Every morning forty gardaí from all around the city assembled at Coolock garda station for an early conference at 6.30 a.m. and then set off at 7 a.m. But a local man living near the station used to tell the protesters what route they were going on. Other protesters used to follow the gardaí to find out exactly where the meter installers would be working that day.

There was a major problem with the legislation the gardaí were working under. Gardaí were told to make arrests under the 2007 Water Services Act, which made it an offence to interfere with the installation of a water meter. Under that legislation, gardaí had to arrest a protester to get his name and address, and then release him from the garda station shortly afterwards. It was completely ineffective as a deterrent. The protesters used to have cars waiting outside Coolock garda station so that a protester could be brought back instantly to the front line. Some protesters were arrested several times per day. There were at least seventy-five arrests made under this Act, but the authorities confirmed this figure could include some people being arrested on 'multiple occasions'.[2]

Gardaí thought it was mad to be using a law as ineffective as the Water Services Act when they had a tried and tested alternative: the Public Order Act. It allowed them to give a direction to a person to desist from an activity, or to leave the area. If they refused to obey, they could be arrested. This was the law that gardaí had been using for years on the streets.

'If that was happening at twelve at night on a main street anywhere, you'd be lifting these lads. You wouldn't tolerate it,' said one garda.

Gardaí did use the Public Order Act to make at least ninety-one arrests during water charge protests.[3] However, there was also a problem using this law, as it could be used only in public areas. When the contractors set up their barriers around the spot on the footpath where they wanted to put in a meter, this square suddenly became a private work space. When protesters jumped in over the barrier to stop the meters being installed, gardaí could not direct them to leave using the Public Order Act.

Garda Chief Superintendent Fergus Healy later gave court evidence that protesters could be asked to move along only if they were outside the barriers. 'It's a "Catch 22" situation we find ourselves in,' he said.[4] After that court hearing, some of the water protesters quoted the chief superintendent's remarks to the gardaí if they tried to get them to move out from behind a barrier.

Garda management did sort out the basic policing problems on the estates within a few weeks. They put in twice as many gardaí, so that they could rotate. There were proper breaks. And an inspector was put in charge of the unit instead of a sergeant.

Protesters kept recording the gardaí on their smartphones. Clips started to appear on YouTube showing gardaí pushing protesters. Gardaí complained that these clips were edited and did not show the full picture. 'You would see a guard pushing at a fellow. But you would never see the crowd pushing the guard before that,' said one garda.

In frustration, some gardaí started filming the protesters on their own smartphones. They developed other techniques. One was to call out the name and address of the water protester, which stopped the protester putting that video online.

Still, the gardaí knew that the videos uploaded by protesters were undermining their authority in the community. 'It set a bad precedent. This is what you can do now. Fellows wouldn't have shoved a camera in your face before,' said one garda.

In response, gardaí in the Dublin Metropolitan Region's Northern Division were given official body cameras to wear during the protests. Gardaí were instructed to inform protesters that they were being recorded. There were usually two gardaí per unit with the body cameras, which were little square devices on their chests.[5] It was one of the first times gardaí had ever used body cameras. It had been inspired by the protesters' use of smartphones.

At the time, there were riots in the US by black protesters about police brutality. At one Irish protest, gardaí heard a protester shouting: 'Kick them in the shins, that's what they are doing in America.' It worked both ways. Some gardaí claim they kicked back.

Gardaí knew that they could not go back to the days of the 1980s when their predecessors would have given the protesters a 'clip around the ear'. But they found it to be a very frustrating experience to just have to tolerate it. 'The more the gougers get away with it, the more they run amok. The more they will push it and push it,' said one garda.

However, Socialist Party TD Joe Higgins insisted that people in these communities were right to use their 'people power' to fight back. 'There were verbals in heated situations. But communities were really angered by the fact that the guards were sent in, in large numbers, to support Irish Water. People were angry and they were righteously angry,' he said.[6]

There was high unemployment in some of the estates, which meant there were protesters available Monday to Friday. The garda view of the protesters was mixed. They believed there were 'some decent protesters' but 'some real gougers' as well. They suspected some of the protesters of orchestrating others, pushing young fellows to the front and staying back themselves. 'There were a lot of innocent eejits they were riling up,' said one garda. During one protest, a man in his thirties was throwing bollards in the air. Gardaí warned him that he was going to get arrested, while the fellows putting him up to it would not be. He started crying, but he eventually calmed down and stopped.

There were older gardaí who were convinced that there was a 'sinister fringe' involved in directing some of the protests. They talked between themselves about the burning down of the British Embassy in Dublin in 1972 after British paratroopers killed thirteen unarmed protesters on the streets of Derry. At that time, there were IRA members at the back, directing operations.

A garda spokesman said that the policing of the protests had been 'onerous and difficult' for its members. He said they had encountered 'considerable resistance' when trying to allow meter installers and their vehicles to move in and out of sites.[7]

Gardaí were also baffled as to why they were being sent to support meter installations in some of the working-class estates in the first place. 'None of those were ever going to pay their water charges. They wouldn't pay their TV licence or their dog licence,' one garda source said.

Garda management made another change which helped to compensate for some of the verbal abuse that front-line gardaí were getting from the protesters. They started to pay more overtime. But that was of little use to gardaí who came from the local area. They did not want to be policing the protest because they knew the protesters personally or had family members living there. Some of them were able to shrug it off. There was a community policeman who knew all the protesters and that used to infuriate them. He would laugh it off when they told him that they used to get on well with him. His response was: 'I get on well with ninety per cent of the estate.'

There were, however, more serious incidents. Some of the gardaí got followed home. Others had threatening messages posted on their personal

Facebook accounts. A couple of patrol cars had their tyres slashed. A female garda had her home address put up on the Internet.

Minister for Justice Frances Fitzgerald said that there had been very few reports of gardaí misbehaving, despite the fact they were receiving 'an awful lot of abuse'. She added, 'It was personally incredibly challenging for gardaí. I thought they showed remarkable resilience in the face of provocation.'[8]

As the protests grew and grew, gardaí believed it was becoming impossible to protect the meter installers without risking a major public order incident. And they did not want to further damage relations with the community. Towards the end of November 2014, gardaí in the Dublin Metropolitan Region's Northern Division were told by management to let the protesters at it. The gist of it was: 'If they want to block the meter installers, let them block them.' From then on, gardaí stopped pulling and dragging protesters out of the holes dug for meters. And their response times slowed down. 'Our hierarchy were afraid to get involved. They were very aware it was so political,' said one garda.

Independent Dublin South Central TD Joan Collins had been arrested in Crumlin for protesting against the installation of water meters. The judge in the case ruled that the state had not provided sufficient evidence to support the charge.[9] But she always kept talking to local gardaí because she had a 'fairly good relationship' with them. She was not surprised to see their pivot on the policing of the water protests. 'The guards actually pulled out because they said they weren't going to put their members under that sort of pressure because of the resistance of their community. It wasn't just lefties or political activists, it was ordinary people,' she said.[10]

Collins was a long-term left-wing activist, having been one of those expelled from the Labour Party in 1989 along with her partner, Dermot Connolly. Both of them had made the point to gardaí that while they were policing meter installations, there were armed drug barons driving around in big cars with bulletproof vests, flaunting their lifestyle and attracting the unemployed youth. The protesters used to tell the gardaí: 'It's easy [to] arrest me. Go up and arrest your man up there who has a machine gun.'[11]

Irish Water soon found out about the new garda policy. Whereas they had previously been able to get a rapid garda response if contractors were under siege from protesters, now it could take an hour or two hours or even longer.

The company would be told politely that gardaí were on other vital duties and were not available right away. The meter installers were going mad because they could not do their work.

One day, with the meter installers heading home early, Derek Byrne and other members of the Dublin Says No group decided to have a party outside a house in Ayrfield at Halloween. They put 'Born Slippy', the dance track by British electronic group Underworld and made famous by the *Trainspotting* soundtrack, playing on a beatbox. The protesters all started dancing around eating jelly babies. A local garda came up to the driveway of the house to find out what was going on. 'Ah, the illegal rave is busted,' said Byrne. 'Here, hide the jelly babies.' The garda headed off.[12]

There had also been protests against water meters in council estates in Bray in Wicklow. A large force of gardaí arrived with meter installers at the Fassaroe estate in Bray in the run-up to Christmas. This 600-house estate had gone through tough times since it was built in the 1970s. There were around 100 residents protesting at the entrance to the estate. They had put up a sign: 'You are now entering Free Fassaroe – get out and support to keep it meter free.' There was a twenty-four-hour picket. Sinn Féin Councillor John Brady told the senior garda in charge that forcing the installation of the meters in the estate could damage relations with the community. 'Irish Water won't be around in six months, but you will still be here,' he said. The gardaí pulled back and the protesters slow-marched the meter installers out. 'We were singing Christmas carols,' said Brady.[13]

Former justice minister, Frances Fitzgerald, confirmed that the gardaí had decided to pull back as the protests became 'hot and heavy'. She said, 'They were very prudent in their approach. There was never a wish to get into a confrontation. It would just be provocative and it wouldn't be without a price.'

Water charge protesters submitted complaints about the garda policing of the water charge protests to the Garda Ombudsman. The majority related to incidents in north Dublin. The Garda Ombudsman examined videos from protesters and from the gardaí's own body cameras as part of its investigation into twenty-three complaints. 'No clear evidence of garda misconduct was shown in the majority of the videos and in some cases they showed that the actions of the gardaí concerned were proportionate,' it stated.[14] One investigation file about a complaint of assault on a female by a garda was sent to the Director of Public Prosecutions for consideration. No prosecution resulted.[15]

The clashes between gardaí and protesters in the estates in Edenmore, Ayrfield and along Tonagee Road had created tensions. But there was a different type of protest being carried out in Cork, where an entire island had risen up against water charges.

42

THE ISLAND THAT SAID 'NO'

Cobh was to become famous in the anti-water charge movement. The town is located on Great Island in Cork city's harbour. There are only two ways of getting on and off the island – by going over a bridge or by getting a ferry. It had no sewage treatment plant so raw sewage was being discharged into the harbour.

The key figure in the protest movement was Karen Doyle, a married mother with no history of involvement in trade unions or party politics. She had stayed involved after her first anti-household charge meeting in the Commodore Hotel in the town in 2011. The disintegration of that campaign had not put her off. She felt that the campaign against water charges would be different. 'A few of us would always say that water is the one the Irish people will not go for. We knew there would be massive resistance to it. And we seemed to be the only ones who knew it,' she said.[1]

Cobh is a town of great history: the last stopping point for the *Titanic* on its doomed voyage, a former base for the British Army, and the birthplace of Olympic athlete Sonia O'Sullivan. But it was also a former industrial town. The giant cranes of the Verolme dockyard were a local landmark and a reminder of how 1,500 people had once worked there before it closed in 1984.[2] Out in the bay lies Haulbowline island, the site of the Irish Steel plant which closed in 2001 with the loss of 400 jobs.

Socialist Party Councillor Mick Barry said he could recognise the former trade union shop stewards when they stood up to speak at protest meetings in Cobh. 'You had a history of industrial work and a trade union tradition of solidarity. And you had a distinct community on an island. I think those two things fused to make Cobh a powerhouse in the anti-metering campaign,' he said.[3]

Cobh was identified early on by Irish Water as a place where there could be resistance to water meters. 'A lot of residents consider themselves islanders. They have an island mentality,' said one former Irish Water staffer.

Karen Doyle and the Cobh Says No to Austerity group were waiting for the meter installers to come onto their island. They had called the Ballyphehane/ South Parish Says No group for advice about what to do. Then, in September 2014, the action began.

Doyle got a phone call from a member of the group to say that Irish Water's contractors J. Murphy & Sons were on Paddy O'Sullivan's Place, opposite Cobh Ramblers football stadium. The street was named after local IRA volunteer Paddy O'Sullivan, who had been a member of a Cork flying column in the War of Independence. He was captured by the British Army in 1921 and executed.

Doyle drove up to Paddy O'Sullivan's Place and spotted a man in a van looking at a stopcock. She and another group member started knocking on doors, telling residents: 'They are going to start installing meters, do you want one?' The majority of people didn't want one. The man in the van agreed to leave.

At this stage, Cobh Says No to Austerity was a tiny group of around ten to fifteen people with its own Facebook page. But word of the start of water metering spread around the town. That night Doyle went to the group's regular weekly meeting in the Great Island community centre, which is just 400 metres from St Colman's Cathedral. She thought there was another event on because all the parking spaces around the centre were taken up. When she started to climb the stairs to 'Room 13', their regular venue on the first floor of the centre, there were people standing on the stairs. There were eighty people inside and outside the small room. They had come because they remembered the Cobh Says No to Austerity group's weekly protests against the €100 household charge and water charges in the town's streets. 'I'm so glad we kept up that walking on the white line and being visible because we never knew if people realised we were there or not till that night,' said Doyle.

Cobh Says No to Austerity quickly organised a rota of protesters to keep watch on the only two ways that Murphy & Sons personnel could get onto the island. The first was the road route, which connected Cobh to Fota Island and the mainland. 'There was a watcher at Fota Road – he would say there are four trucks, two vans, a compressor, before he went to work. This would be at 5.30 a.m.,' said Doyle.[4] She would be waiting herself as the contractors' vans and trucks came on Fota Road to Belvelly Bridge, the only land connection to the island. The second watcher was located near the Carrigaloe port, in case the contractors used the ferry from Glenbrook outside Cork city to make the four-minute crossing to the island. And there was a third person on duty each morning, on Ticknock Hill, to see where the contractors went once they got onto the island. 'By the time Irish Water got into our town, we knew the direction they were going, we knew the roads they were taking and we were able to alert certain estates to get out, which they did,' said Doyle.

Group members followed the Irish Water contractor vans in their cars. If they were in front of the van, they would slow right down to a crawl to give estates enough time to organise themselves. The local taxi drivers were also providing information. The contractors usually had white vans. Local protester Anthony Sheridan said they were stopping every white van to check if they were involved in metering. 'Some of them would say, "Lads, I was here yesterday, I'm cleared." I thought it was amazing you could have ordinary people acting as policemen, really,' he said.[5]

That was something that other water protesters experienced as well. People who had been left powerless as the recession hit now had a sense of power. But the campaign still would not have worked if the people of Cobh were not against the water meters. The campaign went into estates, knocking on doors and inviting people to join street meetings. Doyle saw people out at 8 a.m. in the Rushbrook Manor estate in Cobh, raising their hands to take votes about what to do. 'I had never seen anything like that and maybe I never will. It really gave people a sense of democracy. They really felt they had a say,' she said.

At those meetings, they took votes on what to do when the meter installers turned up. The usual decision was that people who wanted a meter could get one – but those who did not would be supported. 'There was going to be no hard feelings because we all have to live together and I thought that was really important,' said Doyle.

She dropped off and collected her teenage children from school every day and in between helped to keep watch at an estate for meter installers. Red and white posters started to appear on the porch doors and windows of houses in Cobh with the slogan 'No consent – no contract – no meter here.' It was a way for people to protest without having to go outside their front door.

***

Then, on the morning of 30 October 2014, Doyle got a phone call telling her that the Murphy's workers were starting to install meters in the Woodside estate in Rushbrook Manor in Cobh. It was now Halloween and the decorations were up on houses around the estate. She met a man there who frantically told her that he '100 per cent' did not want a meter. But he had to leave his house for a work meeting. Doyle asked the contractors to put meters into the houses on either side of the man's property, because they had no 'anti-meter' posters on their windows. 'I was met with stony silence. Under no circumstances were they budging,' she said. Doyle stood on the stopcock at the request of the homeowner who was going to work. The foreman asked her to please move or he would have to call the gardaí. 'There's no way I'm going to move because I promised I wouldn't,' said Doyle. 'And ye made a promise that ye are breaking.' This claim of a broken promise refers to the fact that her group had always believed that no household would be forced to get a meter against their will.

The gardaí arrived and warned Doyle and two other members of Cobh Says No to Austerity that they faced arrest for obstruction under the Water Services Act 2007 if they did not move off the stopcock.[6]

By that time, word had gotten out around Cobh about what was happening. Around 100 people had come into the estate to watch the standoff. The owner of the house was there, saying he did not want a water meter. There was complete silence and shock when gardaí arrested Doyle and her two fellow protesters and put them in their squad car. In a show of defiance, a woman came out of her house with a child on her hip and stood on a stopcock. Others did the same. Doyle said it sent out a message that they were all willing to be arrested. 'There was just this really peaceful silence in protest. It was pretty powerful,' she said.

The Cobh Says No to Austerity group had enjoyed good relations with the gardaí up to that point. The approach of the gardaí in Cobh had been different to that of the gardaí involved in policing the anti-water meter protests in Edenmore and Ayrfield on the northside of Dublin. They did not pull protesters away from standing on stopcocks. Doyle and her two fellow protesters were treated gently when they were arrested. When they were brought into Cobh garda station, the joke was 'Here's the Cobh Three' and they were offered a cup of tea and released an hour later. 'Our guards really seemed to get what community policing was. I felt respected by them. I think everyone would agree they were pretty decent,' said Doyle.

She and other members of the group did not know why it had been different in parts of Dublin: 'When we saw the violence happening in Dublin, I do think people were frightened of that. They said, "We don't want that, that's not us." I said, "Well, whatever's happening in Dublin, there has to be a breakdown in communication."'

Doyle had never been arrested before. Her mother, Kit Stoat, was waiting for her outside Cobh garda station when she was released. She gave her daughter a big hug and said, 'Well done.'

'Obviously being her mother, I was a bit nervous. I just knew she wasn't going to back down,' Kit said.[7]

Karen Doyle also had strong support from her husband, Chris. 'He's been so great, really. So many times I said, "I'm giving it up." He'd smile and say, "Naah, you're not done."' But she had to come home to her three teenage boys and explain why she had been arrested. 'I wanted to just say that sometimes you do have to take a stand against what you would see as an injustice and I felt the theft of our water was a big injustice,' she said.

Doyle found herself being interviewed by a TV reporter from *NBC News*. 'In her forty-three years, mother-of-three Karen Doyle had never gotten so much as a parking ticket. But a couple of weeks ago, she found herself being hauled off by police in the Irish seaport of Cobh,' the report said. NBC could not resist mentioning the rain. 'It's no small irony that water has become the central controversy in Ireland, a country of 4.5 million, surrounded by an ocean, that stays a lush green thanks to 150-plus rainy days per year.'[8]

The Murphy's contractors did return on another occasion at night-time to the same Woodside estate where Doyle had been arrested. Within ten minutes, there were eighty protesters out there. They slow-marched the contractors out of the estate, singing the chorus from a Bananarama hit song: 'Na Na Na Na, Hey Hey Hey, Goodbye'. 'It took us about forty-five minutes and they didn't come back,' said Doyle.

***

After Doyle's arrest, Cobh Says No to Austerity changed tactics. There was a collective decision by representatives of the various parts of the town to have a picket on all of the estate entrances to keep the contractors out. Doyle said it had been an 'own goal' for the contractors to have abandoned their previous practice of giving householders a choice about getting a meter. 'If they had kept up the agreement, they definitely would have got a hell of a lot of more meters installed in Cobh,' she said. Every estate gathered money to buy tents and shelters for people picketing at the estate entrance. One estate bought a second-hand caravan. Another estate had a horsebox.

They turned into community hubs for residents. Locals would be out from 6 a.m. onwards. They used to pay a few euro each into a kitty every week for food supplies and cylinders of gas for heating. There were a lot of women on the pickets because they were at home caring for their parents or their children. They would bring down stews, soups and sandwiches. Another local woman used to fill up the back of her car with flasks of tea and sandwiches, driving around to the pickets outside different estates in Cobh. Local protester Vivienne Farrell said the women on the front line made a difference. 'We always said it was the ladies pushing the buggies that would win the day,' she said.[9]

There were humorous homemade posters erected at the estate entrances. 'Hands off our stop cock – No to meters' and 'Splish splash – I am taking my bath'. The protesters put up adverts on one of the safety barriers left by the contractors for a 'bill burning barbeque – as sponsored by Murphys and Irish Water'.

By Christmas, the 'No consent – no contract – no meter here' posters were on the windows of the majority of houses in Cobh. Forty-two estates and streets in Cobh came out against water charges. 'The town was almost on strike till Christmas,' said Doyle.

Taking part in the pickets at the entrances to estates gave people a sense of purpose. Doyle met one man who had suffered from depression. He told her: 'I'm really well because of this. I am getting out of my house and I'm talking to people and I feel I have somewhere to go in the morning.' There were discussions on politics and the state of the country. Just like in Dublin, the pickets helped to bring back the tight-knit community spirit that had been lost over the Celtic Tiger years.

Doyle's parents grew up at a time when neighbours lived in each other's pockets, but she herself felt it had gone too far in the other direction. 'Because so many people became so isolated back in those Celtic Tiger years, when it was all flash and holidays and people on the never-never. You didn't know your neighbour, until then,' she said.

Taoiseach Enda Kenny had frequently spoken of his desire for a re-creation of *meitheal* – the old Irish tradition of neighbours coming together to bring in the harvest. This was what he had seen himself growing up in Mayo. His government's water charges plan was uniting towns like Cobh, just not in the way he had expected.

The Murphy & Sons' contractors kept coming but managed to install very few meters. The Cobh group had a trump card, again due to the island's geography. They had told Irish Water that they would block the Belvelly Bridge if necessary to stop water metering. That would have stopped all road traffic getting on and off the island. 'If they closed the bridge, it would have been unacceptable from our point of view. It was threatened,' said an Irish Water source.

Cobh was a write-off for Irish Water. On the political front, too, its troubles were growing. It had recently been heavily criticised by the minister who had helped to set it up.

43

NOONAN POURS COLD WATER

Irish Water's head of communications, Elizabeth Arnett, got a phone call at 6 a.m. from the government press secretary, Feargal Purcell, on 7 October 2014 informing her that Irish Water was under attack from the man who had steered through the legislation to set it up.

Former minister of state Fergus O'Dowd was frustrated that his internal warnings about the Irish Water project had not been heeded. And he was very disappointed that he had been sacked by Taoiseach Enda Kenny during the summer reshuffle. Now he had written an article in the *Irish Independent* about Irish Water.

'I warned the department at a high level meeting that it was going to be an unmitigated disaster if there was not enough engagement with the public and that has proven to be the case,' he wrote. He went on to criticise the fact that senior executives in Irish Water would be entitled to bonus payments, saying they should be scrapped. 'It was a key concern of mine that Irish Water did not become another cosseted quango with a bonus culture … Sadly, the opposite has happened. Irish Water has come across as arrogant and uncaring, demanding money and PPS numbers without explaining why all this is necessary.'[1]

Purcell discussed with Arnett what to do. He already had an idea. Kenny was due to launch a social welfare strategy that day. Purcell's plan was to pre-announce the forthcoming income tax cuts in the budget, now just a week away, to distract the media from O'Dowd's criticisms of Irish Water.

It worked, to a large extent, because the media always loves stories about tax cuts or tax increases. 'Budget will start process of cutting back tax, says Kenny' was the headline in *The Irish Times* the next day. However, there was still anger in government and Irish Water at O'Dowd's article. But none of his criticisms were misplaced. The communication campaign for water charges had been poor. And the existence of a bonus scheme for Irish Water staff had created huge anger amongst a public that was experiencing job losses and wage cuts.[2] 'I just felt they weren't doing it right. Nobody has ever challenged that,' said O'Dowd.[3]

Labour was also under pressure from one of their own. The SIPTU president, Jack O'Connor, a long-term Labour member, was calling on the government to set a date for a referendum to ensure that Irish Water could never be sold off to the private sector. That was a big fear of the council water service workers whom SIPTU represented. It was also a growing issue for voters. It never happened.

O'Connor complained later that he had no influence on the political approach of the Labour Party during its time in government. 'I learned, sometime during Joan Burton's period as leader, that the best way for me to persuade them to do anything was to urge them to do the opposite. There was an absolute contempt for what was perceived as an old-style cloth-capped trade unionist,' he said.[4]

The government did examine the possibility of having a referendum to guarantee that Irish Water would remain in public ownership. 'But we didn't think of a wording that people would accept,' said a government source. Tánaiste Joan Burton and Public Expenditure Minister Brendan Howlin thought that having a referendum was a mad idea. 'We wanted to get away from talking about water – not have a referendum that would give a platform to our enemies. The whole thing was tactically inept,' said a senior Labour source.

Despite the widespread privatisation fears, there was no secret plan in the government to sell off Irish Water. Kenny's economic adviser, Andrew McDowell, who had come up with the idea of Irish Water, told people that it was a 'total red herring'. His priority was getting Irish Water off the state's books so that it could borrow like the ESB. Labour's Eamon Gilmore said it had never come up. 'In fairness to Fine Gael, they never advanced the idea of privatisation,' he said.[5]

Even the Department of Finance, which was always suspected of wanting to privatise as many state assets as possible, was not interested. It had been burned by the privatisation of Telecom Éireann under former Taoiseach Bertie Ahern's Fianna Fáil–Progressive Democrats coalition government. That had involved the sell-off of not only Telecom Éireann's retail business but the crucial telephone network as well. When the state wanted to put high-speed broadband fibre optic cables on the phone lines for its rural broadband plan, it found itself having to negotiate with Eir, the new private owners. A senior official in the Department of Finance said they did not want to repeat that experience by selling off the country's water pipes.

The government's focus was now on getting the October budget through. It was Finance Minister Michael Noonan's first post-austerity budget. Just as Kenny had flagged up, there were tax cuts for the first time in six years. The top rate of tax was cut from forty-one per cent to forty per cent and more lower income workers were exempted from the Universal Social Charge. Noonan was delighted. But when he went into the Fine Gael parliamentary party meeting during budget week, all the TDs were talking about was water charges. 'It ruined the budget for him. Noonan went into an epic sulk, a week-long one, like only he could,' said a Labour source.

Noonan had always put an emphasis on telling little stories in his budget speech to try to bring voters along with him.[6] But his attempts to control the narrative in the recent budget had failed due to water charges. Joan Burton noted that Noonan had included a €100 income tax break for people who paid their water charges in the budget. 'But of course, tax breaks only apply to people who pay tax. A huge amount of people in Ireland who are lower paid, don't pay any tax,' she said.[7]

***

The government went into crisis mode after the budget. It was desperate to get the issue of water charges off the table. There were a series of meetings of the EMC, at one of which Noonan made a dramatic intervention. He told the ministers and advisers that the government had come into office with the biggest majority ever. It had got out of the bailout and started to fix the unemployment problem, so it should be able to get a second term. But Noonan warned that water charges were getting in the way of that and that the government should no longer go ahead with them.

His change of heart came as a complete shock to Andrew McDowell, and to Mark Kennelly, Enda Kenny's chief of staff. 'Their jaws dropped,' said a government source.

Noonan had now adopted the same position as the government secretary general, Martin Fraser, who was also in the room. Another senior civil servant,

John Callinan, later to play a key role in the Brexit negotiations, was listening too. 'Fraser and Callinan realised it was significant,' said the government source. It was not a comfortable position for Fine Gael to be out of step with the views of Fraser, their most senior civil servant.

Enda Kenny kept listening without giving away his own position. But McDowell was not going to give up on the Irish Water project that he had devised. He believed that if the government caved on this issue, it would have to cave on everything else. Environment Minister Alan Kelly said: 'Andrew McDowell would have been very strong on water charges, that we had to drive this home.'[8]

McDowell had been described by a former government special adviser as someone you would hate to play poker with because 'he keeps his cards very close to his chest'. He was seen as a guard dog in government for protecting core Fine Gael policies. When Labour had wanted to increase the Universal Social Charge for people earning over €100,000 in the budget for 2013, McDowell led the Fine Gael resistance. Education Minister Ruairí Quinn wrote in his diary that 'the Labour ministers were told that the Government could collapse because of the intransigence of Fine Gael, who are dominated by Andrew McDowell'.[9]

Labour suspected that McDowell was going to get Noonan back in line with the official Fine Gael position on water charges. Sure enough, when the EMC met again a week later, Noonan's tune had changed. He did not repeat his call for water charges to be suspended. 'Fine Gael did a full push-back job on Noonan. They got to him,' said a Labour adviser.

The metering programme made it harder for the government to pull back. Irish Water's contractors had already installed 475,000 meters in the ground. The government would be accused of wasting hundreds of millions of euro on the meters if water charges were cancelled.

But the government was now going to come under even more political pressure to do just that, due to the outcome of the Dublin South West by-election.

44

THE SOCIALIST TRIUMPH

The Dublin South West by-election might never have happened if the leadership heave against Enda Kenny had succeeded. One of the ringleaders in that ill-fated 2010 campaign was Fine Gael Dublin South West TD Brian Hayes. He was not completely cast into the wilderness like other rebels after the 2011 general election. Kenny put him in as minister of state at the Department of Finance. But it was clear to him that he would not be made a cabinet minister as long as Kenny was leader. So Hayes decided to run in the European Parliament elections instead in 2014, and got elected as an MEP for Dublin. That was why there was a by-election in Dublin South West in October 2014.

The Socialist Party were rank outsiders because they had got just five per cent of the vote in the constituency in the 2011 general election. Some claimed that former MEP Paul Murphy was a parachute candidate for the Socialist Party in the Dublin South West by-election. But their previous candidate, Councillor Mick Murphy, an engineer from the village of Killenaule in Tipperary, was fully supportive of putting Paul Murphy forward instead of him. 'Paul was just after the European elections. He had the profile,' he said.[1]

Mick Murphy never usually gambled, but he could not resist the 8–1 odds the bookmakers were giving Paul Murphy for the by-election. He put down €50. Others in the party who had put down earlier bets had got odds of 15–1. Mick Murphy believed they would be able to outmanoeuvre Sinn Féin's candidate, Councillor Cathal King, who was the clear favourite to win. 'We felt we could do this. It's like going to battle with a dinosaur. Sinn Féin are completely inflexible,' he said.

Paul Murphy had spent three years in the European Parliament in Brussels, having taken over Joe Higgins' seat when the latter got elected to the Dáil in 2011. He had paid his water charges in Brussels on the grounds that it was established practice over there. He had lost out in European elections in May, and felt very little pressure running in the Dublin South West by-election because he did not think he would win. He told the national committee of the

Socialist Party in the Teachers' Club on Parnell Square that it was going to be a two-election strategy. 'We thought that Sinn Féin had such a commanding lead that it would be very difficult for us to win. Our strategy was to do well in the by-election and then win a seat in the following general election,' he said.[2] This was what had happened in 1996 when Joe Higgins missed out narrowly in the Dublin West by-election which led to the abolition of water charges two months later. He ran again in the 1997 general election and won a seat at the expense of Labour's Joan Burton.

***

Paul Murphy saw Joe Higgins for the first time at a protest against low pay in 1998 when he was fifteen. That was at the time of the anti-globalisation movement and the Battle of Seattle.[3] He had grown up in Goatstown in a middle-class family. His father, Kieran, was a senior manager with the Irish division of the food company Mars. He had died from cancer when his son was just eleven years old. Did the loss of his father influence Murphy's political career? 'I really have no answer to that. I like to think that I'd probably have turned out similar. And I wouldn't have a sense of it that it has been a driving factor,' he said. 'But of course people aren't very good at analysing themselves.'

Paul Murphy joined the Socialist Party when he went to study law in UCD in 2004. He was one of the 500 students who blockaded the then minister for education, Noel Dempsey, in the UCD veterinary building for four hours when he came to open it. At the time, Dempsey was trying to bring in third-level fees. 'I was one of the organisers of the protest. We were at the various entrances to the building. There was quite a lively student movement at that time,' said Murphy. The young student was subsequently arrested at protests organised by the bricklayers' union BATU against a construction company which was building student accommodation in UCD. He was also arrested for protesting against the Corrib gas pipeline in Rossport, although he was never charged with anything.

Paul Murphy had been the director of elections in Dublin South West for local Socialist Party Councillor Mick Murphy in 2011. 'I knew all the key people and I knew the area very well,' he said. Running under the banner of the 'Anti-Austerity Alliance', he planned to focus on the abolition of water charges but was unsure about how effective it would be.

During public meetings in the by-election campaign, he realised that water charges was indeed the most powerful campaign issue. He and Joe Higgins turned up for a public meeting in Jobstown community centre in mid-September, which attracted around eighty people in a room designed for fifty. Some Sinn Féin councillors turned up at the meeting to disrupt it. Paul Murphy said one of their arguments was that boycotting the water charges would not work. 'What they said went down extremely badly with the crowd, and people turned on Sinn Féin at the meeting and had a go at them for not supporting non-payment, for not being in principle opposed to water charges,' he said.

The TV series gripping the nation at the time was RTÉ's *Love/Hate*, an urban crime drama with a relentless body count. It was airing to audiences of up to one million people every Sunday night. Its portrayal of a disintegrating society matched the national mood of doom and gloom after years of recession. That was the backdrop to the by-election in Dublin South West, one of the poorest constituencies in the country. There was a couple interviewed on RTÉ News in the Square shopping centre in Tallaght during the by-election. The woman said they were walking around with empty bags because they could not afford to buy anything. 'We're coming up here to keep warm because we can't put the heating on in the house,' she said.[4]

The Anti-Austerity Alliance held another anti-water charge meeting in Firhouse, where Paul Murphy and Joe Higgins were the double act again. Higgins told the crowd that it could repeat the impact of the 1996 by-election in Dublin West, which he had almost won, by electing an anti-water charge TD. 'You can shock the establishment,' he said.

Paul Murphy said the crowd loved it. 'You could just tell this was working. We made the point to people – what difference does one extra Sinn Féin TD make in the Dáil? The entire establishment expected Sinn Féin to win.'

The by-election was becoming a two-horse race.

Fianna Fáil's candidate was Councillor John Lahart, an able politician who had learned a lot from his years working with former Fianna Fáil minister Tom Kitt. However, he could not articulate any party position on whether to keep or abolish water charges, because Fianna Fáil still had not developed one.

Fine Gael's candidate, Senator Cáit Keane, was finding it tough too. When Minister for Justice Frances Fitzgerald was canvassing for her in an estate in Tallaght with a handful of party supporters at night-time, a group of water protesters heard about it and started following her around from door to door. 'We were chased out of the estate. People were following us with loudspeakers. That was the end of the canvass,' Fitzgerald said.[5]

Former Labour minister Pat Rabbitte was canvassing for his party's candidate, Councillor Pamela Kearns, in Templeogue. The water charges had just come into force and Irish Water was sending out letters reminding people to send back their registration forms. Rabbitte came up to the door of a house. He couldn't see a bell to ring so he grabbed the lid of the letter box and rapped it. There was an envelope in it, which fell to the floor. A big man came out in a T-shirt and stooped down to pick up the letter. It had the distinctive blue and white Irish Water logo on it. 'So you're not happy about fucking imposing water charges, you're going around delivering the bills yourself,' he told Rabbitte.

Sinn Féin had realised that water charges was the big issue, after spending the first six days talking about housing. The party made a lot of mistakes during the campaign. The biggest one came on 8 October 2014.

Party leader Gerry Adams and Mary Lou McDonald were promising to scrap water charges in their alternative budget plan in the Alexander Hotel. A reporter asked them if they would be paying their water charges. Adams and McDonald were caught off-guard by the question. They both said they would pay their water charges. Sinn Féin had been burned by its experience of boycotting the bills during the anti-bin charges campaign in the early 2000s. The councils in Dublin imposed the unpaid bin taxes on people's houses instead. The Sinn Féin representatives who were calling for boycotts got blamed.

Now, Sinn Féin was getting it in the neck from water charge protesters who saw their willingness to pay as tacit support for water charges. It was little consolation that Sinn Féin Dublin South Central TD Aengus Ó Snodaigh had said at the same press conference that he was not paying his water charges. All the focus was on Adams, the leader, and McDonald, the leader-in-waiting. Sinn Féin's Denise Mitchell, who had won a seat on Dublin City Council in the local elections in May, was shocked when she saw it on television. 'I remember watching that, saying, "What the hell?" I thought it was a goof. It was really a strange one,' she said.[6]

Sinn Féin environment spokesman Brian Stanley said Adams and McDonald had not been briefed properly. 'Our position was that we were resolutely opposed to charges. But we weren't calling around to grannies in the pensioners' bungalows ordering them not to pay,' he said.[7]

McDonald released a statement a week later to say that she would now not be paying her water charges. Sinn Féin put up Cathal King posters all over the constituency, saying the party was 'totally opposed to water charges'. But the damage was done. One Sinn Féin TD said privately that McDonald's and Adams' original promises to pay their bills represented a turning point in the by-election. 'It gave the Socialist Party a strong attack line to say we were weak on water. It did us significant damage,' he said. Adams later had a meeting with Sinn Féin members in the constituency. They complained about his promise to pay his water charges. Given Sinn Féin's reputation for secrecy, this rare internal criticism of the leader never leaked out.

Sinn Féin's Cathal King was still the favourite to win the seat, but then his campaign suffered another blow. A Sinn Féin supporter created a 'fake' screen grab of a Facebook conversation where 'Paul Murphy' told another person that his criticisms of Sinn Féin's stance on water charges were dishonest. 'I know Sinn Féin may block water charges if they get elected, but I'm not a member of Sinn Féin so politics kicks in and I say what I have to say in order to gain support!' he purportedly said.

Paul Murphy was on a stall in the Square in Tallaght when he saw a Facebook post about him being widely shared by Sinn Féin representatives, including the deputy leader McDonald. He started to panic in case people actually believed it. He knew that the page was a fake because he had said nothing of the sort. And the page was using the photo of him taken from his personal page, rather than his official campaign account. 'It was all bad spelling as well. You can say many things about me, but I have good grammar,' he said. He went home to do some more research on the page and started asking questions online about the Sinn Féin supporter who had supposedly received the message from the fake 'Paul Murphy'. The supporter's cover image on Facebook featured a mural of Gerry Adams, and his page had comments complaining about Socialist Party leaflets. Murphy put up a post on Facebook:

> *A fake screen grab of a conversation that I supposedly had with a SFer is being circulated at the moment by prominent SF members.*
>
> *It is a fake, appears to be a photoshop. Extremely low dirty tricks that should be withdrawn immediately. Please share widely.*

Paul Murphy got on RTÉ's *This Week* show to talk about the fake posting. Cathal King had to appear as well, denying he knew anything about it. It turned into a PR disaster for Sinn Féin. McDonald apologised for sharing the fake post. 'I am happy to apologise to Paul Murphy for any offence or distress this may have caused,' she said in her Facebook post.[8]

Murphy's campaign team recanvassed all 10,000 homes in west Tallaght the day before the vote. Sinn Féin responded by canvassing the same 10,000 houses as well.

All the candidates gathered for the by-election count in the National Basketball Stadium in Tallaght on Saturday 11 October 2014. Despite the campaign setbacks, Sinn Féin's Cathal King topped the poll with over 7,300 votes. Paul Murphy was in second place with around 6,500 votes.

In the Dublin West by-election in 1996, Joe Higgins had narrowly lost because the Fine Gael transfers went to Fianna Fáil's Brian Lenihan Junior. But this time, to Sinn Féin's amazement, large numbers of middle-class Fine Gael voters in the Templeogue part of the constituency gave their second preferences to Paul Murphy. He got the majority of the transfers from Fine Gael Senator Cáit Keane and independent Ronan McMahon (a former Fine Gael member based in Templeogue) when they were eliminated.

Afterwards, Sinn Féin would regret concentrating on traditional strongholds like Tallaght and not doing any canvassing in Templeogue. 'We spent too much time on the Tallaght end and left places like Templeogue in the south end,' said one Sinn Féin TD.

For Paul Murphy, it was a moment of unexpected triumph. 'The message to government is to axe the tax or watch your vote collapse,' he said after his victory.

For Fine Gael, it was a self-inflicted wound. 'If Brian Hayes had never gone to Europe, then Paul Murphy would never have got that exposure,' said one Fine Gael minister.

The turnout for the Dublin South West by-election had been poor, at just under thirty-five per cent, compared with sixty-seven per cent in the 2011 general election. But what mattered was that an out-and-out anti-water charge candidate had been elected. And the impact was going to be magnified by the protest march that was taking place in Dublin's city centre that very same day.

45

TAKING TO THE STREETS

On the very same day as Paul Murphy's by-election victory, the Right2Water protest march took place in Dublin city centre. The combination of the 500,000 fliers that had gone around the country, the public meetings and the social media postings had succeeded beyond the wildest expectations of Mandate union organiser Dave Gibney and Unite's political officer Brendan Ogle.

Gibney and Ogle had told gardaí at a pre-protest meeting in Store Street garda station that they were expecting between 10,000 and 15,000 people on the day. They were surprised to be told by gardaí that they were expecting 20,000. But there were signs on social media that the protest was going to be much bigger. Gibney was tracking the number of visits to the Facebook page in the week leading up to the first march. 'On the week of the march, our weekly reach was nearly one million people on our Facebook page, even though we got no media attention,' he said.[1]

The march had become about much more than water. It was a way of telling the government to stop – not just water charges, but also any further cuts or tax hikes. Water charges had come into force on 1 October 2014. The first bills were not due until January 2015, but they were already generating real fear. Families with children who were going to college had realised by now that they would get no free water allowance for them when they came home. They believed, with some justification, that they would get a huge water charges bill. Older people were also terrified: 'They were talking about not being able to have their grandchildren visit because they would use too much water,' said one Fianna Fáil politician. Now some of those pensioners were arranging to travel from all ends of the country to the Right2Water march in Dublin. They all had their free travel passes from the government, which some of them took particular pleasure in using.

On the day of the protest, 11 October 2014, the plan was to start the march at the Garden of Remembrance, go down O'Connell Street and D'Olier Street and then turn onto Westmoreland Street. Gibney said that route was chosen for a reason: 'We asked people to wear blue so that it would look like a teardrop from the sky,' said Gibney.

Gardaí ruled out allowing a Right2Water drone to take a picture of the 'teardrop' of marchers from the sky. However, the teardrop idea would not have worked anyway, because the number of protesters was beyond all expectations.

Gardaí told the organisers that they needed to extend the march's route because it was so big. The stewards at the front, carrying the Right2Water banner, kept going from D'Olier Street up to Nassau Street, then right onto Kildare Street, where protesters put stickers on the gates of Leinster House. They carried on to St Stephen's Green, all the way around to Aungier Street and South Great George's Street and back to Dame Street and College Green. 'It was at that point that the front of the march met the back of the march,' said Gibney.

The protest caterpillar was now five kilometres long.

The Right2Water organisers had ordered two stages: one outside the General Post Office (GPO) on O'Connell Street, and the other close by, outside the Garden of Remembrance on Parnell Square. It was impossible for many marchers to get to either of them due to the numbers on the streets.

The star performer on the GPO stage turned out to be the young Leitrim poet Stephen Murphy, who bounded up to perform his poem 'Was it for this?' He had written it just a few months earlier, as part of a project to give a 'more modern twist' to W. B. Yeats' 'September 1913'. He decided to get it out on the Internet because his first child, Rowan, had just been born and he would not have much time for any live performances. 'By the time I'd finished it and recorded it up at the cottage in Leitrim, Rowan was already two weeks old and napping in the car around the side of the barn,' he said.[2] The poem went viral.

Before he started reciting it on the GPO stage, he shouted out to the crowds: 'Let's just see how many people are here' and then started to chant: 'From the River to the Sea'. The crowd responded: 'Irish Water will be Free'. This was an Irish version of the Palestinian slogan – 'From the river to the sea, Palestine will be free.' Murphy did the chant again. The crowd got a bit louder. 'Ah, that's bollocks. Can you not do better than that? One more time,' he asked.[3]

His poem was an attack on the gardaí, the Catholic Church, Fine Gael, Fianna Fáil, the 'dogs in our government', the bank bailout and emigration.

It also included a section about water privatisation, which the crowd really responded to:

When the sycophants and the psychopaths
clap backs within the Pale
With an onus on the bonus
for the speedy firesale
Of our water and electric
that could both be ours for free
With a slight recalculation
of our own priorities.
If instead of paying billions
for a debt we never owed
We invested in renewables
and let the future flow.[4]

The Troika had been amazed at the lack of public demonstrations in Ireland against the cutbacks and tax increases. But water charges had become 'the last straw' for people who had been slow to anger. People on the Right2Water march freely admitted that they had many more grievances than just water charges. As The Rubberbandits put it: 'The Irish Water Protests are as much about water as the Boston Tea Party was about Tea.'[5]

The march was a huge morale booster for the 'Says No' groups from all over the country who were attending it. They had all been involved in their own individual protests. Now they knew they were not alone.

Karen Doyle and members of Cobh Says No to Austerity were there. 'Wow, they came from every single corner, every village, every town and every city. That was pretty special,' she said.[6]

The group were carrying a huge banner, which had been knitted by eight women in Cobh. The creator was Rose Brien-Harrington from Cobh, who was not able to take part in the protests for health reasons. She was in a knitting club in Cobh library but the library did not want anything to do with the banner. 'So we had to do it underground – at home or in cafés,' she said.[7] There were mini-figures of gardaí, water meter installers and protesters sewn onto the banner. And there was a flock of vultures with politicians names on them – such as Enda Kenny, Joan Burton and Alan Kelly. The banner got global attention when the BBC featured it in their coverage of the Right2Water protest.

The protesters passed the statue of Sir John Gray, erected in the middle of O'Connell Street to commemorate his delivery of clean water for the city in the nineteenth century through the Vartry water scheme. *The Sunday Business Post* columnist Colin Murphy later wrote: 'As John Gray looked down from his pedestal at the marchers on O'Connell Street, it might have occurred to him that the last occasion water brought so many Dubliners onto the streets was his funeral.'[8]

The size of the Right2Water march meant it had a much bigger political impact than Paul Murphy's by-election victory. An Irish Water source said the politicians panicked when they saw 100,000 people on the Right2Water march. 'These were not loonies, they were the plain people of Ireland. The TDs copped that, once they saw their supporters on it,' he said.

It reminded senior politicians in Leinster House of the PAYE tax marches. The biggest one had been in 1979, when an estimated 150,000 PAYE workers marched down O'Connell Street to protest against paying almost all the taxes, while others were let off.[9]

The size of the Right2Water protest helped to explain why Irish Water was failing to get households to cooperate when it came to signing up for bills. It had sent out 1.5 million registration packs requesting customers to confirm their details and their PPS numbers. Less than half of them had been returned.

It is common practice for a losing team in sport to sack the manager in the hope of turning their fortunes around. There were people in government now thinking of sacking Irish Water Managing Director John Tierney.

46

THE SACKING PLAN
THAT FAILED

Joan Burton had become the target of increasing protests due to her position as Tánaiste. She was ambushed at a community mediation report launch at the Northside Civic Centre in Coolock in early October 2014. Derek Byrne filmed her with his Fuji FinePix S series digital SLR camera when she was walking out to her state car. 'Have you any shame, Joan?' he said.[1] He had his camera up to her face. 'She saw me and my camera. Everyone always commented on my expensive camera,' he said. Water charge protesters surrounded Burton's official car, holding homemade placards with slogans like 'No Water Tax' and 'No Water Meter Here'. Gardaí quickly cleared the protesters out of the way. Burton was driven off by her garda driver, Barry Martin, who had escorted her to the car. Burton found the protesters' tactic of shoving their phones close to her face to be 'very unpleasant'. 'That actually is an invasion of your personal space. There was never a sense they were going to hit you with it. It was going into your eye,' she said.[2]

A week later, Burton was asked about the garda policing of the water charge protests in the Dáil by independent TD Joan Collins. The Labour leader, fresh from her experience at the Northside Civic Centre, insisted that gardaí had acted with extraordinary patience and courtesy to protesters who had been giving them a hard time. 'All of the protesters I have seen seem to have extremely expensive phones, tablets and video cameras. A core part of the campaign is to video every single second,' she said.[3] The protesters were annoyed by Burton's comment because they took it to mean that they should not be able to afford the phones. She said she was picking up on the fact that there were 'more cameras there than Hollywood'.

The protests were becoming more intense and the tabloids were starting to refer to the 'hated water charges', just as they had described the 'hated USC'. It was natural for the government to start looking for someone to blame. John

Tierney became the prime target. Government advisers talked about getting rid of him. 'Sacking him was discussed,' said a Labour source.

The first sign of trouble for Tierney came at a Fine Gael parliamentary party meeting in Leinster House. Fine Gael Kildare North TD Anthony Lawlor was frustrated about Irish Water's communications on water charges and believed Tierney was the wrong man for the job. He called him a 'gobshite'.[4] Lawlor had never meant this to become public, but he should have known that colourful comments in parliamentary party meetings were usually leaked to the media. Within twenty minutes he was getting calls about it from reporters. Lawlor knew he had to try to repair the damage. He got Tierney's mobile number from Phil Hogan and rang him to apologise in private. He also apologised on his local radio station, KFM.

It got worse for Tierney. There was a front-page story in *The Sunday Business Post* on 19 October 2014 saying that the government was planning Tierney's exit. 'Government plots heave against Irish Water bosses' was the headline. Ervia (formerly Bord Gáis), the parent company of Irish Water, was staying ominously quiet on Tierney's position amidst all the speculation. *The Irish Times* reported that Ervia Chairwoman Rose Hynes and Ervia Chief Executive Michael McNicholas would not comment on whether they were happy with the performance of Irish Water or Mr Tierney, claiming it was standard practice not to offer such comments.[5]

Tánaiste Joan Burton said that Tierney had been chosen for his ability to communicate with the councils. 'Fine, he was very good at doing that. But really I think for something like a major utility like water and its establishment, you need an engineer to be able to explain why we have to do it this way. It's like "Trust me, I'm a doctor,"' she said.

Given the noises coming from government, Tierney was supposed to meekly accept his fate as a sacrificial lamb. 'John was supposed to be fired. It didn't work out the way it was supposed to,' said an Irish Water source.

Tierney refused to go. 'My intention is to do the very important job I was asked to do by Ervia eighteen months ago,' he said when contacted by *The Irish Times*.[6]

'Tierney's as tough as nails. He defended his corner very strongly,' said a Labour source.

Fianna Fáil leader Micheál Martin told Taoiseach Enda Kenny in the Dáil on Tuesday 21 October 2014 that it was 'shabby and sleveen' to undermine Tierney with leaks to the media about him losing his job. However, by then the government knew that Tierney was not going anywhere. Kenny publicly backed him. 'I have every confidence that John Tierney can do his job,' he said.[7]

The next day, Tierney went with Elizabeth Arnett, Irish Water's head of communications, and Michael McNicholas for what was billed as a crunch meeting with Environment Minister Alan Kelly in Leinster House. Kelly had a general discussion first with them all. Then he said he wanted to meet McNicholas on his own and then Tierney. Kelly knew that Tierney was popular with the staff in Irish Water. He did not blame him for the backlash against water charges. He saw no reason in calling for his head and then having to spend months trying to find someone to replace him. At the two-hour meeting, Kelly told Tierney: 'There'll be no management changes.'

Kelly said later he was aware of the 'hullabaloo' over Tierney's job. 'I never once looked at firing John Tierney. It never entered my lexicon whatsoever. Whether it entered the views of other members of the government, you'd have to ask them that,' he said.[8]

There was a large crowd of reporters, photographers and TV camera crews waiting expectantly outside Leinster House for Tierney to come out. Michael McNicholas had already left to attend a scheduled meeting, which he ended up being forty minutes late for. That left Tierney and Arnett, who emerged to face the waiting media scrum. 'It was a very good meeting with the minister. We covered all of the issues,' said Tierney.[9]

He and Arnett were hemmed in by the sheer number of reporters and photographers there. One government official used to say that when the 'media pack starts running, it keeps running'. Water charges and Irish Water were now a big story.

Within two weeks, Tierney was wheeled out again, this time in Irish Water's headquarters. He delivered a personal apology, in the hope of regaining some public support. 'I want to apologise to our customers for mistakes that have been made,' he said. Tierney and Arnett stood with their heads bowed while Alan Kelly promised to make changes to water charging that would 'reflect the concerns of the people'.[10]

Tierney followed up his public apology by sending letters to all 166 TDs in the Dáil and sixty senators in the Seanad to apologise for the 'shortcomings' in how Irish Water had communicated with them. 'I acknowledge that this has fallen well below the standards of service that you expect, or that we had set ourselves,' he wrote. As part of the new approach, there were Irish Water clinics for TDs and senators every Wednesday in Leinster House at 4 p.m.

By now, Tierney had been alerted to the fact that his home address in Dublin had been published online by water charge protesters, along with the home addresses of the entire Irish Water board. 'Because Irish Water know where everybody on this island lives we thought it only fitting that you fine people know where the directors of this private company live,' stated a Facebook post which contained all the addresses.[11] Irish Water got word of a planned protest march to Tierney's home on 25 October 2014. It sent a private security guard to the house to provide protection for six hours.[12] Tierney's home would later be attacked, a detail which never became public. No one was ever arrested in relation to this incident.[13]

One senior Irish Water executive said the external intimidation and threats had put people in the company under horrendous personal pressure. 'We had people who weren't able to take public transport because of the threats they were receiving. There was a lot of stuff happening that got very personal and very, very scary,' the executive said.

Given the pressure he was under, it was understandable that Tierney looked utterly miserable when he made a public appearance beside Kelly at the Irish Water call centre in Cork. Kelly said he dealt with Tierney on a day-to-day basis. 'I found him fine. I found John very hard-working and as a human being, quite a decent person. I think the pressure he was under, I think some of the stuff wasn't very fair or nice for him,' he said.[14]

The staff in Irish Water had been recruited from councils, the private sector and Ervia (formerly Bord Gáis). At the start it was all one team. But the divisions between Tierney and McNicholas were beginning to spread. 'The atmosphere started to change. Those who came from Ervia started to club together and the new arrivals to Irish Water were clubbing together,' said one Irish Water source.

Tierney had held on to his job. But he was sidelined in terms of public appearances. Fine Gael wanted someone who would be a better salesman for water charges. They settled on Tierney's boss, Michael McNicholas. He had a private sector background through his work in National Toll Roads and he was more comfortable dealing with the media than Tierney. A senior government source confirmed the strategy of getting McNicholas to take over media appearances from Tierney. 'We felt that Michael was more light on his feet [responding to questions] and could deliver the message better,' he said.

The hostility to Irish Water had gotten so bad that staff who went on nights out would avoid telling anyone where they worked, just like Anglo Irish Bank staff had done after the bailout. And at least one Irish Water staff member with the company logo on her van had started to park it away from her house at night. She was afraid of being targeted by water charge protesters.

The emotions being whipped up by water charges were to peak outside a garda station on the northside of Dublin. It found itself under siege.

47

THE GARDA STATION SIEGE

Taoiseach Enda Kenny was launching twenty new jobs at the Sports Surgery Clinic in Santry. It had been founded by the brother of former Manchester United star and Irish international Kevin Moran.

It was early November 2014. Water charge protesters quickly started to spread the word on Facebook pages about Kenny's arrival. There were rumours that billionaire businessman Denis O'Brien was attending the event with Kenny as well. A post on the Facebook page of the republican socialist party Éirígí declared: 'Flash Protest Underway Against Enda Kenny and Denis O'Brien at Santry Sports Club [*sic*] in Northwood.'[1]

It was a phantom Denis. The Sports Surgery Clinic later confirmed that O'Brien had not been there, had not been invited and had no connection whatsoever with it. Nevertheless, there were rowdy scenes as Kenny arrived in his state car at the clinic.

Ciarán Heaphy, the Éirígí member who worked as a milkman at night-time and went protesting in the daytime, was there. 'A good few dozen of us went up and were protesting. We decided to block him in,' he said.[2] There was a sit-down protest on the road outside the clinic. The gardaí lifted and pulled the protesters out of the way of Kenny's state car. Some of them were women, which was something that always infuriated protesters. 'That's a woman,' shouted a protester. 'Are you proud of yourself, are ye?'[3]

'The guards got very, very heavy. We were thrown off the road,' said Heaphy. A phalanx of gardaí walked alongside Kenny's state car to keep the protesters away. 'Detectives of Ballymun, we know who you are!' shouted one protester. 'Get back in your piggywagon and get back to your station. You're not wanted here.'[4]

Gardaí arrested three protesters. The protests continued even after Kenny had left. A group of sports medicine specialists from Australia, New Zealand and South Africa had been attending the launch of the clinic's new research foundation. They were delayed from leaving the clinic for twenty minutes by protesters doing a slow walk in front of their bus. Eventually, the bus got out after the gardaí cleared a route for it.

Heaphy said Éirígí decided to call a protest that evening outside Coolock garda station, where the three arrested protesters were being held. 'We made a call to all the water groups to hold protests against the garda treatment of water protesters,' he said.

There were unruly scenes outside Coolock garda station that night. From 7 p.m. onwards, there were hundreds of protesters outnumbering the gardaí in the station. 'It was like *Fort Apache, The Bronx*,' said one local TD in reference to the Paul Newman thriller where the local police station was isolated and surrounded by hostile locals.

Gardaí were not that surprised because the water protesters had been threatening to do it for a long time. 'They were telling us: "We're going to follow you to the station. We're going to follow you home." We didn't think they would have the audacity to do it,' said one garda source.

The protesters started up their familiar chants: 'From the river to the sea, Irish Water will be free' and 'Shame, shame, shame on you'. The road outside the garda station was completely blocked due to the number of protesters. Lots of them were holding placards saying 'No Water Meters here'.

Lines of gardaí stood shoulder-to-shoulder at each of the two entrances to Coolock garda station to keep the protesters out. The protesters were shouting and chanting in the darkness. The only illumination came from the main light mounted on top of the garda station. Just across the road was a Cadbury's factory, churning out 18 million Dairymilk bars per year with workers on duty twenty-four hours a day, seven days a week.

A garda inspector called Eddie Hyland tried to negotiate with the protesters. He asked them to organise a slow march away from Coolock garda station. He was popular with rank-and-file gardaí and was doing his best to get on with the protesters. Then he got blindsided by somebody and belted on the jaw. Hyland went up to the protesters. 'I've been assaulted,' he said. He pointed his finger at someone. 'That man will be arrested.'[5] Some of the protesters told Hyland he was wrong. 'No one assaulted ye,' said one. But the swelling on the side of Hyland's jaw was already visible.[6]

Rather than retreating to the garda station, Hyland just took the belt on the jaw and carried on. He and a line of gardaí stood outside the entrance to the station compound. One of the gardaí repeatedly called out the name of one of the water protesters and told him to 'go away'.[7]

After the assault on Hyland, gardaí responded by using pepper spray against protesters. Video footage posted by protesters themselves shows one of them calling gardaí 'fucking scumbags', with guards holding up their pepper spray canisters again. Derek Byrne was there videoing the events. 'Spray me, I'm on camera doing nothing,' he said to a female garda. 'I don't care,' she replied. 'I don't give a shit either,' said Byrne. The Garda Síochána Ombudsman Commission found that the use of pepper spray was justified.[8]

By now, there were twenty-five garda squad cars outside Coolock garda station. A local anti-water charge group, Kilmore/Coolock Says No to Water Meters, posted an appeal on their Facebook page for more protesters to turn up: 'Bodies needed at Coolock garda station now riot squad mobilising.'

Heaphy said there was a bit of 'pushing and shoving' at the protest outside Coolock garda station. 'A couple of people were pepper-sprayed. That was pretty much it. It wasn't that exciting,' he said. 'It was the fact that 400 citizens said we're not taking that sort of abuse and stood outside the garda barracks demanding to know "Why the violence?"'

Gardaí who had finished their shifts were unable to leave the station because it was completely surrounded by protesters. They had to wait in the station watching television. Martin Scorsese's film *The Wolf of Wall Street* was a station favourite. Some of them were frustrated because they were late collecting children or were supposed to be home to let their partners go on shift work.

A group of youths started throwing stones. Some private cars belonging to gardaí in the station yard were damaged. The cost was later paid for by the force after they submitted their claims. Heaphy said the youths throwing the stones had come down to the garda station on bikes. 'A couple of the women knew them and took them away,' he said.

The protest ended at around 11 p.m.

Minister for Health Leo Varadkar said later on Newstalk 106-108 that there was a 'very sinister fringe' to some of the water charge protests. 'They abuse the gardaí. They break the law. They engage in violence. And also they spread all sorts of information. And what I am worried about is that it is only a matter of time before someone gets hurt,' he said. Varadkar did not single out any one group or party as belonging to the 'sinister fringe'. But

Prime Time reporter Mark Coughlan reported that two of the protesters were local members of Republican Network for Unity, the political wing of the republican paramilitary group Óglaigh na hÉireann.[9]

The following day, there was another significant development. GMC/Sierra obtained an order establishing a twenty-metre 'exclusion zone' for protesters when water meters were being installed by its workers in the estates around Coolock garda station and elsewhere. The court heard evidence that some water charge protesters had followed some of the water meter workers in a 'highly threatening and intimidatory manner'. GMC/Sierra's operating manager, Neil Corrigan, told the High Court that he believed the protests were being 'carefully orchestrated by persons who are seeking to use the installation of water meters as a means to generate and provoke civil disobedience'.[10]

The twenty-metre exclusion zone was a new tactic to allow contractors to put in meters without being stopped by protesters. But of even more importance, and arguably on what everything depended, was the public's reaction to the new water charges plan being drawn up behind the scenes. It was the last chance to save the Irish Water project.

Part Four

WATER FALLS

48

WATERING DOWN
THE CHARGES

The Unite trade union's political organiser Brendan Ogle was worried when Phil Hogan left for Brussels. He said the environment minister was the gift that kept on giving in terms of motivating protesters and getting people worked up. 'And then my worrying ended when the government replaced him with Alan Kelly of Labour,' he said.[1]

Kelly knew that the political bulldozing of Phil Hogan had not worked. He and his officials in the Department of the Environment had been working flat out on a new water charges plan to try to break the back of the protests. 'Alan Kelly had learned. He had seen what Phil had done. Alan Kelly is many things, but he is not stupid. Suddenly, he had to be the salesman,' said one Fine Gael minister who had worked with him.

The scale of the opposition was even clearer after the second Right2Water protest on 1 November 2014. It was estimated that 150,000 people turned out in 106 different locations around the entire country. The intention was to really get the message through to government TDs. It worked. One Fine Gael minister looked at the picture in his local paper of the march in his town. He was able to pick out three of his own supporters at the front.

Minister of state at the Department of the Environment Paudie Coffey also spotted some friends of his when RTÉ sent down a camera crew to the Right2Water march in his hometown of Portlaw in Waterford. 'It just showed to me the media were obviously picking me out. Why would they go to a small village in County Waterford, only for the minister of state was from there?' he said.[2]

Coffey had made headlines because of his decision to give a key job to a political ally. Fine Gael Councillor Hilary Quinlan, who was based in Waterford city, was the president of the councillors' lobby group, the Association of Irish Local Government. He had been appointed to the Irish Water board to give councillors a voice in November 2013. The water charges controversy contributed to Quinlan losing his seat in Waterford city in the local elections, although he still retained his position on the board. Then Coffey got his job as minister of state for housing. He wanted a trustworthy ministerial driver who would not repeat the private and personal conversations he was having on the phone in the back of the car. He decided to hire Quinlan. 'I needed somebody to drive me. He was a loyal supporter of mine that I could confide in politically,' he said. Coffey never thought about what it might look like.

All hell broke loose when *The Irish Times* reported that Coffey's driver was on the board of Irish Water.[3] Fianna Fáil called on Quinlan to step down from the board. Coffey eventually made the same request to his friend. 'That was something I'd regret all right. The person involved had the highest integrity. He continued to drive me and support me. We remain good friends,' he said.

Work was now ongoing in government to come up with a comprehensive 'package' to deal with the public concerns about the cost of water charges, the PPS numbers and privatisation. 'We felt we had to do something to try to alleviate people's concerns. The public weren't buying into it to the levels we would have liked to see,' said Coffey.

***

At the start of November 2014, Tánaiste Joan Burton deliberately put out the figure of €200 as the maximum water charges bill for a family. It was what she believed would work. It was also revenge on Fine Gael for having leaked their preferred figure to the media the previous April. 'The Taoiseach and I are very much on the same page,' she told reporters.[4] That was not the case, as was clear in the Dáil when an embarrassed Enda Kenny said that Burton had made her remarks 'in a personal capacity'.[5]

By this stage, Kelly and other government ministers were facing regular anti-water charge demonstrations outside the gates of Leinster House. 'I walked through protests outside on a couple of occasions. I got punched and hit once,' he said.[6]

The government wanted to reduce the water charges as much as possible. The complicating factor was that reducing the bills too much would see Irish Water lose income and fail the dreaded Eurostat test. Irish Water would be classified as the government's problem child and it would not be given the independence to borrow its own money.

Department of Finance Secretary General Derek Moran and Department of Public Expenditure Secretary General Robert Watt were meeting week after week, crunching the numbers. 'We were trying to reduce the charge to make it more acceptable,' said one senior civil servant. There was dissatisfaction among civil servants in the Department of Finance and the Department of Public Expenditure that they were being lumped with the task of sorting out the Department of the Environment's problem. 'We were badly let down by [the Department of the] Environment. There was no leadership shown,' said one senior civil servant involved in the process. However, these two lead departments had been enthusiastic supporters of the plan to get Irish Water off the government's books. They, too, had to share some of the responsibility.

Kelly said most of the civil servants in the Department of the Environment were 'pretty good'. They had been working at this stage for four years on turning the Irish Water project into reality. Kelly found there was a 'huge workload' on the head of the department, Secretary General John McCarthy, and the head of its water sector division, Maria Graham, because there were so few senior staff in that area. 'I thought they were excellent and I've great time for them. I did feel there was probably too much pressure on them as well,' he said.

The officials prepared more than forty pages of public documents with the help of Irish Water on just how bad the water system really was. No government had admitted this before. The aim was to convince the public of the need for them to pay water charges to upgrade the infrastructure. There was particular emphasis on the forty-four locations where raw sewage was being discharged into seas and rivers. Everything was going to be put into one big announcement. Kelly was fired up for his speech to the Dáil to announce the revised water charges package. 'I felt this was one we had to do well,' he said.

***

Alan Kelly began his speech to a relatively full chamber. 'Colleagues, this is a significant moment for the country …' Taoiseach Enda Kenny, who was sitting to his right, lifted up his glass of water and took a sip. Kelly continued on. 'We as a government have made mistakes, but now we face a critical choice.'[7]

The government had realised the previous water charges had been too confusing, so it wanted the new regime to be simpler. It wanted to get rid of the opposition claims that families could face bills of €1,000 per year. Kelly announced that charges would be capped for four years, even though this effectively made the hundreds of millions spent on water meters redundant.[8] 'The capped charges will be €160 for single adult households and €260 for all other households, until 1 January 2019,' he said.

Then Kelly announced that these bills would be cut by a further €100 by the introduction of the water conservation grant. But there was no requirement to spend the money on a rain barrel or to get a plumber to fix any leaking taps. And people who had not paid their water bills could claim it.

The water conservation grant was to become like Fine Gael's 2016 general election slogan 'Let's Keep the Recovery Going', a concept so bad that nobody afterwards wanted to claim credit for it.

Fianna Fáil leader Micheál Martin said the game was over for water charges after that announcement by Kelly. 'I personally objected to the idea where you send out a bill on the one hand and a cheque in the other. It was farcical,' he said.[9] It created a credibility gap for the government.

Kelly said it was not his idea and it was the one thing he would have changed in hindsight. 'I think we could have done other things, like credits for people who were doing conservation things,' he said.

The water conservation grant was borne out of the government's desperation to reduce water charge bills without failing the Eurostat test. It could not just reduce the bills by €100 because this would reduce the public income that Irish Water was getting. So it had to come up with a disguised way of reducing the bills, which was the water conservation grant. For some extra cover, the Department of Social Protection was pulled in, even though it had never wanted anything to do with water charges. It could not use Irish Water's database of customers. So it had to set up an entirely new process to register more than one million households.

Kelly said later he had been assured by Finance Minister Michael Noonan that the new water charges package would pass the Eurostat test and keep Irish Water off the government's books. 'I had to take the advice of Michael Noonan that time. I was told that we could keep this off the balance sheet,' he said.

In his Dáil speech, Kelly announced that he was scrapping the requirement for people to provide their PPS numbers when registering with Irish Water. The date for water charges themselves was being pushed back to 1 January 2015. And the legal right for Irish Water to reduce people's water to a trickle would be removed.

Kelly said afterwards that there was no point in the government even pretending that the 'trickle' threat was possible. 'You could take off the lid [of the meter] and twist the nozzle and turn it back on. A child could do it. It was crazy, the idea of threatening people. There was always a sense of moral authority and doing the right thing,' he said. The new sanction was to impose annual late payment fines of up to €60 on people who did not pay their water charges.

All of the key elements in the Water Services Bill that had been guillotined through the Dáil the previous December had now been thrown out. The 'generous free allowance' of water for every household previously announced by Phil Hogan had been scrapped, as part of the shift to lower capped charges. It had been a case of *dá mhéid í an deifir is mó an mhoill* (the more haste, the less speed).

The opposition started to heckle Kelly more loudly as he neared the end of his speech. He began shouting to make himself heard over the din. He talked about the 'legacy' he wanted to leave. 'Unlike some in the House, I want my legacy to be one of achievement, not of destruction,' he said, pointing over in the direction of the opposition.

Much of the subsequent media coverage focused on Kelly's use of the word 'legacy'. That was not what he'd intended. Afterwards, Kelly said to his special adviser Jim McGrath, 'How did we not see that word?'

Socialist Party leader Joe Higgins said that Kelly had antagonised people and made them more determined to resist water charges. 'But it didn't matter who the minister for the environment was [who was] bringing in water charges. They could have been the most charismatic individual on the face of this earth and they would have faced the same opposition,' he said.[10]

Kelly had asked people to give the new water charges package 'a fair hearing'. But the protests against contractors putting in meters continued to increase. And in some instances, they were becoming violent.

49

METER ATTACKS

The cabinet had decided to meter the entire country in December 2011. Now the workers who had to get down on their hands and knees to put in the meters were getting the backlash. There were protesters pulling down barriers and standing on stopcocks to prevent meters being installed. There is no suggestion that any of the water charge protesters named in this book were engaged in such behaviour, but there were attacks by some protesters on meter installers.

The most comprehensive account came from a memo prepared by Irish Water's Managing Director John Tierney. He had been asked for it by minister of state Paudie Coffey, who was getting ready for a Seanad debate on Irish Water in 2014. 'The more information the better,' an official in the Department of the Environment told Tierney.[1]

Tierney got back within four hours with a lengthy memo put together by his staff. His memo stated that fifty assaults had been reported to Irish Water including:

- Team members punched, kicked and bitten by protesters
- Hot water thrown at team member
- Team members hit with objects, including shovel and hammer
- Team members hit by a vehicle.[2]

The memo summarised some of the other difficult situations that water meter installers had found themselves in. They had been surrounded by protesters, who refused to let them leave. In some cases they had been spat at by protesters and had glass, stones and even fireworks thrown at them. They had been put under surveillance by protesters. Their names and home addresses had been discovered on social media and their families had been targeted.

There was more. The memo stated that contractors had been followed by protesters from sites, 'including on public transport'. The tyres of contractors' vehicles had been slashed, some of them outside their homes. And metering barriers had been vandalised and burned at sites.

The memo also complained about the verbal abuse that water meter installers were getting, and the videoing of them by protesters. 'There has been a heavy and persistent level of online intimidation of individual team members with videos and photographs uploaded to social media sites encouraging increased levels of cyber and physical abuse towards metering team members,' it said.

As a result, water meter installations had to be abandoned, which in the view of Irish Water was 'unfortunate for the wider communities at these locations'. The memo also sounded an optimistic note that households would eventually recognise that the meters would help them manage their meter bills and detect household leaks.

Many of the meter installers had been among the construction workers who had lost their jobs after the property crash. Irish Water had found it easy to meet its target of keeping twenty per cent of the 1,300 meter installation jobs for unemployed workers. One meter installer, speaking in the shadows to protect his identity, described how desperate he was for work on RTÉ's *Prime Time*.[3] 'It's my job. Like, I have a wife and a child and a mortgage. You know, I need the job,' he said.

The meter installers found it very frustrating to have their work disrupted by protesters. That was visible in an encounter between an installer and a protesting resident in an estate in Baldoyle. 'Why aren't ye off fucking annoying somebody else? We're only doing a job,' said the installer.[4]

The man Irish Water hired to run the metering programme was Kevin McSherry. He was described by colleagues as a tough northerner whose family had always stood up to any intimidation during the Troubles. He got weekly updates from contractors of how many meters were going in, and where. During the installation programme, McSherry had been in a shop discussing that he was working for Irish Water. When he came out, a group of at least six youths were shouting 'Irish Water scum'. Two of the tyres on his car had been slashed. 'I can't understand why anybody would protest against the working man. If somebody wants to protest, then you're welcome to go walk to the Dáil or walk on O'Connell Street, but don't attack the working man who's there to do their daily job,' he later told RTÉ's *Prime Time*.[5]

Under Article 40 of the Irish Constitution, protesters have the right to 'assemble peaceably and without arms'. But the water meter installers felt that protesters who assaulted and intimidated them were not behaving 'peaceably'. In Clarecastle, in County Clare, a man came out of his home armed with an airgun, which usually fire pellets and can cause severe injuries. He pointed it at the contractors who were putting in meters outside. The workers jumped out of the holes in the ground and fled. The man's complaint was that he could not have a shower because the workers had switched off the water on the street to install the meters. Then he walked down the road and threw the airgun into the river. Judge Patrick Durcan later fined him €250 in court, saying the man 'did a very, very foolish thing'.[6]

GMC/Sierra complained that its 477 workers in Dublin city were being subjected to a continuous aggressive campaign of 'intimidation, bullying and harassment' by protesters.[7] This had been going on since the summer but had 'intensified since September'. It had to stop work in certain locations.

An Irish Water executive said the staff working for the contractors were fantastic despite the treatment they got from some protesters. 'One of the things that is absolutely incredible is that no contractor ever assaulted or abused a member of the public. There was intimidation and abuse. Nobody ever reacted,' he said.

In response to the protests, GMC/Sierra hired private security firms such as Guardex, a Kildare-based company founded by Eamonn Gibney, who served in the Army Ranger Wing for fourteen years. These security staff had been trained in courses such as 'responding to threats and violence' to identify risks and control their own responses. One of their main jobs was to video the water charge protesters in Dublin to use as evidence in court. That made them obvious targets.

On a single day in September 2014, one security guard was headbutted by a protester in one incident, and pushed by another protester in another incident. Later, another protester threatened to cut the security man's face with a knife.

The justice minister at the time, Frances Fitzgerald, said the anti-meter protests were stopping Irish Water contractors from doing something which was 'agreed government policy'. 'Irish Water was having incredible difficulties going into areas. It was anarchy,' she said.[8] Fitzgerald also said that the gardaí were worried about the potential risk to the safety of the public. 'There was extreme concern about the safety of everyone. There were children being brought to the protests, and babies,' she said.

Fine Gael was supposedly a party of 'law and order', so Fitzgerald was horrified at what was happening during the meter installations in some council estates. She had watched some of the videos put up by the protesters on YouTube. 'The ugliness of it. The anger. The behaviour was outrageous. It's the level of aggression from the protesters,' she said.

For years, ministers had travelled to public events around the country with very light security – or none at all. But that was all changing due to the intensity of the water protests. At one stage, Fitzgerald was contacted by a fellow cabinet minister who was concerned about their own safety. 'I told them that they needed to go to the gardaí. I think there were probably a few ministers who had to get extra garda protection,' she said.[9]

The most controversial water charge protest of all was about to happen in Jobstown.

50

NO PRIVATISATION

The Right2Water march in Dublin in October 2014 had succeeded in uniting the working-class communities who were physically stopping water meters with the middle-class people who were refusing to pay their water charges. There had been an even bigger turnout for the second protest in November.

But the Jobstown protest on 15 November damaged that cross-class union. The protesters' own YouTube footage of Tánaiste Joan Burton and her assistant trapped in a car and then a jeep for over three hours was there for all to see. Unite's Brendan Ogle incurred the wrath of some of the protesters later when he strongly criticised what had happened. 'It was also so counterproductive and damaging that nobody in their right mind would have set out to do such damage intentionally,' he wrote.[1]

The Herald newspaper followed up the Jobstown protest by revealing that a dissident republican was there on the day. 'Senior gardaí have said they are concerned that sinister dissidents had infiltrated water protest marches,' it said.[2]

Dave Gibney of the Right2Water campaign believed it was 'nonsense' to suggest that IRA members were running the water protest marches. He wondered if an IRA man turned up at a GAA match would there be stories about the IRA running the GAA? 'It was very frustrating; in our eyes that was deliberately being done to split the working class and everybody else from the movement. And it worked,' he said.[3]

This was not new. It was always comforting for the authorities to imagine there was some arch-criminal behind all the protests. There had been suggestions from gardaí in the 1980s that the anti-drugs marches in Dublin were a front for the IRA, due to the involvement of Sinn Féin activists. But gardaí eventually realised these were marches that had broad community support.

The gardaí were playing catch-up again. Jobstown was a wake-up call about how little intelligence they had on the water charge protesters. They set up what was called 'Operation Mizen' to monitor the activities of the protesters on their Facebook pages. A garda spokesman said it was prompted by safety concerns about 'the coordinated and organised behaviour of a small cohort at some protests who engaged in aggressive and violent actions against elected representatives, other public figures, Irish Water workers, gardaí and the public'. Operation Mizen used information publicly available on 'social media and other channels' rather than surveillance. 'No public representatives or any member of the public are subject to surveillance or profiling by Operation Mizen,' the garda spokesman said.[4]

Leo Varadkar said later that he believed his 'sinister fringe' phrase had been helpful to the water charge protesters. He said he knew there were a lot of people involved in the protest who were genuine and decent people who were opposed to water charges. 'But there was a sinister fringe too and a nasty element. As is often the case, you get misrepresented and it's made out that by referring to the sinister fringe, you really secretly meant everyone. I actually meant the sinister fringe,' he said.[5]

The phrase was starting to stick. The height of this came when Fine Gael Tipperary North TD Noel Coonan compared some of the water protesters to 'ISIS' in the Dáil. Government ministers such as Michael Noonan started to come up with a new phrase to frame the water charges issue. 'We govern for the reasonable people, and the reasonable people were upset by the way in which it was handled,' he said. An academic study later found that in the space of a single week in November 2014, Taoiseach Enda Kenny and four of his key government ministers repeatedly used the phrase 'reasonable people' in the media.[6] There appeared to be a concerted effort to split the 'reasonable people' in the water charge protests from the 'sinister fringe'.

The Right2Water campaign started to get some emails from people saying they had been on the first march on O'Connell Street but would not be coming to the next one on 10 December 2014 because they were being run by republicans. There were also other emails from people pulling out after the Jobstown protest. 'It definitely did have an effect on the numbers,' said Gibney.

It was a worrying time for the Right2Water campaign because it was hoping that the 10 December march outside the Dáil would be big enough to send a strong anti-water charge message to the government. It needed a boost.

It got one from Russell Brand. The British comedian and actor had already made a video about Irish Water which had gone viral. His team offered Ogle an interview with Brand in his townhouse in London's East End while he was over there on business with Unite. 'It was to appeal to young people,' Ogle said.[7]

Brand put in a typically flamboyant performance in his interview with Ogle. 'You, the Irish people, fought to kick the British out of your country. Now your own government are ripping you off over water. Get onto the streets,' he said.[8]

One of the Labour special advisers could not resist sending a text message to Ogle after this unusual liaison. 'What was it that first attracted you to the millionaire comedian Russell Brand?' he asked him.

Gibney thought at first that it was a 'nightmare' when he got the video of the interview from Ogle. 'I find some of these things that Russell Brand and other people do a bit cringeworthy. But in fairness, it gets attention and the media cover it, so it worked,' he said. The headline on the *Irish Times* story about the video was: 'Russell Brand urges Irish people to take day off for water protests'.[9] Digital analytics showed that it became one of the newspaper's top ten most viewed stories about Irish Water.

***

The anti-water charge movement had produced chants and poetry and now it had a celebrity endorsement. But there was no protest song. That was about to change too.

It started during a session in a roadside pub called Campbell's Tavern, two miles outside the town of Headford in County Galway. It had a music-mad owner who was able to attract a crowd from all over Galway and Mayo. There were gigs in the function room at the back and regular jamming sessions for musicians on Sundays. When Ed Sheeran came to play in Galway city, he made the half-hour journey to Campbell's Tavern to meet the musicians there.

At the end of November 2014 a group of professional musicians turned up at the pub to celebrate the show they had put on at the Electric Picnic festival in Stradbally, County Laois a few months earlier. They included Noelie McDonnell, a singer-songwriter from Tuam who had a hit with 'Nearly Four' about his young nephew in 2008. The musicians started talking about writing a song about the water protests. The water charges themselves were not the main issue because most of the people in the area were paying for water for years on group water schemes. Rather, they missed fellow musicians who were no longer playing gigs with them because they had been forced to emigrate for work.

Filmmaker Eamon de Staic, who was there on the night, said there was a frustration with austerity in general – the Universal Social Charge, the property tax and now water charges. 'The government were making us pay for bailing out the banks and the national debt ballooning,' he said.[10]

He had been talking about the one issue that everyone did agree on – the threat of Irish Water being privatised by stealth. The government had insisted time and again that there was no plan to privatise Irish Water. But it would not bring forward a referendum to guarantee in the Constitution that Irish Water would remain in public ownership.

De Staic's brother Aindrias came up with a catchy chorus for a song: 'No privatisation – Irish Water, Irish nation'. Then he asked some of the other musicians who were in Campbell's Tavern to write a verse each. The bones of the song were worked out that night. Eamon de Staic said it was a 'shamtown reggae rock'. That was a homage to Tuam, a music-mad town that had produced The Saw Doctors and a 1980s reggae band called Too Much for the Whiteman. The musicians agreed to come back a week later to Campbell's Tavern to finish the protest song.

De Staic turned up with his camcorder and got the musicians to do it seven times. He recorded them playing in the kitchen of the pub, so that they could use the tap as a prop in the video. 'It was recorded in forty-five minutes. The musicians just wanted to make a statement, to put it out there,' he said.

The name of their loosely formed band was the same one they had used for the Electric Picnic gathering of musicians – the Rolling Tav Revue. That was a tribute to Bob Dylan's 'Rolling Thunder Revue' tour with a travelling caravan of musicians, and of course to Campbell's Tavern.

The next day, de Staic brought the footage on a USB stick to a friend and got him to upload it to YouTube. Within twenty-four hours, it had 5,000 hits and it kept going.[11]

It was distinctly Irish with violins and guitars. But it also had the reggae sound and the beat of a cajon drum. The end of the YouTube video for the song featured an appeal for people to turn up to the third Right2Water march. 'Let's show them,' it said.

The Right2Water campaign picked up what was happening and invited the members of the Rolling Tav Revue to play at their protest on 10 December.

The 'No Privatisation' song had a verse about having '50,000 people marching on the streets'. Now the band were playing in front of at least 30,000 people on the large stage at the Merrion Street side of Leinster House. Aindrias de Staic was belting out the words, as well as playing the violin.

> *Enda Kenny, not a penny, we won't pay at all,*
> *Cause corruption of your policies is worse than Fianna Fáil …*

Aindrias de Staic had gone to protests in Galway about the jailing of the Rossport Five, while his brother Eamon had been at the protests in Rossport itself. The song lyrics linked the garda policing of the protests against Shell's Corrib gas pipeline in Rossport in Mayo to the recent protest in Jobstown.[12]

> *From Rossport to Jobstown,*
> *the 20 meter ban*
> *police brutality is Black and Tan.*[13]

The crowd loved it. Donal Gibbons, who was playing the guitar, had helped to come up with a line on the cryptosporidium outbreak that had left Galway city without water for three months in 2007.

> *But the government are fighting a fight they're gonna lose*
> *Charging us for water that we can hardly use*
> *The chloride, the fluoride, the cryptosporidium*
> *Flush them out cos it's time to get rid of 'em!*[14]

Every one of the Rolling Tav Revue was a professional musician, so playing to the crowd was not a new experience. But Gibbons said they still found it amazing to get such a response for a song only written a week earlier. 'It was great. They were all singing it back to us,' he said.[15]

The Right2Water organisers had brought along actor Martin Maloney, who plays Eddie Durkan in the *Hardy Bucks*. Maloney had grown up in the same hometown of Swinford as the Ervia chief executive, Michael McNicholas. Maloney helped out by playing on the cajon drum for their song, because they were short a drummer on the night.

A beaming Brendan Ogle was singing along with the Rolling Tav Revue on stage. He had asked for the phone numbers of the anti-water charge protesters involved in some of the 'Says No' groups, so that he would no longer be a stranger to them. He met Audrey Clancy, a prominent protester in the Edenmore Says No group, and Derek Byrne from Dublin Says No to arrange a meeting with them in the Edenmore House bar. Now the two of them were up on the stage with Ogle, dancing along to the music. They had pink high-vis vests on, in tribute to the 'Pink Ladies' in Dublin who were on the water protests.[16]

Ogle introduced Clancy to the crowd first and then handed her the microphone. 'I always knew we were not the frightened Irish. We are now, for sure, the fighting Irish,' said Clancy.[17]

Derek Byrne was wearing sunglasses under his trademark baseball cap. At this stage, he was one of nine protesters under a court order to stay twenty metres away from water meter installations. He told the crowd they had already broken the injunction. 'They thought that bringing us to the High Court would scare the life out of us. We were not afraid … We don't give a damn about injunctions,' he said. Byrne told the crowd to put the pressure on the TDs in their local communities and let them know there was nowhere to hide. 'If Enda Kenny doesn't get the bloody message today, that it's time for him and the rest of the parasites in that open prison behind me [Leinster House], we will come back in January and we will throw them bloody out,' he said.[18]

There had been grumblings from some of the left-wing political activists about the number of artists on stage for the three-and-a-half-hour event. Brendan Ogle recalled some of them telling him: 'I don't want to go to a rock concert, I want to go to a protest.' His response was that it was about keeping the movement as broad as possible.

From his office in Leinster House, Environment Minister Alan Kelly could hear the line-up of musicians playing songs for the protesters. He joked to his advisers that he was going out to join Glen Hansard and Damien Dempsey, two of his favourite musicians, who were singing 'The Auld Triangle'. Kelly was heartened, though, to hear Fr Peter McVerry praise him from the stage as the only person in the government who knew how to solve the homelessness crisis. Kelly had spent hours talking to McVerry about the possible solutions. 'I will always remember him for that. It wasn't the popular thing to do,' he said.[19]

Another notable sight was that Sinn Féin had lots of party activists in the crowd, holding green Sinn Féin flags and handing them out to others. It was a show of force by the party after being beaten by Paul Murphy in the Dublin South West by-election two months earlier.

After the protest, the Rolling Tav Revue musicians went to O'Donoghue's pub on Merrion Street, which has photos of Ronnie Drew and Luke Kelly on the wall. They had a few pints with Damien Dempsey, Glen Hansard and Martin Maloney. Eamon de Staic, who was there with the band, said they were happy that the message of the song came across. 'Whatever happened, our water supply cannot be privatised,' he said.

However, the figure of 30,000 protesters on the mid-week march outside the Dáil was well down on the previous two marches, which had been held on Saturdays. Fewer people were able to go to it. The government saw it as a sign that the cheaper water charges that had been announced were softening the opposition to the charges. 'The third march was the least impactful. We thought it was dying a bit,' said a Labour adviser.

Meanwhile, there was another tactic being used to deal with the protesters who were continuing to block meter installations. It involved the courts, and the prisons.

51

LOCKED UP

Damien O'Neill was a karate instructor who ran a security company. He was a relative latecomer to the water protests. He only started in October 2014 when his wife, Anita, told him that her mother had been 'pulled down the road' by gardaí during protests against the installation of water meters in the estate where she lived in Donaghmede in north Dublin. 'Will you give a hand out?' she asked him.[1]

O'Neill had never been on a protest in his life. He turned up the next morning at the Foxhill estate in Donaghmede to meet his brother-in-law. The meter installers were already there. 'What do I do?' he asked. He was told to 'Stand on that shore and don't move.' The meter installers came and put a barrier around him. He refused to move when the gardaí asked him to. Then the gardaí shoved him out. O'Neill kept protesting. In the afternoon, he jumped over a barrier put up by meter installers outside the house of an elderly man who did not want a meter. He was subsequently arrested.

O'Neill was soon to become known to gardaí because he kept turning up at protests around the city. He cut a distinctive figure because he was tall – over six foot two inches – and strong from regular gym sessions. He was one of the protesters named by Irish Water's Dublin city contractor, GMC/Sierra, when it applied to the High Court to get a court order to keep protesters twenty metres away from meter installations.

The Dublin Says No group called on people to turn up in O'Connell Street on 15 September 2014 to protest against the first set of injunctions. Derek Byrne, who was one of those facing an injunction, was amazed when 5,000 people turned up. They marched around the city centre and over the Ha'penny Bridge. 'I've never seen so many people march across the Ha'penny Bridge. 'I was terrified. If this bridge collapses, how am I going to explain it?' said Byrne.[2]

The marchers ended up back outside the GPO on O'Connell Street, the location of the headquarters of the leaders of the 1916 Rising. 'We were all full of adrenaline. This was great. People were ecstatic. Hundreds of us marched into the GPO,' said Byrne. He hopped up on one of the customer counters in the GPO and read out the 1916 Proclamation. Thrusting his fist into the air, he finished up by shouting a warning to the government. 'Our power is greater than the power of the people in power.'[3] Then the protesters left the GPO and started marching again.

Damien O'Neill was one of the protesters who was brought to court in September 2014 along with Derek Byrne. He refused to sign the injunction, which would have prevented him from going within twenty metres of a meter installation. The next day, meter installers working on an estate in Donaghmede sprayed a line in red paint which was twenty metres from their workstations. O'Neill broke the injunction straight away. 'I drove my car straight through it,' he said.

There was a worker behind a barrier with a consaw. O'Neill and another protester jumped over the barrier and pulled the consaw off him. He could see the private security guards with their cameras. 'We knew straight away they were filming us breaking the twenty-metre rule,' he said.

Soon other protesters were doing the same. 'Once we broke it once or twice, then everyone broke it. So the twenty-metre rule meant nothing,' said O'Neill.

There had been several protesters put in jail in Rossport during the protests against Shell's Corrib gas pipeline. Some left-wing activists believed the jail sentences had helped the state to break the resistance against the gas pipeline. But the threat of going to jail was not putting off the water charge protesters. O'Neill was one of around seventy protesters who blockaded fifteen workers from the GMC/Sierra company in the Grangemore Park estate, Donaghmede, on 30 October 2014. This was the same day Karen Doyle was arrested for standing on a stopcock in Cobh. The protest began at around 1.30 p.m. and continued even after 5 p.m., when workers would have normally finished. O'Neill said that people who had been at work during the day wanted to continue the protest.

'It came to a stage, we blocked the vans, we just blocked everything and then we wouldn't let them out in the evening,' he said. The installers eventually left at 1 a.m., which was almost twelve hours after they first entered the estate. The *Irish Independent* reported that the incident was supervised by gardaí, 'who did not make any arrests or intervene to free the workers'.[4] O'Neill maintained the workers could have left earlier, if they had been willing to leave their vans behind. He also said they had not been left without food. 'They were in McDonald's across the road in the Donaghmede shopping centre. There was no one ever stopping them going home,' he said.

When the workers returned the next day to fill in holes for safety reasons, they were met by another fifteen protesters and had to be given a garda escort to their workstations.

By now, the anti-meter protests were seriously hampering the work of the meter installers. GMC/Sierra had planned to install 500 water meters in areas around Dublin over a number of days in November 2014 but only 200 were installed.

O'Neill was found to be in breach of the court order to remain twenty metres away from meter installations in November 2014. He got a suspended sentence of twenty-eight days. Around this time, a mystery man invited O'Neill to have a cup of coffee with him while he was trying to stop meters being installed in Stoneybatter in the north inner city. 'There's money in it if you stop protesting,' the man told him. 'No,' said O'Neill. But the man persisted. 'What do you want?' O'Neill said he would give up the protests if he got his back garden concreted. 'Where do you live?' asked the man. 'Croke Park' said O'Neill, whose actual home was in Coolock in north Dublin.

***

Four months later, in February 2015, O'Neill and four other water protesters were put on trial in the Central Criminal Courts of Justice complex in Parkgate Street. Mr Justice Paul Gilligan said the video evidence he had seen revealed that the actions of the defendants were designed to 'generate and provoke civil disobedience'. 'It is both unfair and cowardly that the workers who are installing meters are subjected to ongoing harassment and intimidation on a daily basis,' he said.[5]

The protesters noted that the barrister prosecuting the case on behalf of meter contractor GMC/Sierra was none other than Jim O'Callaghan, the brother of RTÉ presenter Miriam O'Callaghan. He was running for a Dáil seat as the Fianna Fáil candidate in the Dublin Bay South constituency.

O'Neill got a fifty-six-day jail sentence for breaching the twenty-metre rule, as did another protester called Paul Moore from Mount Olive Grove in Kilbarrack in Dublin. Derek Byrne of Dublin Says No, activist Bernie

Hughes from McKelvey Avenue in Finglas, and pensioner Michael Batty from Edenmore Avenue were all sentenced to twenty-eight days in jail each for breaching the twenty-metre rule. Michael Batty – known as Meter Mick – never served any time in jail because he was on holidays in Tenerife at the time for health reasons. That provoked much comment online. 'I go every year. I'm a chronic asthmatic,' he said.[6] He was slagged afterwards about it by Derek Byrne, who did have to do jail time. 'I was drinking my piña coladas and he won't let me forget it,' he said.

A crowd of water charge protesters blocked a prison van which came out the side of the courts complex to stop O'Neill, Byrne and Moore being brought to jail. But it was the wrong van. The authorities had instead brought the three men out the front of the complex in another van.

None of them had ever been in prison before. Damien O'Neill recalled how he was stripped down and searched when he got to Mountjoy Prison and then given prison clothes which were too big for him. He was pleased to find that his prison cell was warm and had a TV with sixteen channels. A day later, however, he was moved to Wheatfield Prison in Clondalkin with Paul Moore and Derek Byrne. The authorities wanted them out because the water charge protesters were disrupting traffic with demonstrations outside Mountjoy on the North Circular Road in support of them.

Byrne had taken to wearing a baseball cap with 'Je Suis Derek' printed on it. He had been inspired by the 'Je Suis Charlie' slogan which had been used worldwide to proclaim free speech after the terrorist attacks on the *Charlie Hebdo* magazine in Paris. He had a national profile at this stage because he had insulted President Michael D. Higgins the month before. Higgins had been targeted by water protesters after he signed the second Water Services Bill on Christmas Day in 2013 without referring it to the Supreme Court for consideration.

Byrne turned up to protest when Higgins and his wife, Sabina, visited the Coláiste Eoin secondary school in Finglas, which was celebrating its fiftieth anniversary in January 2015. He called Higgins a 'midget parasite' as he was driven out, and videoed the entire exchange. The story about what he had called Higgins was not reported until a week and a half later. The only reason it came out was that someone sent the video footage of the protest to journalists and uploaded it to YouTube as well. That was Byrne himself. 'I leaked that video. We needed the publicity. How else are you going to get publicity? By the president getting abuse from a protester,' he said.

Byrne was accused of damaging the water charge protest movement. Soon afterwards, it emerged that he was going to be prosecuted. But he saw it as a way to publicise the upcoming marches against water charges, even if it did damage his reputation. 'I would be very happy to sacrifice my reputation. Every journalist in the country wanted to talk to me and every time they spoke to me, they always had to report on one thing – there was a protest in Dublin city centre,' he said.

Late Late Show host Ryan Tubridy played Byrne's YouTube footage for Paul Murphy TD to comment on.

'So, do you approve of that protest?' he asked.

'No,' said Murphy. 'I condemned it repeatedly, so I don't know why you want to talk about it because I've been in the media repeatedly condemning the protest, right?'[7]

Murphy was unhappy with the questioning and put up a tweet after his *Late Late Show* appearance: 'Afterwards, Ryan showed me a video from ISIS and asked me what I had to say about it.' The tweet was a joke, but even some people in his own party thought he was serious. 'It's probably my most retweeted tweet ever,' said Murphy.[8]

Now in Wheatfield Prison, Byrne wanted a transfer back to Mountjoy Prison's Training Unit. It was easier for his family to visit him there than going out to Wheatfield. Byrne told O'Neill and Moore that he was going on a hunger strike to get his prison transfer. But when O'Neill got to his cell, there was a chicken curry waiting there for him. He shouted out to his fellow protesters in the nearby cells. 'Lads, I'm not going on any hunger strike. I'm eating me food.'

There were newspaper reports that Byrne had been seen stuffing down food during his three-day hunger strike in prison. Byrne denied this. 'If I was on a hunger strike, I was on a hunger strike. I don't need to prove it. I don't give a shit what people outside think,' he said. Byrne was put in a cell with a convicted armed robber, who was taking drugs. 'I'm not going to run him down, he gave us a lot of help. He was smoking sleeping tablets and heroin. I was in a cell for three weeks with a guy doing this,' he said. Byrne read a book about Che Guevara's fight in Africa and a biography of Charles Stewart

Parnell while he was locked up. He refused to do any jobs. 'I'm not a criminal, I'm not working,' he said.

But O'Neill and Moore agreed to clean the prison gym, which entitled them to use it every day instead of the three-day-a-week limit for prisoners doing no jobs. O'Neill enjoyed doing two-hour sessions per day because the gym was part of his regular routine. 'I'd go anyway. I still do. Any chance I get,' he said.

The culture in the prison wing was not to ask what anyone was in for. But the other prisoners knew the water charge protesters. 'Me mam said to look after you,' one of them said. Another prisoner complained that the protests outside Wheatfield by supporters of the jailed protesters were making it harder to throw drugs in over the prison wall.

***

O'Neill, Byrne, Moore and Bernie Hughes got out of prison after twenty days. O'Neill's barrister, Jane McGowan, had been up late at night identifying flaws in the case that led to his jailing. She found errors in the committal warrant that sent them to prison. 'She's responsible for us getting out of prison,' said O'Neill.

When they were released in March 2015, they all went to Edenmore House pub to celebrate. Byrne then went to visit his partner, Siobhán Walsh, in Cashel in Co. Tipperary. He had met her for the first time the previous year when she invited him to take part in a water charge protest there. They hit it off.

Byrne filmed Walsh following Environment Minister Alan Kelly around a housing estate in Cashel shortly after his release from prison. Kelly said that he had carried on canvassing regardless. 'The only thing that happened in Cashel was this girl followed me around for a short period of time. That was it. Of all the personalities you know in Leinster House, do you think I'm the type of person who would stop?' he said.[9]

Kelly was a high-profile target for protesters. He had travelled to Carrickmacross in County Monaghan to open a new water treatment plant on the top of Nafferty Hill.[10] There was only one route in and out. Around eighty protesters were waiting at the Ballybay roundabout for Kelly's car. They were only letting local cars through. Kelly managed to escape thanks to a lift from the local council chairman. 'I got into the back of his car, and went down, and they didn't notice anything. They were waiting for my car, but I was gone,' said Kelly.

While he was in prison, Byrne had released a statement promising that he was going to visit Kelly when he got out. The day after his release from prison, he called into Kelly's constituency office in Clonmel. 'Just tell him that Derek Byrne, jailed water protester, was here looking for him,' he told one of Kelly's office staff. Byrne marched into Kelly's constituency office in Nenagh with Siobhán Walsh later in the month to talk to the minister, but Kelly was not there. Clearly, Byrne's desire to protest had not been broken by his jail time.

GMC/Sierra never tried to prosecute any more water charge protesters for breaching the twenty-metre rule after that. The court tactic had failed. The rate of meter installation in Dublin was dropping sharply.

Now the focus was shifting to another key statistic – the number of people who had paid their first water charge bill.

52

THE BOYCOTT OF THE BILLS

Irish Water was under attack on three fronts. The anti-meter protests had slowed down the installation of water meters. The Right2Water marches had shown that opposition to water charges was broad and deep. And now the water charge bills themselves were about to be boycotted.

Due to the success of Joe Higgins' tactic of using a boycott of bills in the 1990s to defeat the previous round of water charges, his party believed that another boycott would defeat water charges again. For that reason, Anti-Austerity Alliance TD Paul Murphy was desperate to find out what the payment rate was for the first one million bills issued by Irish Water in April 2015.

He complained to Taoiseach Enda Kenny that he had not got the information in May 2015. Kenny started talking to Murphy as if he was an infant. He told him to ask Irish Water for the information on the bills instead of expecting him to 'spoon feed' him. 'I advise him to toddle along to the audio-visual room [in Leinster House] at 4 p.m. today where Irish Water will give him the answers to any questions he wishes to ask,' he said.[1]

Murphy turned up to get the bill payment figures he was so keen on from Irish Water. The room was jammed. Irish Water's head of communications, Elizabeth Arnett, put down her bag. 'I'd like to thank you all for toddling in,' she said. The TDs present tried not to laugh. Arnett, of course, had no bill payment figures for Murphy. But the two of them got on relatively well, even though Murphy wanted to abolish the company for which she worked. 'Elizabeth Arnett wasn't incompetent. She was faced with defending something that was unpalatable for the majority of the population at that particular point in time,' said Murphy.[2]

While he was publicly calling for the bill payment figures, the government was privately asking Irish Water for the same thing. The head of the Department of the Environment's water division, Maria Graham, sent a letter to John Tierney on 19 June 2015 to ask him how many had paid their water bills. 'I would be grateful if you could update me as soon as possible on the degree to which collections thus far are aligned with expectations,' she wrote.[3]

Tierney had devastating news for her. Just 44.5 per cent of households had paid their first water bill. Tierney tried to portray it in the best possible light by saying it was a solid start. 'As a new utility sending out bills for the first time, this progress compares well with other utility collections experience. We are satisfied with the rate of collection to date but obviously are monitoring progress closely,' he wrote.[4]

The reality was that more than half of Irish Water customers were boycotting their bills. As one former Ervia official put it, the man on the street was now wondering if he was a fool to pay his water bill given the level of non-payment. 'That's the problem for the government. That's got into the public consciousness,' he said.

Murphy said the three pillars of the water charge protest – the anti-metering protests, the big marches and the boycott of bills – were working in tandem. 'The protests gave people the confidence to refuse to pay. And non-payment gave a very strong rock for the protests. So things fed off each other. At the centre of it was the boycott,' he said.

***

The debates at the government's newly established Public Water Forum gave an insight into why the bill payment rate was so poor. Its chairman, Dr Tom Collins, said there was no support for Irish Water's plan to turn people from citizens into water customers. 'Almost to a person, the forum found that language offensive. As citizens of this state, there are entitlements that are derived from our citizenship rather than our place in the market,' he said.[5]

The Public Water Forum members believed that water should be free for people's basic needs with charges only allowed for wasteful use. But Collins acknowledged the irony that people were willing to pay voluntarily almost as much for water in the supermarket as Irish Water was trying to collect through compulsory domestic charges.

'Irish people were spending €214 million on bottled water per year. That was €47 for every man, woman and child in the country for twenty-five litres each. People were prepared to pay for it when it was presented one way and not when it was presented another way,' he said.

Due to the poor bill payment rate, Paul Murphy and his political mentor Joe Higgins became even more convinced that the Right2Water movement should back the boycott of water charges. That caused a row with Brendan Ogle, now the key figure in the movement. He did not want to alienate people like his eighty-four-year-old mother, who had paid every single water bill. 'We were trying to broaden the movement. They were trying to narrow it,' he said.[6]

Murphy said they persisted in their campaign because they believed the boycott was the best way to defeat water charges. 'It would have bolstered the non-payment figures significantly and given people the confidence not to pay,' he said. Ogle complained that he and fellow Right2Water coordinator Dave Gibney got abuse on social media from 'comrades' on the left.[7] He believed that the 'ultra-left' had deliberate plans to take over Right2Water and sideline the unions like Unite and Mandate that were financing it. A senior figure in the Anti-Austerity Alliance insisted it had only wanted the bill boycott. 'The idea you can control a mass movement is just nonsense,' he said.

Ogle took on the big two unions in the public sector – IMPACT and SIPTU – at the conference of the Irish Congress of Trade Unions in Ennis in early 2015. They were used to winning votes there because they had the most members. Ogle put down a motion to abolish water charges and to call for a referendum on Irish Water. SIPTU's Jack O'Connor and IMPACT's Eamon Donnelly argued instead for a bigger free water allowance which would cover every person's needs. Ogle managed to convince the Northern Ireland unions to back his motion because they had an anti-water charge campaign of their own. He won by nine votes.[8] 'It was the first and only time that SIPTU and IMPACT lost a vote at an ICTU conference,' said Ogle. The abolition of water charges was now the official policy of the Irish trade union movement.

The government believed that the negative media coverage of Irish Water was influencing the low level of bill payments. Irish Water was tracking the coverage. It found that Irish Water got twice as much coverage as homelessness, the health service and electricity pylons combined. Around sixty per cent of the coverage was classed as negative, thirty-five per cent as neutral and five per cent positive. Irish Water's Jerry Grant would later say that the media coverage was 'unprecedented and extremely negative'.[9] One frustrated government special adviser described it in even more colourful terms. 'It was like fighting the wind with a sword,' he said.

Irish Water's Elizabeth Arnett infuriated the water charge protesters by regularly insisting on the airwaves that people would pay their bills. However, she was well regarded in government for her willingness to go out and bat for Irish Water. 'She was fighting a very good fight,' said one government adviser.

But her position was repeatedly undermined by government policy U-turns. She had been sent out to explain the free water allowances for children in May 2014. Then she was sent out again in July 2014 to explain why those free allowances had been reduced. The same happened with the requirement for Irish Water customers to provide their PPS numbers to claim their free water allowances. Arnett was defending this in the media in September 2014. Two months later, she was explaining why it had been dropped.

'Elizabeth Arnett was sent out to look like a complete eejit. She paid a heavy price,' said one public relations expert who worked with her. It culminated with Arnett being sent, with Fine Gael TD Andrew Doyle, on to *The Late Late Show* to debate water charges with Richard Boyd Barrett and Paul Murphy. 'No other politician would put their head up to do it,' said the public relations expert.

RTÉ's coverage of water charges was also starting to raise hackles in government. There was nothing particularly surprising about this: governments throughout the ages have felt they were being unfairly treated by the media. The biggest focus was always on RTÉ because, as the national broadcaster, it had significant influence on setting the news agenda. The government press secretary, Feargal Purcell, a former army officer from Kilkenny, was sent out to meet RTÉ's head of news, Kevin Bakhurst. Purcell told Bakhurst that the government felt Irish Water was not getting a fair hop of the ball. Purcell had got his staff to do an analysis of the media coverage of the eighteen or so announcements that Irish Water had made about new projects. These were 'good news' stories. Not a single one of them had been covered. 'We were shouting into the valley of the deaf,' said one Fine Gael source.

The government always believed that RTÉ had under-reported the growing public anger about water charges in the first half of 2014, when sites like the Mirror.ie, TheJournal.ie and Broadsheet.ie had run endless stories about it, and so overcompensated. 'They felt they had to catch up,' said the same Fine Gael source.

There was one RTÉ move which particularly infuriated the government. A list of the locations and times for local Right2Water protests on 1 November 2014 was put up on the RTÉ News website. Fine Gael TD Jim Daly later complained that RTÉ was promoting demonstrations as if they were St Patrick's Day parades.[10] Former communications minister, Pat Rabbitte, said RTÉ was acting as a 'recruiting sergeant' for the far left and Sinn Féin.[11] RTÉ's government critics did not know that the leaflets, the public meetings and the Facebook posts of the Right2Water campaign had played a much bigger role in the huge turnouts at the protest marches.

The government was also annoyed when RTÉ and TV3 news cameras were set up outside an event that Taoiseach Enda Kenny was attending in Dublin. They filmed his entrance and exit with protesters jeering in the background – but they didn't go inside for Kenny's speech.

However, the water charge protesters were just as annoyed with RTÉ. When Kenny visited the Blackpool shopping centre in Cork city for a jobs announcement in November, 500 water charge protesters turned up in the lashing rain to boo him. They shouted 'Out, Out, Out' as Kenny stepped out of his black Audi state car. After Kenny went in, the protesters booed the RTÉ camera van. 'RTÉ were very much seen as players on one side,' said Socialist Party Councillor Mick Barry.[12] RTÉ would later argue that the fact it was getting criticised by both sides meant it must have got it about right.

In a case of unfortunate timing, RTÉ was lobbying the government to bring in a new broadcasting charge while all the water charge protests were taking place. It would have replaced the TV licence and would have stayed at the same price of €160 per year. But it would have brought in more revenue for RTÉ because it would apply to households that had no TV but were watching programmes on laptops, tablets and smartphones. RTÉ needed the money because its advertising revenues had dropped during the recession and audience figures were dropping due to the rise of services like Netflix and YouTube. Also, the evasion rate for paying the TV licence was up to twenty per cent.

However, the resentment in government about RTÉ's coverage of the water charges meant that the broadcasting charge was off the table. Communications Minister Alex White said there was no way that the government was going to agree to anything that would assist RTÉ in its financial position. 'There was just zero sympathy for the case. People would just look at their shoes when it was raised. And that's just the Labour people. Fine Gael, with some exceptions, were worse. Michael Noonan in particular was quite hostile towards RTÉ,' he said.[13]

There was no love lost between RTÉ and Noonan, given that the station had broadcast a four-part drama series about the hepatitis C scandal in the run-up to the 2002 general election, which had put the spotlight on his role as health minister at the time.[14]

However, White said it was the water charge protests that really killed off the plan to bring in a broadcasting charge. 'There was no stomach for trying to persuade the public given the experience of the water charges,' he said.

Several government ministers saw a connection between the TV licence fee and water charges. They believed that the same twenty per cent of people who refused to buy TV licences were also among the most vocal opponents of water charges. Tánaiste Joan Burton described them as a group of people in Ireland who fly below the radar. 'They are extremely averse to paying any tax and, in fact, they actually don't want the state to know anything about their financial affairs,' she said.[15]

Irish Water was now paying the price for the failure to start communicating with the public well before water charges were introduced. As the controversy grew, there was no media appetite for the story about infrastructure problems in the water service. It was all about the battle over water charges. 'Once the media pack starts running, it keeps running. Communications became impossible,' said a government source.

Fianna Fáil had been undecided about where it stood on Irish Water up to this point. Now party leader Micheál Martin was about to announce a decisive shift.

53

FIANNA FÁIL BACKS THE PROTESTERS

Irish Water was struggling to get people to even register to pay their bills. One million had not signed up. Then, during Leaders' Questions in the Dáil, Enda Kenny introduced a character who was to become famous. The man with two pints. 'The man who stopped me with the two pints in his hand last week and shouting about the cost of water that he couldn't pay for,' he said. 'And I said to him, what he was holding in his hands would pay for water for him – because I know him – for nearly ten weeks,' he said.[1] The water charge protesters were soon gleefully pointing out that Kenny had been talking in the Dáil about meeting another man with two pints two months earlier. He had told that particular man that his two pints would cover his water bill 'for a couple of weeks'.[2]

Repeated inquiries of Kenny's inner circle and his contacts in Mayo failed to reveal the name of the man with two pints. The charge against Kenny was that the man was a figment of his imagination. It would not be the first time that a politician had fortuitously bumped into a man whose situation just happened to support the point he was making. Kenny and other ministers kept using the line that water charges would cost families only €3 a week. But Kenny's supporters insisted that he knew lots of fellows with two pints in Mayo and elsewhere. 'I've no doubt it happened. Enda engaged with people in that way,' said a key supporter. Kenny used it as part of his 'folksy approach' to particularly thorny issues when discussing them with ministers, according to former government special adviser John Walshe.[3] Kenny would often say: 'Last week I met a farmer …' Or it could be a 'businessman in Crossmolina or a teacher in Ballina'.[4]

Kenny was convinced by the argument being strongly put by his economic adviser, Andrew McDowell, that water charges were needed to fix the crumbling water infrastructure. 'We have not measured up for the past forty or fifty years and it is time to deal with it,' he said in the Dáil.[5] Throughout all the protests, Kenny's faith in water charges remained unshaken. Growing up in Islandeady, he had seen how valuable water was and how people were willing to pay for it through group water schemes. 'Enda was irrepressible. He believed water charges were the right thing to do. Because of where he comes from, he couldn't get why this was ideologically a problem,' said a key supporter.

But Kenny had noticed that Fianna Fáil was beginning to shift its position on water charges after the Dublin South West by-election and the large Right2Water march in Dublin in October 2014. Fianna Fáil leader Micheál Martin had asked him if it was time to consider 'suspending' water charges. Kenny quickly pointed out that Fianna Fáil had not included any proposal to suspend water charges in its budgetary submission a week earlier, or in its latest Dáil motion on water charges. 'It seems that Fianna Fáil members are scared witless of the guys on their right-hand side and they are scared witless of the guys to the left of them,' he said.[6]

At this stage, Martin had no clear policy on water charges after three years on the opposition benches. Fianna Fáil Environment Spokesman Barry Cowen had been dancing on the head of a pin during the period. Rather than coming out against water charges, he said they should not be introduced until the water service was fit for purpose. 'That was our nuanced position,' he said.[7]

It didn't help that the water charge protesters now had a singing priest to add to their ranks. Fr Brian O'Fearraigh from Gaoth Dobhair in County Donegal had torn up registration forms for the €100 household charge campaign.[8] Now he was opposing water charges as morally wrong. He featured in a video for the 'Water Protest' song as the lead singer. It became one of the most viewed stories on the *Irish Daily Mirror* website. It was like something out of *Father Ted*, the classic Channel 4 clerical sitcom which was still being repeated. Fr O'Fearraigh, a big fan of the show, had put in some references in the video. He was holding placards in the video with the words 'Down with that sort of thing' and 'Careful Now' on them. There was also an Alan Kelly lookalike calling to the door looking for votes. The message in the song was clear, ahead of the impending general election.

So be off with your meter and be in no doubt,
A vote put you in and a vote put you out.[9]

Left-wing parties were starting to believe that their dream of a left-wing government might actually be achievable at the next election. 'You could definitely sense the opportunity it was presenting to the splinters, the smaller socialist parties,' said Cowen. Fianna Fáil TDs had seen their own supporters protesting on the Right2Water marches. However, it was going to be difficult for Fianna Fáil to switch to all-out opposition to water charges. After all, it had signed off on the introduction of water charges and nationwide water metering in September 2010. It had supported the bailout deal in November 2010, which also committed to water metering. Micheál Martin had voiced no objections to any of this.

However, his close supporters always pointed out that this had been a very difficult time in Martin's life personally as well as politically. His seven-year-old daughter Leana died from a heart condition in Great Ormond Street Hospital in London in October 2010. He and his wife, Mary, had also lost a young son, Ruairí, as a baby in 1999. He was facing a hostile electorate at a time when other Fianna Fáil ministers were announcing their retirements. 'If he had walked away, no one would have questioned it. He's had huge tragedy, but he never dwells on it and he never discusses it,' said one senior Fianna Fáil TD. But Martin decided that he was going to stay involved and won the Fianna Fáil leadership contest after Brian Cowen stepped down. 'He made up his mind at the end of 2010. He loves his country. And he was determined to bring the party back,' said a Fianna Fáil source.[10]

Martin acknowledged later that his party had signed up to water charges. But he said he had always been wary of them due to the history of opposition to them. He compared it to John B. Keane's famous play about the 'Bull McCabe' and his determination to keep 'his land'. 'It's a bit like *The Field*, in terms of revelations about the Irish psyche and land. Whatever it is about water, there's something,' he said.[11]

After the Dublin South West by-election, Martin knew his party was in mortal peril of losing out on the votes of middle-class and urban working-class voters due to the water charges issue. They had been reliable Fianna Fáil supporters before deserting it in droves in the 2011 general election. He got his party to carry out research on what revenue was coming in from water charges and whether meters were getting people to conserve water.

'What are we getting from this? Are we getting conservation? No. Are we getting any substantial revenue? No, it's costing us money. And it's also potentially radicalising an increasing degree of middle ground opinion that doesn't need to be radicalised,' he said.

Martin made his big move at the Fianna Fáil Ard Fheis in April 2015. He promised to abolish water charges and Irish Water itself. It was hugely significant. If Fianna Fáil got into government at the next election, Irish Water could be doomed.

Fianna Fáil's sudden shift caught the government off-guard. 'We thought they would be responsible. We were always surprised at how far they went. It was madness to call for the abolition of Irish Water,' said a Labour adviser. The government had also expected Fianna Fáil to be afraid of alienating its many rural voters. There had been a rural backlash when water charges were abolished by the Rainbow Coalition government (Fine Gael–Labour–Democratic Left) in Dublin in 1996. It had led to the formation of the National Federation of Group Water Schemes, which managed to get funding for the sector from Fianna Fáil's minister for the environment, Noel Dempsey. This time, some rural people were unhappy that their urban cousins were getting off again. But by now, the National Federation of Group Water Schemes had built up a good working relationship with the Department of the Environment. It kept working quietly on getting increased funding for group water schemes to compensate for any sudden abolition of water charges in urban areas.

Fianna Fáil's sudden enthusiasm for abolishing Irish Water did not go down well with the 700 staff there. Fianna Fáil's alternative plan was to have a national coordinating body of 100 people, which meant that 600 of them would lose their jobs.

Ervia Chief Executive Michael McNicholas voiced some of that frustration during a speech at the MacGill Summer School in Glenties in County Donegal in the summer of 2015. It was being held in the Highland Hotel in the village. McNicholas explained how Irish Water was going to address the many failings in the water service. 'The Vartry tunnel is in imminent danger of collapse since 1987 and no money has been invested in it,' he told the crowd.[12] Fianna Fáil Environment Spokesman Barry Cowen was in the audience in front of him and so was Sinn Féin Finance Spokesman Pearse Doherty, who had published a draft bill to abolish Irish Water if his party got into government. McNicholas delivered a message to both of them. 'We are very committed to delivering this plan. That's provided we are still around after the next election, I should say,' he said.

There were claims afterwards that this had been a joke on McNicholas's part. But video footage of the speech showed that he was deadly serious and no one laughed. McNicholas did admit that Ervia and Irish Water 'came up short' when it came to communicating with the public. 'We could have been clearer about how unfit the water infrastructure is, how much was needed to be done to fix that infrastructure, and the scale of the investment that was needed to do that,' he said.[13]

McNicholas had been fighting to deal with complaints about a 'bonus culture' at Irish Water. As a former ESB man, he managed a decent joke about how there had been complaints about pay rates for the workers building Ardnacrusha. 'But back then, the complaint was that they were paid too little – at least some things have changed,' he said.

Taoiseach Enda Kenny needed a garda escort on his way into the Highland Hotel for his speech at the MacGill Summer School. Water charge protesters were jeering him from behind barriers set up to keep them away from the hotel entrance. He did get a laugh with his opening line: 'Thank you for the warm welcome in Glenties – both inside and outside,' he said. But there was a dig later about the Glenties protesters being unemployed in his comments to reporters on his way out. 'I would assume that all of these people across the street want to work and I hope we can give them that opportunity in the future,' he said.[14]

There was a common assumption in government that the protesters were only able to do what they did because they were out of work. Due to the recession, many of them were. But jobs were no longer nine-to-five. There were milkmen, security guards and taxi drivers who could hold down their jobs while they were protesting.

Many of those protesters were also complaining about a new issue that would cause further trouble for Kenny. It was the sale of Siteserv.

54

SITESERV

Independent TD Catherine Murphy had organised 'the leprechauns' during the campaign against water charges in the 1980s. This was the group of plumbers who would re-connect people's water supply if they were cut off for not paying their water charges. Murphy said her phone number was on the leaflets distributed to people living in her Kildare constituency.

'I organised people to do it. It was done late at night. Ours were known as leprechauns,' she said.[1] The nickname came from a case where residents in Meath were prosecuted for having their water supply reconnected. They said they just woke up and their water was running again. The judge in the case quipped that it must have been a group of leprechauns that were giving people back their water.[2]

In 2014 Irish Water was dealing with a new variant of the 1980s leprechauns. They were called the 'water meter fairies'. They were going around removing water meters at night. In Dublin north-east, forty meters were taken out overnight in one estate. Irish Water meters were used at a children's community fun day in the Edenmore estate. There were DJs playing and there was food. Sinn Féin activist Denise Mitchell, who had won a seat on Dublin City Council in the local elections in May 2014, said it was organised for protesters and their families to have some downtime. 'Instead of welly throwing, it was meter throwing. All the children had anarchist masks on throwing the meters – whoever won was getting a medal,' she said.[3] These anarchist masks were modelled on Guy Fawkes, who had attempted to blow up the House of Commons in 1605. The mask had been worn in the film *V for Vendetta* in 2006 by a freedom fighter who was taking on an evil dictatorship and it had since been adopted by protesters around the world.

The anti-metering protests had slowed down the rate of meter installations in the Dublin city area by Irish Water's contractors GMC/Sierra. Its workers had been getting in 5,000 meters per month in the early months of 2014. A year on, they could not get in more than 500 per month. The grim totals were being sent by Irish Water's metering programme team to the Department of the Environment in the Custom House: 466 meters installed in Dublin city in May; 371 meters in June; 148 meters in July. A temporary uplift to 314 meters in August. Then back down to 89 in September. It was a collapse.[4]

***

Catherine Murphy TD had been on all the Right2Water marches throughout 2014. She was chatting to people as she walked along, trying to find out why they were there. The metering contracts kept cropping up. 'That was a huge issue,' she said. Murphy started looking at how the metering contracts were awarded. They had been given the all clear by KPMG in an independent assessment and signed off as legally compliant by law firm A&L Goodbody.[5] She saw nothing wrong with them. 'It looked to me like it was a robust enough process,' she said.

Then she started to look further back at the history of a company called Siteserv, whose subsidiary Sierra was doing water meter installations in partnership with construction firm GMC. And Murphy found that Siteserv had owed €150 million to the former Anglo Irish Bank in 2012. The IBRC, which was winding down Anglo for the state, agreed to write down this debt from €150 million to €45 million when Siteserv was sold in March 2012.[6] The new owner of Siteserv was Millington, an Isle-of-Man-registered company controlled by businessman Denis O'Brien. Siteserv's subsidiary Sierra went on to win four of the eight water metering contracts in July 2013 in partnership with GMC. Their joint venture was called GMC/Sierra.

Murphy submitted nineteen different parliamentary questions to Finance Minister Michael Noonan about the deal. She followed up with requests for documents on the sale of Siteserv under the Freedom of Information Act. 'It was 100 per cent the water charges marchers that prompted that, and what people were saying,' she said.

Murphy next decided to raise the Siteserv deal publicly in the Dáil during Leaders' Questions with Taoiseach Enda Kenny in December 2014. 'Why did IBRC choose to accept a bid from Denis O'Brien's Millington for Siteserv when it was actually the lowest of the bids and resulted in a loss to the State of €105 million?' Kenny said he did not have an answer to her question.[7]

During this time, Irish Water was carrying out research for a €650,000 advertising campaign it was planning. It asked a panel of specially selected people, known as a focus group, what words they associated with Irish Water. 'Denis O'Brien' and 'Paul Murphy' were two that cropped up. 'Topaz', a chain of garage forecourt stations controlled by O'Brien, was also mentioned. Other words were 'controversial', 'tainted image', 'staff bonuses' and 'Phil Hogan'.[8]

By May 2015 Catherine Murphy was no longer a lone voice on the Siteserv issue. Fianna Fáil brought forward a Dáil motion calling for a commission of inquiry into the sale of Siteserv and other companies by the IBRC. Fianna Fáil leader Micheál Martin told the Dáil that the sale of Siteserv was an important issue of public interest. 'A subsidiary of this company subsequently went on to win three contracts linked to water metering, totalling €62 million each,' he said.[9]

The government bowed to the pressure and set up the inquiry in June 2015.[10]

Another potential big blow was coming. Eurostat was about to pronounce its verdict on whether Irish Water was really independent from the government.

55

IRISH WATER'S EU TEST

The Department of the Environment was awaiting a decision about Irish Water from the EU's statistical agency, Eurostat. The civil servants in its Custom House headquarters, with its sixteen-foot statue of commerce on the green dome overlooking the River Liffey, were very nervous. They feared that Eurostat was going to rule that Irish Water was indeed on the government's books, thereby undermining the foundations of Irish Water.

The new lower water charges of €60 for single-person households and €160 for households with two or more people announced in November 2014 were well below what the government's semi-state watchdog, NewERA, had recommended in a confidential report on passing the Eurostat test in 2013. 'Based on current cost assumptions, minimum average charge required to meet test, allowing for some headroom, is €300,' it said.[1]

Indeed, the Troika had already privately warned the government that Irish Water was now in danger of failing the Eurostat test. Then the media found out about it. The government was enraged at this latest water leak. The Department of Finance summoned Troika inspectors to its Merrion Street headquarters for an urgent meeting and told them to 'butt out' of local political debate, according to an *Irish Times* report.[2] Finance Minister Michael Noonan sent a letter to EU Economic Affairs Commissioner Pierre Moscovici saying that the comments about failing the Eurostat test were 'entirely unhelpful' and had served to 'undermine the credibility of the government's decision on water'.[3]

Despite all the danger signs, one senior official said the Department of Finance and the Department of Public Expenditure remained very gung-ho about Irish Water passing the Eurostat test. Tánaiste Joan Burton said the mood began to change when Eurostat officials in their Luxembourg HQ started sending back more questions. 'Once that process began, I think there was a sense of red flags, that this is not as much of a sure thing as it might be,' she said.[4]

The bad news for the government landed on 28 July 2015. Eurostat did not believe that Irish Water, a newborn state company, was fully independent. It saw the influence of the parent – the government – everywhere. Irish Water would have to continue to live at home rather than getting a place of its own.[5]

Finance Minister Michael Noonan described it as embarrassing. Environment Minister Alan Kelly was on holidays in Kerry, his wife's home county, when the news broke. He had to do a phone interview with RTÉ's Sharon Ní Bheoláin on the station's *Six One News.*[6]

Sharon Ní Bheoláin: 'It's evident that the government has been putting a brave face on this all day long. They're saying "nothing to be seen here", but to the man and woman watching at home, this is really the latest chapter in the omnishambles that has been Irish Water.'

Alan Kelly: 'I wouldn't agree with that at all, Sharon.'

Kelly had said that the Eurostat decision did not change anything. But everyone in government knew it did. 'That was certainly not a good day. It was another blow,' he said later.[7] In hindsight, Kelly accepted that the rush to get Eurostat to declare Irish Water off the state's balance sheet had been the wrong strategy. 'If we had kept it on [the government's] balance sheet and planned it out over a number of years, that was the right thing to do,' he said.

Government officials had always insisted that the campaign to boycott water charges would not affect Irish Water's chances of passing the Eurostat test. They were completely wrong. Eurostat specifically noted the 'situation of public disquiet over water charges' and the high uncertainty about how many bills 'will never be paid'.[8] Eurostat was not fooled by the government's attempt to disguise the true purpose of the €100 water conservation grant. It counted it as a state payment to Irish Water, saying the grant was clearly intended to provide partial compensation to householders for water charges. The government's decision to cap water charges for four years also played a role in Irish Water failing the Eurostat test. Eurostat said that the prices for water were not 'economically significant' when these caps were in place. It noted there was 'considerable government control over Irish Water' such as over the size of water charges and board appointments. All of this meant that Irish Water failed the Eurostat test on multiple grounds.

The government had insisted that Irish Water was charging households and businesses more than fifty per cent of its operating costs. But Eurostat found that Irish Water was getting as little as thirty per cent of its operating costs from customers. The rest was being paid by the government.

'There was a lot of irritation with Eurostat in government. But it found that Irish Water didn't have a robust independent commercial structure. It's hard to disagree with them,' said a government source.

It was a hammer blow for Irish Water. It was set up to borrow billions independently of government. Now it would have to get out the begging bowl again. It would have to compete for funding with all the government departments that had new schools, roads and housing to build.

The economist Jim O'Leary later concluded that the desire to pass the Eurostat test meant that water charges were higher than they might have otherwise been.[9] Leo Varadkar agreed with him. He said that the desire to pass the Eurostat test had led to a decision on the level of charging that was just wrong: 'The holy grail was to get it off balance sheet because that would give us an extra €700 million of fiscal space and all the infrastructure costs would be off balance sheet. The desire to do that above all things was the foundation of many of the policy mistakes,' he said.[10]

Meanwhile, the water charge protesters were planning a big publicity stunt to remind the government that they had not gone away. It was going to be in the home of the GAA, Croke Park, during the All-Ireland football semi-final between Dublin and Mayo.

56

THE HILL 16 PROTEST

The Right2Water organisers were trying to keep the numbers up. They posted around fliers for the march on 29 August 2015 declaring: 'We haven't gone away, you know.'[1] Tens of thousands turned up on the day, which showed the reduced water charges had not taken away all of the public anger. The government insisted that there would be no more changes to the charges.

After the march, three protesters had an idea about how to keep the Right2Water cause in the public eye. Damien O'Neill, who had continued to protest against meter installations after being released from jail, and two fellow protesters got a giant Right2Water flag from Brendan Ogle. They met the morning after the march in the Ayrfield car park and folded the flag up carefully into a holdall bag. They wanted to get it into Hill 16 in Croke Park, where Dublin were playing Mayo in an All-Ireland football semi-final.

O'Neill was ruled out as the transporter because they feared he might be recognised. So one of the other protesters volunteered instead. He dressed up as a tradesman in a boiler suit, so that he would look like a guy dashing into the game from work. He got in through the turnstile and, once in Hill 16, took the flag out of his bag.

The Dublin supporters in Hill 16 had a tradition of passing around a giant Dublin flag before matches. Now they held up the 'Right2Water Right2Change – equality-democracy-justice' flag for several minutes before it was put away. It was a clear sign of just how strong the anti-water charge sentiment was.

O'Neill said the protester was tracked down by gardaí at the stadium. 'He was thrown out of Croke Park with the flag,' he said. The GAA condemned the display of the Right2Water banner, with a spokesman saying the organisation was opposed to 'political acts on GAA property'.[2]

There were more protests outside Leinster House. Security had been stepped up there after TDs and senators had been blocked by protesters from getting out the Kildare Street gate. Gardaí started to erect large metal barriers to keep protesters away from the gate. They were also watching what the protesters were saying online.

At one point, Derek Byrne of Dublin Says No was chatting online with fellow water protester Damien Farrell of Éirígí, who was still fitting in protests between his taxi work. As a joke, Byrne posted up his message. 'Tomorrow I'm not going to be outside Buswells [Hotel] at one o'clock,' he wrote.

Buswells Hotel is just outside the Kildare Street entrance to Leinster House. It is a very popular meeting place for politicians, journalists and members of the public due to its location and its unobtrusive staff. The next day, there were reports that the Dáil was on lockdown for a water charge protest. The metal barriers had been put up to block off the streets, and gardaí from Pearse Street station were out in numbers.

But Byrne and Farrell did not show up at 1 p.m. Neither did anyone else. Byrne was listening to the news with great amusement. 'This was me and Damien Farrell having a laugh online. That's how much they were watching us,' he said.[3]

Farrell himself was finding it harder as 'the flying column' continued their protests against metering into the winter of 2015. 'It was a tough winter. It was driving rain, like needles,' he said. He was still getting up at 6 a.m. and going on patrols with two or three cars to spot the meter installers. But on a few occasions, he claims that some of the contractors would tell them where they were going. It was usually if a long weekend was coming up or if rain was forecast for the next day. They would tell us, "We're going to be here tomorrow." They [the contractors' supervisors] stopped telling them [where they were going the next day] because they felt the information was being passed from the workers to us.'[4]

Once the protesters showed up, the supervisors for the contractors knew there was no prospect of getting meters in and would tell the workers to head home. The protests hit the contracting companies in the pocket because under a clause in the metering contract, Irish Water paid them only for 'meters installed'.[5] However, it was later reported in *The Sunday Business Post* that Siteserv, whose subsidiary company Sierra was doing the water meter installations in partnership with construction firm GMC, had settled a multi-million-euro dispute with Irish Water over who would pick up the cost of delays and video surveillance associated with the installation of water meters.[6]

The protests were not just occurring in Dublin; meter installations had ground to a halt in many working-class estates around the country. Contractors had been stopped from installing meters in the Cranmore estate in Sligo town, for example, which was the largest public housing estate in the West of Ireland. They got about thirty homes metered, but there were still at least 370 homes left by the time they were forced to pull out.

A high-level government group, made up of Irish Water staff and government advisers, identified Dublin, Donegal and Waterford as the hotspots for anti-water metering protests. Irish Water was even beginning to provoke protests in Dublin's wealthiest suburbs. When contractors put down meters in Dartry, they added two houses to one meter. An elderly man, a strong Fine Gael supporter, phoned local TD Lucinda Creighton saying he was trying to prevent Irish Water from installing water meters. 'They are putting one meter for my house and the house next door. Myself and my wife are going to have to pay for that.' Creighton said he was fulminating.[7] Actions like this further eroded support for water charges.

However, the metering of middle-class estates continued at pace. There was a sign of the class divide in two estates built either side of the community school in the small suburb of Ballinteer on the southside of Dublin. The Broadford estate to the south of the school had around 800 houses, mainly semi-detached and middle class. It was metered, despite protests by Éirígí Chairman Brian Leeson, who lived in the estate. 'There wasn't four locals who came out when we were blocking them,' he said. But it was a completely different story in the neighbouring Hillview estate to the north of the school, which was built by the council. It was only about a quarter of the size, with 250 houses, but when the water meter installers turned up, around eighty local residents came out to protest. 'They got in and they didn't get out. They were eventually let out. They never got a single meter in there,' said Leeson.[8]

The reason there was more resistance in council estates was simple. People were poorer, so water charges were a bigger threat to their income than they were for middle-class people. And unemployment was higher, which meant there was a pool of people available to protest during the day.

The Dublin 8–Dublin 12 campaign was happy that they had stopped the majority of metering in their own area. But they discovered the limits of their influence when they started protesting against the installation of meters in the suburbs of Terenure and Templeogue. 'There was little to no support because it's a very middle-class community,' said Farrell.

Damien O'Neill had a similar experience. He found it very frustrating when he spent two days supporting anti-meter protesters in Dún Laoghaire. A defining moment came when they were trying to stop a meter going in outside a mansion. The woman of the house emerged with sandwiches. 'She walked by us and gave them to the workers,' said O'Neill. 'I said afterwards: "Never again."'[9]

Anti-water meter protesters found it hard when the residents turned against them. One member of the Crumlin Says No group put it like this: 'Sometimes you might get a bit of a negative response I suppose or go into an area sometimes that's a bit more leafy ... and they are not into resisting the meters. It does demoralise you a bit.'[10]

The Ballyphehane/South Parish Says No group in Cork city believed that trying to stop meters in such areas was futile. Group member Keith O'Brien said the best tactic to stop meters was to get the support of residents well in advance of the contractors arriving. 'What was going on in Dublin was counterproductive to try to stop as much meters as possible. They were running into estates and they were stopping people where they wouldn't have support. So while they were doing this big piece here, there were meters going in up there,' he said.[11]

The Ballyphehane/South Parish Says No group had a twenty-three-man garda task force following them in squad cars. The task force set up checkpoints, which the group saw as an attempt to turn the community against them, because it delayed local drivers going to work. But it had unexpected benefits. 'They caught a couple of burglars. They had stolen goods in their cars,' said O'Brien.

The contractors from J. Murphy & Sons were not getting any meters installed in Ballyphehane. It was very hard for them to go unnoticed. The group had a text alert system that was connected to 1,200 phone numbers in the area. People were willing to give tip-offs because many of them simply could not pay water charges. 'When you were knocking on doors, they'd open the doors and you'd see exactly what these people were living on, which was basically nothing,' said O'Brien.

Irish Water wanted to start metering in other areas of Cork city, but it was concerned that the Ballyphehane/South Parish Says No group would follow the contractors wherever they went. Group members John Lonergan and Donal O'Sullivan were invited to a meeting with senior Irish Water staff and contractors from J. Murphy & Sons. Lonergan said they were offered a deal of no more metering attempts in Ballyphehane on condition that they did not protest elsewhere: 'What they wanted was us not to follow them to the northside of the city or anywhere else. I agreed that I wouldn't.'[12]

However, Lonergan's thinking was that there was nothing to stop the rest of the group going protesting if they wanted. He said that Irish Water had honoured the agreement. 'They never put a water meter anywhere in Ballyphehane,' he said.

57

THE FINAL DAYS OF
WATER CHARGES

Ervia Chief Executive Michael McNicholas was the man doing the public relations work for Irish Water now, in line with the government's wishes. He gave the media briefings in October 2015 on Irish Water's six-year business plan, which included raising €1.8 billion in water charges from households.

But almost half the country were still not paying their water charges. The government had been knocked back when just 44.5 per cent of people had paid their first water bill in April 2015. That only increased to fifty-five per cent paying the second bill in October 2015. McNicholas put a brave face on it publicly by saying that it was always going to take time to increase the payment rate.

Irish Water hired the Behaviour & Attitudes company to find out why customers were refusing to pay their water charges. Householders were asked if they agreed with the statement: 'Why should I pay the bill when everyone else isn't paying?' Another question was about whether they believed that 'water should be free', which was a common slogan of water charge protesters.[1]

There were around 500,000 households not paying their bills, so Irish Water took action by sending them letters warning of 'late payment charges' of up to €60. Under Environment Minister Alan Kelly's legislation, households who did not pay four water bills in a row could get these fines added on. Irish Water also had the power to eventually seek a court order to recover unpaid water bills of €500 or more from people's wages or social welfare payments. But the fear of getting caught was negligible. 'Once it became established that people were not paying and "getting away with it", then that gave confidence to other people to do it,' said Anti-Austerity Alliance TD Paul Murphy.[2]

Irish Water was running out of time because the general election was fast approaching. The already strained relationship between Joan Burton and Enda Kenny worsened when she insisted that he postpone his plans for a general election in November 2015. She wanted to hang on in government for as long as possible in the desperate hope that the slowly recovering economy would repair some of the damage inflicted on her party by water charges.

When Kenny eventually called the election in February 2016, his handlers had no intention of doing the public walkabouts that had been a strong feature of his previous campaigns. The last thing they wanted to see was TV footage of Kenny being harassed, harangued and filmed by water charge protesters. Instead, he was locked away from the public and confined to set-piece events in factories, warehouses and Fine Gael's dark and gloomy underground election headquarters in the Custom House Quay building in the Dublin docklands.

The results of the election were demoralising for Fine Gael. It had been sure that voters would not put the people who crashed the car back at the wheel again, but Fianna Fáil still went up from twenty-three seats to forty-four seats. Meanwhile, Fine Gael went from seventy-six seats to fifty. Fine Gael insisted after the election that none of the seats it lost were down to water charges. 'We picked up seats in eastern urban areas where the recovery was stronger, and we lost seats in rural areas where water charges weren't an issue. I think we lost seats over life being bad for people over the last few years,' said one senior party figure.

Damien O'Neill, the security company owner who had been jailed for his role in the water protests, ran for the Dáil in the Dublin Bay North constituency. He had tried to reach an agreement with two other prominent water protesters – Anti-Austerity Alliance Councillor Michael O'Brien and People Before Profit Councillor John Lyons – about which of them would run. In the end, all three ran and none of them got elected.

Some of those who campaigned strongly against the water charges did see success in the election, however. Sinn Féin's Denise Mitchell, who had been standing on stopcocks in her Ayrfield estate, did win a seat in the constituency. People Before Profit Councillor Bríd Smith was elected as a TD in Dublin South Central. Anti-Austerity Alliance Councillor Mick Barry, who had been involved in the water charge protests in Cork, won a seat in the Dáil for the first time in the Cork North Central constituency. To his surprise and delight, Irish Water's contractors had started metering Cork city right on the eve of the election. 'I'd like to thank Irish Water. They played a not insignificant role in my election,' he said. Senator Katherine Zappone, who had asked Joan Burton to turn up for the An Cosán graduation ceremony in Jobstown, was elected to the Dáil in the Dublin South West constituency on an anti-water charge ticket. Labour lost its two seats in the Dublin South West constituency.

In fact, Labour was decimated in the general election, going from thirty seats to just seven. Joan Burton held on to her seat in Dublin West but resigned as Labour leader. She attributed part of the reason for the severe Labour losses to the 'ferocity' of the campaign by Sinn Féin and the ultra-left. 'They couldn't have cared less what happened to Fine Gael and Fianna Fáil. The party they wanted to destroy was the Labour Party. They made no secret about it and they spoke about it often,' she said.[3]

Water charge protesters were hoping that Environment Minister Alan Kelly would be one of the many Labour casualties in the general election. He had made things more difficult for himself during the campaign when he told the *Sunday Independent* that, for him, 'power is a drug'.[4] Kelly, however, always believed that the issue of water charges would not damage him as much as people thought. 'In Tipperary, it's quite a rural constituency. There's a lot of people in rural areas, they are paying for water all their lives,' he said.[5]

Kelly was waiting in a packed count centre in the Presentation College in Thurles for the returning officer to deliver the election result. When the returning officer announced he had won the fifth and final seat, Kelly's supporters roared in triumph and they lifted him into the air. Kelly started punching the air with his two hands and roaring, 'Yes.' It was sheer relief after the pressure he had been under. 'I'm not sure if I'll ever experience pressure like it in my life again. There was pressure at government level, there was pressure at departmental level, there was pressure on the lads in Irish Water. There was public pressure,' he said.

Kelly's first stop after his re-election was Borza's takeaway in Thurles. The *Irish Independent* reported that he 'clearly relished his bag of chips, complete with generous helpings of salt and vinegar'.[6]

***

However, Kelly was appalled several days later when he was watching RTÉ *Prime Time*'s coverage of the post-election fallout. He was at home in the village of Portroe, overlooking Lough Derg. Fianna Fáil Environment Spokesman Barry Cowen told *Prime Time*'s David McCullagh that the abolition of water charges was a 'red line' issue for his party in any government formation negotiations.[7]

In the second part of the programme, *Prime Time* presenter Miriam O'Callaghan followed up on those remarks with Fine Gael's Simon Coveney. 'Listening earlier to Barry Cowen, if the price of going back into government with Fianna Fáil was giving up on water charges ... would you do a U-turn on water charges?' she asked.

Coveney responded: 'Well I think we'd certainly be willing to talk about water because it's a big issue for lots of people.'

Kelly could not believe it. He got on well with Coveney, who had been an ardent defender of water charges all the way through. 'Fianna Fáil were chasing Sinn Féin, so they flipped. And then, ultimately, Simon Coveney flipped. That interview on *Prime Time* was the day Irish Water ended up going in the opposite direction. When he opened the door to Barry Cowen, where he said everything was up for negotiation,' Kelly said.

There was real anger at Coveney's comments in Labour. The party had been almost wiped out in the general election. Water charges, which had been insisted on by Fine Gael, had become a millstone around its neck. Now Fine Gael appeared to be willing to walk away from water charges to get back into power. Coveney insisted that he was just reflecting the reality of the political situation after the general election rather than giving up on Irish Water. 'That's a political charge from people who want to pretend that somehow I was the one who triggered a new debate on Irish Water,' he said. 'There was going to be a water debate as part of the confidence and supply agreement, regardless of what was said by me or anybody else for that matter,' he said.[8]

The bill payments had been slowly rising before the general election. Around sixty-one per cent of people paid their third bill in January 2016. An Irish Water staffer said that after Coveney's comments on *Prime Time* in March 2016, the payment of water charges bills 'fell off a cliff'. Just forty-eight per cent paid their fourth water charges bill in April 2016. People who had been paying their bills automatically through direct debits started to cancel them. Almost 30,000 people cancelled their direct debit payments between April and June 2016. But it was not just Coveney's comments. A majority of TDs elected by the voters, whether from Fianna Fáil, Sinn Féin, the Anti-Austerity Alliance, People Before Profit or the Social Democrats and most independent TDs were opposed to water charges. People could now see that the writing was on the wall for water charges.

However, former Fianna Fáil minister Noel Dempsey was very unhappy with Fianna Fáil's demands to get rid of Irish Water and water charges. The diplomatic thing to do would have been to stay silent. That was not Dempsey's style. 'I just couldn't agree with the position Fianna Fáil took. I could understand it. But I couldn't agree with it,' he said.[9] Dempsey went public by writing an article for *The Irish Times* after the general election results to warn against abolishing Irish Water and water charges.[10]

Barry Cowen said Dempsey's intervention might have been 'well intended', but he did not know just how unhappy the electorate was about water charges, having retired before the 2011 general election. 'Noel has been at many a door in his time but he wasn't at too many doors in the last election. So he hadn't the authority or the informed view of the public that we had,' he said.[11]

In Cork city, the Ballyphehane/South Parish Says No group kept the pressure on to abolish water charges and Irish Water. They held a silent protest outside Coveney's family home in Carrigaline in Cork. They were initially standing outside the wrong house until a local person directed them to the correct address. The group held another silent protest outside the family home of Fianna Fáil leader Micheál Martin, which lasted for over an hour. That form of protest had previously been seen as unacceptable. But group member Keith O'Brien said that government ministers were imposing property taxes and water charges on people and then going home to their 'nice cosy lifestyle'. 'We said, "No. You're going to see the consequences outside your house." And it will be peaceful, it will be civil. We were never screaming and roaring outside people's doors,' he said.[12]

Micheál Martin became one of the few senior politicians who actually went to meet a 'Says No' group to hear what they had to say in the Ballyphehane community centre. John Lonergan told Martin that he did not believe Fianna Fáil would honour its election promise to abolish water charges and Irish Water. 'You're backtracking on what you promised in the manifesto,' he said.[13] Martin picked up his party's manifesto and threw it down the table in front of him. 'We're not budging from that,' he said.

Martin was willing to sign a confidence and supply arrangement which would put a Fine Gael-led government in power. But he informed Enda

Kenny that abolishing water charges was a must. 'This has to go if there's going to be any confidence and supply. This is a red line issue for us,' he told him.[14]

Martin said later that he had a very good chat with Kenny about it. 'I went through some of the stuff I was saying about what are you getting in return for it. He accepted that. He knew exactly what I was saying around middle ground opinion being radicalised,' he said.

The talks between Fine Gael and Fianna Fáil now began in Trinity College about forming a government. Fine Gael's negotiating team included two potential future leaders, Leo Varadkar and Simon Coveney. Their supporters believed that Kenny would soon be gone because his position had been weakened so much by Fine Gael's loss of twenty-six seats in the general election.

Martin believed that Kenny had difficulties selling a climbdown on water charges to his own negotiators because the Fine Gael leadership battle was already underway. 'Having Simon Coveney and Leo Varadkar on the one committee to form confidence and supply was a recipe for things being unnecessarily prolonged,' he said. The Fianna Fáil team reported back to Martin that the Fine Gael negotiators were digging in on water charges. 'They just didn't want to stomach it. It just dragged on and dragged on,' he said.

Fianna Fáil's negotiating team during the talks in Trinity College was made up of Environment Spokesman Barry Cowen, Finance Spokesman Michael McGrath, Agriculture Spokesman Charlie McConalogue, and newly elected Dublin Bay South TD Jim O'Callaghan.

The Fine Gael negotiators had thought Cowen, with his image as a tribal Fianna Fáiler, would be the hardest to deal with on water charges. They were surprised to find out that O'Callaghan was much more hard line than Cowen. He had won the third seat in his constituency while outgoing Labour TD Kevin Humphreys and Renua leader Lucinda Creighton lost out. Both of them had supported water charges.

O'Callaghan had been the barrister representing GMC/Sierra when it brought Derek Byrne of Dublin Says No to court for breaching the order to stay twenty metres away from meter installations. Byrne decided to contact O'Callaghan to see if he would contribute to a fundraiser for a woman with epilepsy who was being offered ground-breaking surgery in the US. It would give her the chance of walking instead of being confined to a wheelchair for the rest of her life. When Byrne rang O'Callaghan's office, his secretary said he was not there.

Byrne: 'Tell him Derek Byrne called.'

Secretary: 'Does he know you?'

Byrne: 'I hope so, he sent me to prison.'

O'Callaghan rang him back that evening. 'Put me down for €100.'[15]

It did him no harm with Byrne. He and two other water charge protesters turned up at an election meeting that O'Callaghan was holding in the Hilton Hotel in Charlemont Place overlooking the Grand Canal. They met O'Callaghan on the way in and shook hands with him. 'Jim, no hard feelings,' said Byrne, who stayed quiet for the meeting.

***

Water charges had almost led to the collapse of the Fine Gael–Labour government in April 2014. Now the same issue threatened to prevent the formation of a new government.

Leo Varadkar said some TDs in Fianna Fáil genuinely felt their opposition to water charges had helped them win seats that Sinn Féin might otherwise have won. 'I don't believe that but some of them genuinely do, particularly in Dublin,' he said. That was Jim O'Callaghan, of course. 'I wasn't going to mention any names but obviously your sources are accurate,' said Varadkar.[16]

Varadkar said water was easily the most difficult issue during the three months of talks. 'It wasn't an election on water. I was kind of annoyed to the extent to which Fianna Fáil decided to make it the issue. I remember even in discussions with some of them, they were almost upfront about it,' he said. The phrase Varadkar recalled one of the Fianna Fáil negotiating team using was a 'pound of flesh' – the same demand made by the moneylender Shylock in Shakespeare's *Merchant of Venice*. 'It was the price or humiliation we had to pay and face in order to get a confidence and supply agreement,' he said.

Fine Gael was in a state of panic about having to abolish Irish Water in order to retain power. It was desperate to get any material it could to bolster its case for the company's survival.

Andrew McDowell – Kenny's chief economic adviser and the man who had come up with the idea of creating Irish Water – met Ervia Chief Executive Michael McNicholas on 11 April 2016. He wanted to know the 'long-term benefits' of Irish Water passing the Eurostat test and to discuss 'policy options to address water affordability'.[17] Then Taoiseach Enda Kenny and five cabinet ministers – Michael Noonan, Paschal Donohoe, Frances Fitzgerald, Leo Varadkar and Simon Coveney – met Michael McNicholas and Irish Water's Jerry Grant about the same issues on 18 April 2016.

There were real fears by now among Irish Water staff about whether it would survive. Jerry Grant found that out when he walked the corridors on Fridays, talking to staff. They asked him if it was safe to take out a mortgage, if the company was on the verge of being abolished.

Simon Coveney and Paschal Donohoe, who were part of the Fine Gael negotiating team, privately visited Colville House to reassure the staff that this would not happen. Coveney said Fine Gael would not give in to Fianna Fáil's demand to abolish Irish Water. 'I couldn't have supported that in all conscience. To go back to local authorities providing this service again, when we knew that was a broken model?' he said.

Coveney and Cowen ultimately broke away from the other negotiators to hammer out a complicated process that would lead to the abolition of water charges. It involved setting up an expert commission on water charges, then an Oireachtas committee to examine the findings and then a Dáil vote on water charges which the government had to abide by. Given that a majority of TDs were against water charges, their abolition was now guaranteed. Fianna Fáil leader Micheál Martin was satisfied that Kenny would follow through on this. 'The definitive decision was taken at the start. The rest was a work through,' he said.

Towards the end of the talks, Varadkar gave an interview on the *Today with Seán O'Rourke* radio show about the National Children's Hospital and the state of the talks. He attacked Fianna Fáil for their 'obsession' with water charges. Micheál Martin hit back a week later by revealing that Varadkar had told Fianna Fáil negotiators of his fears that the €460 million spent on water meters could be 'Fine Gael's e-voting machines by ten'.[18]

Martin suspected that Varadkar was distancing himself from Taoiseach Enda Kenny by suggesting that the abolition of water charges was not his policy. However, Varadkar said his comments were nothing to do with the future leadership contest. 'It was so bloody frustrating for the best part of two years, any time I did or said anything, it was all about my leadership plan. I'm genuinely happy to bash Fianna Fáil on occasion: 1) because I believe in what I'm saying and 2) it may go down well with our base and our supporters,' he said.

Varadkar, who had always been in favour of water charges, found it difficult to agree to scrap them as part of the confidence and supply agreement signed in May 2016. 'Part of the price of forming a government and part of the price of doing a deal with Fianna Fáil was to row back on a major reform that we actually got done. I thought it was a real shame from an environmental point of view, from a fairness point of view and from an infrastructure point of view,' he said.

There was a furious reaction from Alan Kelly in the Dáil to the deal secured by Fianna Fáil to abolish water charges. He described the party's actions as 'environmental treason'.[19] Looking back, he said that was the most important speech in his political career. 'In five or ten years, another government is going to have to deal with this again. What's going to happen when we're found to be in contravention of European law? You have to pay fines or else deal with it. Where will Barry Cowen be then and all those other people?' he said.

In total, it took three long months to negotiate a government. In contrast, the end of water charges was brutal and swift.

58

THE DEPARTURE
OF JOHN TIERNEY

John Tierney had been publicly vilified. His house had been attacked. Now he was nearing the end of his three-year contract as managing director of Irish Water.

The newspapers were reporting for a second time that Tierney was on the way out. This time, the reports were accurate. On Sunday 8 November 2015 Tierney sent a late-night email to all Irish Water staff, telling them that media reports about his plans to retire the following April were true:

> *Establishing Irish Water has been one of the most challenging projects ever undertaken in the public sector. It has been delivered because of the calibre and commitment of the people of Irish Water and Ervia and I am very grateful to you all.*
>
> *As I have said on many occasions it continues to be my privilege to work with you.*
> *Best Regards,*
> *John*[1]

John Tierney was finishing his career in the public service at the age of just fifty-seven. But he still wanted to believe that Irish Water would continue on. He emailed all the staff on 16 January 2016 to 'bring them up to speed' on the news that sixty-one per cent of Irish Water customers were now paying their water charge bills.

'These results are a credit to the hard work and commitment of our teams across the organisation all working together to improve the service to our customers and to deliver significant improvements to our water system,' he wrote.[2] Tierney had been sneered at when he spoke about his pride in the

Irish Water staff. But those who worked with him believed that he had been absolutely genuine. 'It was very hard to see John Tierney having to take what he took. He did a really good job. He was always a gentleman,' said an Irish Water source.

Tierney's impending departure made more headlines when it emerged that the government had agreed to a special deal to ensure he got paid his pension earlier than normal.[3] If he had stayed on as Dublin city manager – and some of his friends wished that he had – he would have qualified for a full pension at the age of sixty. But the terms of his Irish Water contract provided for him to get a full pension once it ended. As a result, the government agreed to pay €470,000 to cover the cost of his pension for three years until he got his county manager pension. Tierney also got a severance payment of €100,000 on his departure. He decided to stay largely silent on the matter. In his only public comment afterwards, he said that he hoped that a fair account would be given of the Irish Water staff 'who had gone the extra mile to deliver a very challenging and complex project on behalf of the government'.

'Despite all of the challenges, the organisation is functioning as it was intended, thanks to the hard work of everyone who was involved,' he said.[4]

It was a bruising end for someone who saw himself as a public servant. He had become the personification of all that had gone wrong with Irish Water. Alex White, who was the communications minister at the time, said Tierney was treated unfairly. 'He was made a scapegoat: not the first or only public servant to be treated in this way in these times,' he said.[5]

Former Fianna Fáil minister Noel Dempsey once noticed how the political system and the media moved in lockstep in situations like this. 'It is much easier to sell a newspaper if the story is of an evil individual who can be personally blamed for something – rather than if the story is about a system's failure,' he said.[6]

There was one consolation for Tierney as he adjusted to life after Irish Water. He was still the chair of the Tipperary Supporters Club. And in September 2016 Tipperary shook off their reputation as under-achievers by beating Brian Cody's Kilkenny in the All-Ireland hurling final. In the days afterwards, Tipperary County Board singled out the supporters club 'led by Chairman John Tierney' for their fundraising for the team.[7]

Tierney was replaced as managing director of Irish Water by Jerry Grant, who was to become very popular in the government because of his depth of knowledge about the water service and his ability to communicate it to the public.

59

FLOTSAM

The results of the general election had effectively killed off water charges, with just 30.5 per cent of people paying their fifth Irish Water bill in July 2016. Most people now saw little point in paying when they fully expected water charges to be abolished.[1]

But the funeral procession was to take almost two years. That delay was to cover Fine Gael's embarrassment at having to give up on its grand plan for Irish Water. The first step came when water charges were suspended on 1 July 2016 by the Fine Gael-led minority government, in line with the commitment given to Fianna Fáil in the confidence and supply agreement. Then a very complicated plan was put in place. First, an international water commission was set up. Secondly, its findings would be debated by a special committee of TDs and senators. And then its final report would be voted on by the Dáil and Seanad. Fianna Fáil leader Micheál Martin said his party did not want this at all. 'We got this very elaborate Oireachtas committee structure. And they dragged it out for about two years after that. I think that was foolish. You're wasting a lot of energy and time,' he said.[2]

Fine Gael and Fianna Fáil had deliberately arranged to have eleven of their TDs and senators on the twenty-person committee. They needed the majority vote to control the final outcome. But they could not agree during the months of committee hearings as to what the outcome should be. Sinn Féin Dublin Mid-West TD Eoin Ó Broin noticed the 'non-stop fighting' between the Fine Gael and Fianna Fáil TDs on the special committee. 'For two parties who had set this thing up to try and resolve a problem, the level of hostility was remarkable,' he said.[3]

The other TDs on the committee included several who had been active in the protests: Anti-Austerity Alliance TD Paul Murphy, independent Donegal TD Thomas Pringle and independent Tipperary TD Seamus Healy, who had been standing on stopcocks during anti-water meter protests in Clonmel. They all wanted not just to abolish water charges but to kill off any chance of them ever coming back. Stopping the use of meters was the key. They rejected Fine Gael's revised plan to use meters for a system of excessive charges for those who wasted water. And they would not countenance any further meter installations. That would have left the 880,000 existing meters to rot in the ground. To Fine Gael's horror, Barry Cowen decided to support this plan of no more metering and no excessive charges. Eoin Ó Broin said there was a huge row at the committee between Cowen and the Fine Gael members. 'Fine Gael were left completely isolated,' said Ó Broin.[4]

The Right2Water TDs triumphantly went onto the plinth at Leinster House on 28 February 2017 to announce they had a deal with Fianna Fáil.

Simon Coveney made a dramatic intervention by giving a press conference later that night in Leinster House. He warned Fianna Fáil that ruling out excessive charges would be 'illegal' under EU law because there had to be penalties for wasting water.[5] Fine Gael could live with the abolition of water charges. But it had to keep the water metering programme going because it had already spent €467 million on the meters.

Fianna Fáil leader Micheál Martin felt that the committee was being dragged into the forthcoming Fine Gael leadership battle between Leo Varadkar and Simon Coveney. 'Simon was being paranoid about how whatever subsequent deal would be used against him by Leo Varadkar to undermine his position in terms of the leadership. That was our sense,' he said.[6]

Water charges were now threatening the collapse of the confidence and supply deal between Fine Gael and Fianna Fáil, which was less than a year old. Fianna Fáil backed down the day after Coveney issued his late night ultimatum. Cowen agreed to the excessive charging system and the installation of meters in new homes. He knew why Fine Gael was so desperate about this. 'If they keep metering, there was always the chance of charging in the future. So they were being loyal to their supporters,' he said.[7]

The metering programme had been scaled down since the outcome of the February 2016 general election. Irish Water had got 817,000 meters installed by then. Just 6,000 meters were installed nationwide the following month. Metering was almost halted completely in Dublin city but continued at a reduced rate in other areas. Irish Water started to send in metering reports to the Department of the Environment every two months instead of every month. The last meter under Irish Water's programme was installed on 3

February 2017. The final tally was around 892,000 meters, which was 157,000 short of the target of 1.05 million meters. Around €467 million of the final budget of €612 million had been spent. The leftover €145 million was put into capital projects, with most of it going on new water infrastructure for strategic development sites.

Irish Water's own figures showed that it had actually come close to hitting its metering targets in four regions – the North West (85,000 meters installed), the West (126,000 meters installed), the North East (124,000 meters installed) and the Midlands (118,000 meters installed). The protests in places like Cobh and Ballyphehane had had an impact in the South West, where it got in 132,000 meters out of a target of 162,000. But the worst performance of all was in Dublin City, where the most intense protests had taken place. Just 65,000 meters were installed out of a target of 120,000 – just over half of the target. The metering programme in Dublin County was more successful, with 142,000 meters installed, but that was still well below the target of 190,000 meters.

However, Irish Water now had the metering data to show if people really had reduced their use of water by ten per cent after the introduction of charges, as the cost–benefit analysis had predicted. The answer was a resounding 'No'. The average water usage per person was around 109 litres per day in a metered household before charges started in 2015. That rose slightly to 114 litres of water per person per day in 2015, when charges were in force. And it went up further to 117 litres of water per person per day in 2016, when charges were suspended halfway through.[8]

The special Oireachtas committee on water charges ultimately recommended the scrapping of water charges and a return to the old system of funding the water service through general taxation. It said there should be charges for those who used excessive water. And it called for a referendum to ensure Irish Water was kept in public ownership.

After the Dáil voted to abolish water charges on 13 April 2017, there was a sense of bewilderment among those who had not objected to meters and who had paid their bills. The ones who had shouted the loudest had won. It was the minority ruling over the sixty-one per cent majority who had been paying their bills up to the general election. The *Irish Independent*'s personal finance editor, Charlie Weston, was a voice for this sizeable group. He described himself as one of the 'one million suckers who have paid their water charges'. He went on to say, 'The political agenda has been hijacked by those who want to abolish any tax or charge that they don't like, and instead impose the costs on middle earners. The betrayal of middle Ireland is galling.'[9]

The *Irish Daily Mirror* columnist Pat Flanagan took a completely different view. He said it was the first time in history that the people of Ireland actually rose up and took to the streets at what they deemed was a tax too far. 'Those who stood up to the government's bullying deserve a medal for as we commemorate the Easter Rising they are the true inheritors of the spirit of 1916,' he wrote.[10]

Andrew McDowell had stayed on as Enda Kenny's chief economic adviser in the new minority government. He had always been very loyal to Kenny and used to hate when people brought up questions about the Taoiseach's future. But then he was appointed by the government as vice-president of the EU's European Investment Bank, which was seen as a sure sign that Kenny was on the way out. That eventually happened in May 2017, with Leo Varadkar winning the subsequent Fine Gael leadership battle against Simon Coveney.

***

The one reform that did endure was the creation of Irish Water itself. The senior management there were proud that there was very little turnover among staff during the worst of times. And when the economy started to improve, very few walked out through the double locking door of their Colville House HQ on Talbot Street. Some staff considered themselves fortunate to have seen the creation of a national water company. It might never have happened if such a severe and painful recession had not forced the government to come up with a different approach.

Elizabeth Arnett had moved to the role of head of corporate affairs and environmental regulation in 2016. She left Irish Water the following year to become head of corporate affairs at Ulster Bank. She said it had been a privilege to be a part of the Irish Water project. 'Setting up a national water utility to provide a safe sustainable water service to millions of people was such an important thing to do,' she said.[11]

During his time as managing director, Jerry Grant approved the replacement of cast iron pipes in Fethard, the twelfth-century Norman walled town in Tipperary where he had gone to school. He also gave the go-ahead to a water treatment plant for 7,000 homes in the Fethard area. That was welcome news for forty households in particular who had been on boil water notices for a decade. Grant was clocking up the media appearances, including some very lengthy and detailed interviews with Pat Kenny on Newstalk. The Irish Water media team were analysing the media coverage. It had changed from sixty per cent negative during the water charges crisis to seventy-five per cent positive during the summer drought in 2018.

Grant believed that Irish Water was performing well in serving the needs of the people of Ireland. 'I consider it a great privilege to have been managing director of Irish Water for two and a half years, which enabled me to continue the work that John Tierney and the team had commenced,' he said.[12] Grant went on to say he had enjoyed an 'excellent' working relationship with 'civil servants and ministers', which was crucial to overcoming the challenges Irish Water faced. He stepped down from his position in Irish Water in September 2018.[13]

Later, Grant would give a detailed assessment of the Irish Water project at a water conference in New Zealand. He said the introduction of water charges for households was 'a bridge too far'. He told delegates: 'Hit hard by recession, the public reacted at the "austerity tax on water" and protested against water meter installations, which became the focus of anger.'[14]

There were changes at the top of Ervia too, during this period. Michael McNicholas stepped down as chief executive in May 2017 and was replaced by Mike Quinn, the former head of Bord na Móna. The government decided that it was going to split Irish Water from Ervia in 2023 without giving Quinn any advance warning. He left the company soon afterwards. Still, at least the unhappy marriage between Ervia and Irish Water now had a divorce date.

However, the problem remained for the government of what to do with the 'one million suckers' who had paid their water charges. There had been no refunds given when water charges were abolished by the Fine Gael–Labour government in 1996. This time, the Fine Gael-minority government had been told by the special Oireachtas committee to refund those who had paid their charges.

Irish Water customers got letters in the post from the appropriately named Eamon Gallen, the company's head of customer operations. 'Dear Customer,

Following the Government decision to refund domestic water charges, please find below a cheque,' it said. In total, Irish Water handed back €173 million in customer refunds at a cost of €5 million in administration.

The government also had to increase the payments to group water schemes so that rural households would get free water for the first time in decades. This was another humiliating U-turn. The official government press release disguised the move by talking about 'increased supports for rural water service'. The national media did not pick up the story until months later.

**

Given the public backlash against water charges, there is now an extreme nervousness in government about bringing in new taxes and charges. Taoiseach Leo Varadkar said he was giving a lot of thought to how to increase carbon taxes in the light of the water charge protests.

'When I think of carbon tax, and I want to do it, I reflect on the experience in other countries, France, Australia, you name it, and also our own experience with water charges. You can only govern by consent,' he said.[15]

The failure of Irish Water to prove to Eurostat that it was off the government's books was to have long-term consequences in government. Varadkar said the government had been 'badly burned' by it. 'Now any time we design anything, we almost say to ourselves, "Let's forget about whether it's on or off balance sheet." There was an obsession at the time about being on and off balance sheet, not just water but capital investment, public–private partnerships, all those things,' he said.

Eurostat officials would privately express a certain regret at the consequences of their statistical decision on Irish Water. 'They are not political. They now realise how crucial that decision was for the whole water reform programme,' said a government source.

The influence of the Eurostat decision can be seen in subsequent government policies. The Land Development Agency was set up on the government's books. The entire €116 billion Ireland 2040 infrastructure plan was treated the same way. Minister for Finance Paschal Donohoe said he was not going to set up any new organisation with the sole purpose of getting it off the government's books. 'It shows to me the dangers of designing an organisation that might have a particular balance sheet status, as opposed to designing an organisation to deliver the sort of objective of how we deliver the right service,' he said.[16]

After the failure of water charges, there were several theories about how it should have been done differently. John Mullins, former Bord Gáis chief executive, believed that a flat charge with a gradual roll-out of meters was the way to go. 'If you had introduced the flat charge with social welfare waivers, and you put in the meters over time to detect leakage, and you built up your utility on a steadfast basis, we might be in a very different place today,' he said.[17]

Labour's Joan Burton said her personal view was always that the water charge should have been incorporated as a €50 to €100 element of the property tax.[18]

But the most popular theory among Irish Water's backers is that water charges could still be in place if politics had not 'got in the way'. Labour's Alan Kelly said if water charges had not been abolished, the payment rate would have increased gradually from the sixty-one per cent who were paying up to the general election. 'OK, it would have taken a period of time. But it would be there. The level of investment to be washed down the drain for the sake of populist politics for me will always be something that was completely and utterly a disgrace,' he said.[19]

It is natural for those who had planned and organised and legislated for water charges to argue like this. In their version of history, they would have won the war but for the stab in the back by Fianna Fáil.

In truth, Irish Water was in deep trouble prior to that. There had been no way it could go back to metering the working-class estates because there was organised resistance waiting for it. And for how long would the silent majority keep paying their bills when a significant minority were not? The rapid drop-off in bill payments after the 2016 general election showed that some were reluctantly paying. The electorate had made its decision on water charges by selecting a majority of anti-water charge TDs. The parliamentary system, which had been accused by some water charge protesters of being anti-democratic, implemented this mandate. Former environment minister Phil Hogan was correct in one sense – there had been just one shot to get Irish Water right. But the government missed.

It did so in large part due to the relentless campaign by the water protesters. They managed to rally their communities in a way the government could not. The Right2Water protest marches broadened the movement even further. And the controversial boycott of bills became a more important metric of Irish Water's performance than the monthly updates on the number of meters installed.

Karen Doyle and two other members of the Cobh Says No to Austerity group were convicted of obstructing the installation of a meter under the Water Services Act 2007. They were bound to the peace. Doyle said she had no regrets about taking part in the campaign. 'What the water movement did – and I know it happened in lots of areas as well – people got to know each other again. That's one of the reasons why we won,' she said.[20]

After the suspension of water charges, the 'Says No' groups around the country gradually began to wind down. The Cobh Says No to Austerity group was disbanded in the summer of 2015 due to internal tensions. 'There was one element of it going very far left with the Socialist Party and the majority of us who weren't involved in any political parties at all, I think we wanted to be more broad-based,' said Doyle.[21] She invited twenty-one people to her kitchen after that and all of them turned up. They set up a new group called Cobh Community4Change. They took part in the Yes campaign during the referendum to remove the restrictions on abortion from the Irish Constitution.

Independent TD Joan Collins continued her campaign for a referendum to keep water services in public ownership by publishing her own private bill. She said the water charge protests had shown the power of communities to change government policy. 'If people get organised, they can actually change things. That's a crucial lesson,' she said.[22]

And the protests, in some cases, had a negative effect on the lives of the protesters. For example, Damien Farrell, the taxi driver who was a member of Éirígí, had a 'few bob' before the protests but got into mortgage difficulties because he was protesting so much. He was not in 'massive arrears', but it was enough to have his mortgage sold by PTSB to a vulture fund. He went on to take part in the occupation of Apollo House, an empty, ten-storey building in Dublin's city centre, in protest at the housing and homeless situation. He said that campaign did not have the size and scale of the anti-water charge movement. 'If we had that, we'd be on the pig's back. We're constantly searching for "What was it? What was the magic formula?"' he said. Like many water protesters, he misses the sense of camaraderie and the size and scale of the anti-water charge movement. 'But do I miss the early mornings and the cold? Not a chance,' he said.[23]

Some of the strength of the anti-water charge movement was due to a specific set of circumstances. The charge applied to everyone, in a way that the housing crisis does not. And it was taking place at a time of mass unemployment, public and private sector pay cuts and emigration. Water charges turned out to be one tax too many after the Universal Social Charge, the €100 household charge, the property tax, the private pension levy.

Whatever chance there had been of convincing the public to pay water charges was blown and it was due to a series of factors. Everything was done at breakneck speed to meet the Troika deadlines. The installation of one million meters was given the go-ahead based on a flawed cost–benefit analysis study. The deep political divisions between Fine Gael and Labour on water charges diminished the sense of collective purpose which had helped to drive through the property tax. There were internal divisions between Irish Water and Ervia, due to the strange management structure created by government. The schemes to help people who could not afford the water charges were a disaster. The government could never find a Revenue-style solution to force people to pay their water charges. The calls to retreat from the country's most senior civil servant and its finance minister were ignored. The whole project was swept on by the mistaken belief that Eurostat would deliver the grand prize – an Irish Water which could borrow for itself.

There was also arguably an element of not letting a good crisis go to waste from some politicians' viewpoint. The recession was a political opportunity to do things like the property tax and the water charges that had not been possible before. The Department of Public Expenditure's Secretary General Robert Watt questioned if it was 'uniquely Irish' to push through a change in these circumstances. 'The political system was seeing that this policy wasn't going well. That was pretty clear and it certainly wasn't going to be popular. Why did the system continue to push? It pushed because it didn't believe this type of reform is possible in peacetime,' he said.[24]

***

There was an interesting postscript to the entire saga. President Michael D. Higgins, a keen football supporter, was in the Stade Pierre-Mauroy in Lille, France for Ireland's final group game in Euro 2016. He jumped to his feet when Robbie Brady headed in the winning goal against Italy with just five minutes remaining. There was pandemonium at home. Ireland were through to the knockout stages.

Higgins could not have known that there was a connection between Robbie Brady and the intense water charge protests that only recently had come to an end. Robbie Brady's mother, Mia, had been a water charge protester.[25] His uncle, Pauly Dillon, had been one of the people served with an injunction to keep twenty metres away from water meter installers. And Robbie Brady's young cousin Josh had also been involved in the protests in Ayrfield in north Dublin. He had been diagnosed with Duchenne Muscular Dystrophy, a muscle-wasting condition, when he was four and began using a wheelchair full-time by the age of seven. Derek Byrne of Dublin Says No said he used to be on the front lines against Irish Water in his wheelchair. 'His enjoyment was coming out on the front line with us. But when his wheelchair broke down he couldn't come out, and he used to love it,' he said.[26]

The water charge protesters raised €11,000 for a new wheelchair for Josh through a 'Dancing with the Stars' competition. The gardaí in Coolock sent a cheque for €500. As Josh's health deteriorated, his family were upset when he was brought home from hospital in the BUMBLEance, a special children's ambulance. 'What are you all crying for? I'm the one dying, not you,' he said.[27] He was always calm and easy-going. 'He never once complained or moaned, he always had a smile on his face,' said his uncle Pauly.[28] He was a big Dublin football supporter, so Dublin manager Jim Gavin and players Jack McCaffrey, Brian Fenton and John Small visited him at home, five days before their All-Ireland final against Tyrone in 2018.

Another passion for Josh was playing the EA Sports' FIFA football video game on his Xbox. He wanted to play the new FIFA 19 version but it was not going to be released for another month. After the visit of the Dublin GAA players, the Share a Dream Foundation arranged for Josh to be airlifted to the Irish headquarters of EA Sports in Galway to play an advanced version of FIFA 19.[29] He died two days later at the age of seventeen. That was the same day that Dublin won their fourth All-Ireland football title in a row.

The water charge protests had involved people from all walks of life, protesting against meters, marching on the streets, refusing to pay their bills and singing songs. What had started off as a shallow movement had become very deep.

60

#JOBSTOWNNOTGUILTY

The water charges issue remained in the public eye due to the 2017 trial of Paul Murphy TD and six others who took part in the Jobstown protest on 15 November 2014. Gardaí had conducted dawn raids as part of their investigation and arrested twenty people. There were complaints from Murphy and others about being taken out of their homes at 6 a.m. by a large force of gardaí. Comparisons were made with bankers who had been arrested by appointment at their local garda station. But gardaí privately briefed reporters that they did not want to give the water charge protesters a chance to organise noisy demonstrations outside garda stations.

The youngest person charged was Jason (Jay) Lester, who had been fourteen at the time of the protest. He spent two-and-a-half months in Tallaght Hospital while he was waiting for trial in the Children's Court. 'They put it down to stress. I got out of hospital two days before the trial began. I still got a very good Leaving Cert so I was all right there. But it was something that was over me when I was studying,' he said.[1]

Lester was convicted of the false imprisonment of Joan Burton at Jobstown. His case was later overturned on appeal. 'I was going through a very hard time back then. It was very frightening. But my mam and my dad were there throughout the whole thing, they were very supportive,' Lester said.

Lester is an eloquent speaker who performed strongly on the RTÉ *Claire Byrne Live* show after his conviction was quashed. He turned down offers from Sinn Féin and Fianna Fáil to join their parties. 'Party politics is an infection to me. I don't want to be near it,' he said.

One of the other Jobstown accused was Philip Preston, who worked in a pharmaceutical plant in Swords. He got the award in 2015 for Tallaght Person of the Year while he was awaiting trial. It was for his work as the youth development officer with Tallaght Rugby Club, where he started off coaching rugby to ten children in 2012 before ending up with 100 every week. 'Tallaght is one of the greatest places in Ireland … In the past, the community spirit kinda dropped a little bit during the Celtic Tiger, but now it's back and on the rise,' he said in his award acceptance speech.[2] He died suddenly in 2016 of natural causes, leaving behind a partner and a young child. Socialist Party Councillor Mick Murphy, who was facing charges himself, said that Preston had been helping to calm down people during the Jobstown protest. 'He was a big character. He played a very important role on the day,' he said.[3]

A little after he was charged with the false imprisonment of Joan Burton and Karen O'Connell, Mick Murphy lost his job as an engineer in a pharmaceutical plant in west Dublin, where he had worked for six years and had won the 'Safety Person of the Year' award.[4] While he was awaiting trial, he continued to carry out research to boost his defence for the Jobstown trial. He had access to the garda helicopter footage of the protest, which had been supplied to his defence team. He wanted to get footage of Paul Murphy and himself discussing ending the protest with the crowd in Jobstown, as it could provide vital evidence for their lawyers to argue they were not guilty of the charge of false imprisonment of Burton and O'Connell.

The garda helicopter did indeed capture the images of the discussion on ending the protest, which had taken place at 2.30 p.m. on the day. But given that it was flying high overhead, it did not pick up what was being said. Mick Murphy figured that someone in the vicinity must have been filming it with a smartphone.

'I kept looking [at the footage] until I eventually spotted a fellow with his phone in his hand,' he said. Murphy and others went on the hunt for this man, who was wearing blue jeans and a black jacket on the day. Over the next six weeks, they found three other men who were wearing the same type of black jacket on the day. But none of them was the man with the mobile phone.

Murphy went back to the garda helicopter footage and started to look at it slide by slide. He then recognised who the man was. 'He turns his head to the side. He has a nose that you can't miss, even from 1,500 feet. The minute I've seen it, I said, "That's him,"' he said. The man with the distinctive nose had actually put up the footage of the protest online. But it was on his private Facebook account, so only his friends could see it.

Mick Murphy sent the footage to his legal team. They revealed it for the first time during the Jobstown trial. The smartphone had been a key weapon for water charge protesters. Now it was going to play a crucial role in the courtroom.

Three gardaí had stated in evidence to the court that Paul Murphy had asked the crowd to vote on whether they should let Burton go or hold her there for the night. But the Facebook video sourced by Mick Murphy showed that Paul Murphy never said anything about holding Burton there 'for the night'. Judge Melanie Greally told the jury that video footage was the most reliable account of what happened during the protest because it was not subject to the 'frailties of human memory'.[5]

'In a number of instances, there was garda testimony describing events which are not borne out by the footage and testimony which contradicts what can be seen in the video. Those types of discrepancies may influence how you view the evidence of the particular Gardaí Síochána,' she said.

All the gardaí involved in the case strongly denied giving untruthful evidence.

The legal teams for the Jobstown accused cited many different grounds as to why their clients should be cleared of the charges of false imprisonment of Burton and O'Connell. The Twitter hashtag used by the Jobstown accused was #Jobstownnotguilty.

That was the verdict delivered by the jury after three hours of deliberations.[6]

In the Dáil, Paul Murphy later called for a public inquiry into how the garda evidence conflicted with video footage in the Jobstown trial. But he got a withering put-down from Taoiseach Leo Varadkar. 'It may well be the case that you were not involved in kidnapping, but it was thuggery and your behaviour was wrong. The protest was ugly. It was violent. It was nasty,' he said.[7]

Although years have passed since the Jobstown incident, Paul Murphy and Joan Burton have never spoken to each other about it, or about anything else, since. Murphy said he would not be apologising to Burton about the protest he had taken part in. 'For me, the main apology needed is for Jobstown, from Joan Burton for the cuts that have been implemented,' he said.[8] However, he acknowledged that Burton should not have been hit with a water balloon. 'Yes, things happened that shouldn't have happened on the protest, in particular the water balloon and the stuff coming from outside of the protest,' he said.

There was anger among some locals in Jobstown that the area became a byword for disorder after the protest. Murphy said there were different views about it because no area was homogeneous in political outlook. 'By and large, you would find quite a lot of pride in the area. It became a byword for the struggle against the water charges, which was about working-class communities like Jobstown experiencing their power,' he said.

Burton decided to stop using social media around this time. She had received death threats and acid attack threats on it. 'The thing I found most personally difficult about it, there was a nightmare of trolling on social media, which was horrific. There were threats. I remember being upset,' she said. She did not report the threats to the gardaí, but she did complain to Facebook and Twitter: 'It was all reported to the social media companies, but they never bothered their barney about it,' she said.[9]

One of the conspiracy theories on social media was that Burton had somehow ensured that the Director of Public Prosecutions (DPP) had got the Jobstown protesters charged with the serious offence of false imprisonment. Needless to say, there was never any evidence presented to back this up and Burton rejected it out of hand. 'Nobody in government ever discussed it with me. I never received any technical support or advice from anyone in the government or the DPP's office,' she said.

Burton found people continued to bring up the Jobstown protest every time they met her. She had also not been impressed with Paul Murphy's decision not to give evidence during the Jobstown trial, even though the trial judge pointed out that this was his right. 'He was there when myself and Karen were subjected to ferocious and frightening abuse and treatment. He decided then to join the Carmelites and take a vow of silence when it came to the court case,' she said.

Burton insisted that she would never have been subjected to such a protest by Joe Higgins, who had been in the same constituency as her for years. However, Higgins himself strongly defended the Jobstown protesters. 'Like my colleague Ruth Coppinger says, "What does she expect when she went into Jobstown, a red carpet?" What about the concept that if you are the Labour Party, you should represent the working class, which is what Connolly and Larkin set it up for?'[10] Time had not healed the deep discord between Higgins and the party which had expelled him three decades previously.

61

STILL WATER

Water charges are due to come back in 2020. There will be bills for any 'excess users' – households who use more than 170 per cent of the average demand. The official estimate is that only seven per cent of households will have to pay excess usage charges. Most of them are using large quantities of water because they have leaks in their pipes. Once those leaks are fixed, they should be in no danger of having to pay any water charges. The amount of revenue collected will be tiny – around €40 million over five years. For this reason, (since-departed) Ervia Chief Executive Mike Quinn said he was not afraid that they would lead to another public backlash against Irish Water. 'This is not a revenue collection exercise. It's a conservation exercise. It's such a small proportion of our revenue,' he said.[1]

Water protester Derek Byrne of the now-disbanded Dublin Says No group expects a future government to try to bring in water charges again. 'We will rise again. I am prepared to go back to prison again. There are many more with me who will do it again. We didn't do this for popularity, we didn't do it for fame. We did it because we had to,' he said.[2]

John Gormley, former environment minister, said the state was playing the long game by starting with an 'excess charge'. 'That probably will change over a period of time so the amount you pay will grow. So it will be a gradual process, and then they'll make another effort to introduce charges at some stage,' he said.[3] This is what's known as the 'boil the frog' strategy in politics. The temperature is slowly turned up so that the frog does not notice – and before he knows it, he is cooked. Taoiseach Leo Varadkar said excess charges could lead to the return of a broader water charges regime. 'Let's see how that goes. You could see over time that threshold being reduced and maybe that's the way we should have done water charges in the first place,' he said.[4]

The other potential way for water charges to return, of course, is due to court action by the European Commission. The Water Framework Directive requires countries in the EU to have water charges to pay for the service.

The 'Irish exemption' from water charges secured by the then environment minister, Noel Dempsey, in 2000 is now gone. The government could be forced to re-introduce water charges to avoid heavy fines. The European Commission has warned that the fines for being found in breach of the Water Framework Directive could amount to 'tens of millions'.[5]

Varadkar said the Water Framework Directive could influence the return of water charges. 'We may well find ourselves in breach of European law, and we'll have to perhaps deal with that,' he said.[6]

When Alan Kelly was in the Custom House, he spoke to the EU's Environment Commissioner Karmenu Vella. The clear message he got was that Ireland was obliged to have water charges to comply with the Water Framework Directive. 'I believe the decision to suspend water charges and the way it's now constructed to pay for water, I believe it's outside the law. We are outside the Water Framework Directive. We will have to come into line at some stage,' he said.[7]

The European Commission declined to answer questions about whether Ireland's water charges plan was in breach of the Water Framework Directive. But it is known to be very nervous about taking Ireland to court when it has a weak minority government and when Brexit is endangering the economy. 'They are aware that this government has no capacity to do anything about the European Commission case against Ireland,' said one official who has been in contact with the Commission. 'But water charges will come back.'

Irish Water has been promised €8 billion in funding up to 2028 to pay for new water and wastewater treatment plants, leak repairs and mega-projects like the Shannon pipeline. But John Mullins, former Bord Gáis chief executive, said it was now completely dependent again on the government for its money. 'It's a question of what the exchequer is like. If we get a squeeze on Brexit, and our economy starts to throttle back a bit, will there be scope to put the monies into water infrastructure?'[8]

Varadkar acknowledged that Irish Water's funding would have to be reduced if there was an economic crisis. 'If something went wrong with the national finances, you'll be cutting back capital expenditure all over the place. It wouldn't just be water. It would be across the board,' he said.[9]

His belief remains that water charges are the best way to ensure that Irish Water has the money it needs to fix the ageing network, regardless of whether there is a recession or not. He said that with water charges gone for the foreseeable future, investment in water infrastructure is going to happen more slowly than it would have otherwise. 'We do have an issue with water leakages. We do have an issue with contaminated water supplies around the country, raw sewage still going into rivers and seas. And we do have an issue now in getting Irish Water to connect to new housing [in terms of providing water pipes to new houses]. All those things would be happening more quickly and efficiently had Irish Water happened as we intended,' he said.

Varadkar said he did not expect any party to promise to re-introduce water charges during the next general election campaign. 'I think it is off the political agenda for the foreseeable future. You're probably talking decades, rather than years,' he said.

Irish Water is requiring meter boxes to be put in outside all new houses before it will provide a connection from the house to the water supply. However, there are still forty per cent of homes in the country without water meters. There are no plans to send meter installers back into the working-class estates where they were so strongly opposed in 2014, 2015 and 2016. Varadkar sees this as a long-term project too. 'Again, we're talking decades rather than years,' he said.

The installation of 892,000 meters was a daring move. But it was planned in a huge rush and rolled out at lightning speed. The government was gambling on the protesters being disorganised and weak. But the resistance was greater than expected. Former Irish Water executive Noel O'Keeffe said that meters were only a good idea if there were water charges. 'We have the worst of both worlds. We spent nearly €500 million on meters and we didn't use them for the purpose. Meters aren't meant to measure water, they're meant as a charging mechanism,' he said.[10]

That just leaves the installed meters, where the black and red dials are slowly turning day after day to record how much water is being used in each home. They have brought in no money, which is what they were installed for. For now, and likely for some time to come, they will be the ultimate symbol of public money going down the drain.

TIMELINE

1977: Domestic rates, which fund the water service operated by the councils, are abolished by the Fianna Fáil government.

1983: Fine Gael–Labour government in power. As environment minister, Labour leader Dick Spring gives councils the power to re-introduce water charges. Protests in Dublin halt water charges there.

1993: Under a Fianna Fáil–Labour government, three new councils in Dublin re-introduce water charges. Expelled Labour Party member Joe Higgins leads the protests against them.

1996: Joe Higgins almost wins a seat in a Dublin West by-election due to his opposition to water charges. The Fine Gael–Labour government abolishes water charges in response.

2009: Green Party leader John Gormley gets the introduction of water charges and water meters into the revised programme for government.

2010: Fianna Fáil and the Green Party agree to introduce water charges at cabinet and subsequently in the bailout deal. They are both decimated in the subsequent general election.

March 2011: The new Fine Gael–Labour government promises to introduce water charges with a 'generous free allowance'.

December 2011: Environment Minister Phil Hogan gets cabinet approval to meter one million homes and to set up a new company called Irish Water to take over the water service from the councils.

April 2012: The state gas company, Bord Gáis Éireann, wins the contract to set up Irish Water.

January 2013: John Tierney is appointed as managing director of Irish Water.

March 2013: Bill is passed to set up Irish Water as a subsidiary of Bord Gáis on a temporary basis.

May 2013: Michael McNicholas is appointed as chief executive of Bord Gáis, the parent company of Irish Water.

July 2013: The government approves the signing of service level agreements which will see water workers in thirty-four councils continuing to work for Irish Water for at least twelve years.

August 2013: The water metering programme begins.

December 2013: The government brings through the legislation to introduce water charges and to set up Irish Water on a permanent basis.

January 2014: Irish Water Managing Director John Tierney appears on the *Today with Seán O'Rourke* show.

January 2014: Bord Gáis's retail business is privatised. The remaining parts of the company – which now is left with the gas network and Irish Water – is renamed 'Ervia'.

April 2014: The first water meter installation is halted in an estate in Cork city. A week later the first water meter installation in Dublin is halted.

May 2014: Environment Minister Phil Hogan announces the water charges.

23 May 2014: Labour suffers heavy losses in the local and European elections.

26 May 2014: Eamon Gilmore resigns as Labour leader. Joan Burton takes over shortly afterwards.

4 July 2014: Phil Hogan is nominated by the government to be Ireland's next European commissioner. Labour's Alan Kelly replaces him as environment minister.

30 July 2014: The water regulator, the Commission for Energy Regulation, announces more details about the water charges.

1 October 2014: Water charges begin.

10 October 2014: Anti-Austerity Alliance TD Paul Murphy wins the Dublin South West by-election. On the same day, up to 100,000 people take part in a Right2Water protest march against water charges in Dublin's city centre.

30 October 2014: Karen Doyle of Cobh Says No to Austerity is arrested.

1 November 2014: Up to 130,000 people take part in local Right2Water protests in towns, villages and cities.

5 November 2014: Protesters gather outside Coolock garda station to protest against water charges.

15 November 2014: Tánaiste Joan Burton and her adviser Karen O'Connell are surrounded in a garda car and then a garda jeep for three hours at a water charge protest in Jobstown in Dublin.

19 November 2014: Environment Minister Alan Kelly announces details of the revised water charges regime and the water conservation grant. Charging is pushed back to the start of 2015.

10 December 2014: At least 30,000 people take part in a Right2Water protest outside the Dáil.

April 2015: Fianna Fáil leader Micheál Martin announces that he wants to abolish water charges and abolish Irish Water.

June 2015: Irish Water fails the Eurostat test.

February 2016: The pro-water charges parties are badly hit in the general election. Labour loses thirty of its thirty-seven seats. Fine Gael loses twenty-six of its seventy-six seats. On the anti-water charges side, Fianna Fáil gains twenty-three seats to return with forty-four TDs and

Sinn Féin gains nine seats to return with twenty-three TDs. The Anti-Austerity Alliance and People Before Profit go from four seats to six seats.

April 2016: Fianna Fáil demands the abolition of Irish Water and water charges in government formation talks with Fine Gael.

May 2016: The new Fine Gael minority government announces that water charges are being suspended.

June 2017: Six men are found not guilty of falsely imprisoning Joan Burton and Karen O'Connell at a water charge protest in Jobstown; charges against a seventh man are dropped during the trial.

2017: A cross-party Oireachtas committee recommends introducing 'excessive charges' for those who use more than 1.7 times the average household amount of water. 1.1 million people are refunded water charge payments of €173 million.

2018: The government announces it is going to split Irish Water from Ervia in 2023.

ENDNOTES

1 The Jobstown Revolt

1   Post on public Facebook page of Tallaght Says No, 15 November 2014: www. facebook.com/TallaghtSaysNotoWaterMetering.

2   Public Facebook page of a water charge protester.

3   Interview with Paul Murphy, 17 October 2018, Dublin.

4   *The Irish Times,* 11 January 2017.

5   www.youtube.com/watch?v=tzKz69VkYJE&list=PLgcCe0L6V-TM3QRTyBzn UemxGpq2Cty-z&index=98&t=0s.

6   *Ibid.*

7   *Ibid.*

8   Phone interview with Jay Lester, 10 October 2018.

9   www.youtube.com/watch?v=tzKz69VkYJE&list=PLgcCe0L6V-TM3QRTyBzn UemxGpq2Cty-z&index=98&t=0s.

10 *Ibid.*

11 Later gardaí would identify a middle-aged man as the suspected water balloon thrower. He was picked out in photographs during the investigation – one showing him as 'water balloon thrower' and another as 'water balloon thrower without hat'. No one was ever convicted of the offence.

12 www.youtube.com/watch?v=tzKz69VkYJE&list=PLgcCe0L6V-TM3QRTyBzn UemxGpq2Cty-z&index=98&t=0s.

2 Getting out of the Church

1   Jobstown trial transcripts, evidence of Garda Gavin Cooke, 15 May 2017. The full transcripts of the trial of the Jobstown protesters are available at https://sites. google.com/view/jobstownnotguilty/trial.

2   www.youtube.com/watch?v=65MasJ8DGgQ&list=PLgcCe0L6V-TM3QRTy BznUemxGpq2Cty-z&index=94.

3   Interview with Joan Burton, 29 August 2018, Dublin.

4   Interview with Paul Murphy, 17 October 2018, Dublin.

5   Trial transcripts, closing statement for Frank Donaghy, 22 June 2017.

6   Trial transcripts, closing address to jury from barrister Roisin Lacey on behalf of Scott Masterson, 22 June 2017.

7   Trial transcripts, evidence of Karen O'Connell, 5 May 2017.
8   Trial transcripts, ruling by Judge Melanie Greally, 26 June 2017.
9   Trial transcripts, evidence of Derek Maguire, 15 May 2017.
10 Phone interview with Jay Lester, 10 October 2018.
11 Trial transcripts, charge to the jury by Judge Melanie Greally, 26 June 2017.
12 Interview with Paul Murphy, 17 October 2018, Dublin.
13 https://youtu.be/DN6c2AZ7ES8. This video features clips of interactions between protesters and gardaí.
14 Trial transcripts, evidence of Daniel Flavin, 18 May 2017.

3 Getting out of the Car

1   Interview with Joan Burton, 29 August 2018, Dublin.
2   Trial transcripts, evidence of Michael Phelan, 23 May 2017.
3   Trial transcripts, evidence of Joan Burton, 27 April 2017.
4   Trial transcripts, evidence of Garda Jonathan Ryan, 29 May 2017.
5   *Ibid.*
6   Trial transcripts, evidence of Joan Burton, 27 April 2017.
7   Interview with Joan Burton, 29 August 2018, Dublin.
8   Interview with Brendan Howlin, 12 July 2018, Dublin.
9   Phone interview with Mick Murphy, 19 December 2018.
10 Private video footage supplied to author contained the audio for the protesters' discussion about bringing the Jobstown protest to an end.
11 *Belfast Newsletter*, 21 January 2016.
12 Phone interview with Crispin Rodwell, 31 January 2019.

4 Getting out of the Jeep

1   Trial transcripts, evidence of Karen O'Connell, 5 May 2017.
2   Footage from inside the garda jeep obtained by author.
3   *Ibid.*
4   O'Gorman, Aidan *et al.*, 'A Report on the Policing of Protests in Ireland relative to Human Rights Standards and Good Practices Internationally' (University of Limerick, 2018), p. 55.
5   Trial transcripts, evidence of Gary Farrell, 24 May 2017.
6   Trial transcripts, evidence of John Kelly, 19 May 2017.
7   O'Gorman *et al.* (2018), p. 55.
8   Trial transcripts, evidence of Brian Boland, 17 May 2017.
9   Trial transcripts, evidence of John Kelly, 19 May 2017.

10   Interview with Paul Murphy, 17 October 2018, Dublin.

11   Trial transcripts, evidence of Joan Burton, 27 April 2017.

12   Trial transcripts, closing speech by defence council Padraig Dwyer, 22 June 2017.

13   Garda helicopter footage from the Jobstown incident: https://twitter.com/
     Earl1995Lfc/status/859868564148367365.

14   Trial transcripts, evidence of Karen O'Connell, 5 May 2017.

15   Trial transcripts, evidence of Brian Boland, 18 May 2017.

16   Interview with Paul Murphy, 17 October 2018, Dublin.

17   Garda report to minister for justice on the Jobstown investigation, June 2017.

18   Trial transcripts, evidence of Karen O'Connell, 4 May 2017.

19   *The Irish Times*, 18 January 2018.

20   Garda report to minister for justice on the Jobstown investigation, June 2017.

5 The Source of Irish Water

1   *Irish Independent*, 2 March 2011.

2   UCD Business Alumni profile of Andrew McDowell, January 2017: www.ucd.ie/
    businessalumni/news/inprofile/andrewmcdowellbcomm91msc92mba03/.

3   That ended when Bruton lost his position as policy director after his ill-fated
    heave against Kenny in 2010.

4   *Irish Independent*, 28 February 2011.

5   Fine Gael's NewERA policy in 2009 advocated the creation of Irish Water. Avail-
    able at www.paschaldonohoe.ie/wp-content/uploads/2010/01/NewERA1.pdf.

6   Interview with Simon Coveney, 19 October 2018, Co. Monaghan.

6 A Green Light for Water Charges

1   *Village*, March 2010: https://villagemagazine.ie/index.php/2010/03/inside-the-
    mind-of-john-gormley/.

2   Interview with John Gormley, 21 June 2018, Dublin. All quotes from Gormley in
    this chapter are from this interview.

3   Brian Lenihan speech, 9 December 2009: www.budget.gov.ie/budgets/2010/
    financialstatement.aspx.

4   McMorrow, Conor, 'The Cowen government's water files', RTÉ Blog, 19 Octo-
    ber 2015: www.rte.ie/news/2015/1018/735225-cowen-governments-water-files.

5   Memorandum of understanding between the European Commission and Ireland,
    16 December 2010. Available at http://ec.europa.eu/economy_finance/articles/
    eu_economic_situation/pdf/2010-12-07-mefp_en.pdf.

7 Big Phil

1   Phone interview with Chris Maher, 14 July 2018.

2   *Kilkenny People*, 23 August 1985.

3   Seanad Éireann is the upper house of the Oireachtas, and has sixty members.

4   RTÉ News, 10 September 2014: www.rte.ie/news/special-reports/2014/0910/642699-phil-hogan/.

5   RTÉ Archives, www.rte.ie/archives/exhibitions/1333-memorable-budgets/1343-budget-1995/338362-phil-hogan-comments-on-his-resignation.

6   Minutes of Department of the Environment ministers' management advisory committee meeting, 14 April 2011. Obtained from the Department of the Environment under the Freedom of Information Act.

7   Speech by Phil Hogan at the Institute of International and European Affairs, 14 November 2011: https://youtu.be/SObzkPbtDsA.

8 Water in the West

1   Downing, J., *Enda Kenny, The Unlikely Taoiseach* (Paperweight Publications, Dublin, 2012), p. 20.

2   Phone interview with Martin McLaughlin, 15 October 2018. All quotes from McLaughlin in this chapter are from this interview.

3   That problem was eventually dealt with by the construction of a new wastewater treatment plant in 1983, which turned the Castlebar river from a pollution blackspot into one that had salmon and trout again.

9 Going against the Tide

1   Interview with Brian Stanley, 23 October 2018, Dublin.

2   *Munster Express*, 6 October 1989.

3   https://irishelectionliterature.files.wordpress.com/2010/05/gilmore87fba.jpg.

4   https://irishelectionliterature.com/2010/09/08/one-man-and-his-dog-eamon-gilmore-democratic-left-1997-ge-dun-laoghaire/#more-10388.

5   https://irishelectionliterature.com/2009/11/05/we-buy-our-homes-and-developers-buy-the-big-parties-eamon-gilmore-workers-party-1989-dun-laoghaire/.

6   *Sunday Tribune*, 12 January 2003.

7   *Irish Independent*, 19 February 2011.

8   Which, unfortunately for Labour, turned out to be very accurate.

9   Interview with Eamon Gilmore, 21 August 2018, Dublin.

10 Programme for government, 2011: https://merrionstreet.ie/wp-content/uploads/2010/05/Programme_for_Government_2011.pdf.

11 Department of the Environment management advisory committee meeting, 11 March 2011. Obtained from the Department of the Environment under the Freedom of Information Act.

12 Interview with Brendan Howlin, 12 July 2018, Dublin.

10 The Man for the Job

1 Delany, Brendan, 'McLoughlin, the Genesis of the Shannon Scheme and the ESB' in Bielenberg, Andy (ed.), *The Shannon Scheme and the Electrification of the Irish Free State* (Dublin, The Lilliput Press, 2002), p. 12.

2 *The Sunday Times*, 23 December 2012.

3 John Mullins at Oireachtas transport committee, 21 February 2018: www. oireachtas.ie/en/debates/debate/joint_committee_on_transport_tourism_ and_sport/2018-02-21/3/?highlight%5B0%5D=john&highlight%5B1%5D= mullins.

4 This was the same asset management system that Irish Water would later use.

5 Interview with John Mullins, 16 August 2018, Dublin.

6 When Irish Water tried to map the water and wastewater system, it was staggered at the errors it encountered.

7 Interview with John Mullins, 16 August 2018, Dublin.

8 Oireachtas committee on communications and energy, 29 September 2010: www. oireachtas.ie/en/debates/debate/joint_committee_on_communications_energy_ and_natural_resources/2010-09-29/3/.

9 *Ibid.*

10 *The Irish Times*, 6 October 2014.

11 Meters, Meters, Everywhere

1 Cabinet memo, 12 December 2011. Obtained from the Department of the Taoiseach under the Freedom of Information Act.

2 Department of the Environment, cost–benefit analysis on water metering, September 2011. Obtained from the Department of the Environment under the Freedom of Information Act.

3 Statement to author by the Department of the Environment (now known as the Department of Housing, Planning and Local Government), 16 April 2019.

12 Labour's Bogeyman

1 Dáil debate, 9 March 2011. All Dáil debates and Leaders' Questions sourced at www.oireachtas.ie/en/debates.

2   *Irish Independent*, 22 July 2012.

3   Interview with Joe Higgins, 3 September 2018, Dublin. Unless otherwise noted, all quotes from Higgins in this chapter are from this interview.

4   *The Sunday Business Post*, 10 January 2015.

5   Interview with Mick Barry, 15 November 2018, Dublin.

6   Joe Higgins, Ruth Coppinger, Joan Collins, Clare Daly and Mick Barry all went on to be elected as TDs.

7   TheJournal.ie, 9 November 2014.

8   http://socialistparty.ie/2001/02/water-charges-struggle-lessons-today.

9   *The Irish Times*, 6 April 1996.

10 Dáil debate, 20 November 2014.

11 Interview with Micheál Martin, 10 January 2019, Dublin.

12 The policy was unveiled in the 'Better Local Government' document launched on 19 December 1996: www.kildare.ie/localdev/LocalGovtReform/BETTER%20LOCAL%20GOVERNMENT.html.

13 Interview with Brendan Howlin, 12 July 2018, Dublin.

14 *The Sunday Business Post*, 10 January 2015.

15 Leaders' Questions in the Dáil, 29 January 2003.

13 Awash with Warnings

1   Interview with John Mullins, 16 August 2018, Dublin. All quotes from Mullins in this chapter are from this interview.

2   The Journal.ie, 15 January 2015.

3   Irish Water: Water Metering Strategy, 7 June 2012. Obtained from the Department of the Environment under the Freedom of Information Act.

4   Email regarding Irish Water metering strategy, 8 June 2012. Obtained from the Department of the Environment under the Freedom of Information Act.

5   Maria Graham speaking during public discussion on 'How (not) to do public policy: water charges and local property tax', 13 September 2018, Galway. See 'Response to Jim O'Leary': http://whitakerinstitute.ie/how-not-to-do-public-policy-highlights-from-the-conference.

6   Dublin City Council submission to consultation process on water sector reform (2012): https://www.housing.gov.ie/sites/default/files/migrated-files/en/Environment/Water/WaterSectorReform/Submissions/LocalandRegional Authorities/FileDownLoad%2C31735%2Cen.pdf.

7   Corcoran, Michael, *Our Good Health – A History of Dublin's Water and Drainage* (Dublin, Four Courts Press, 2005), pp. 47–8. The Vartry scheme was the brain-

child of John Gray, from Claremorris in County Mayo, who saw how the dirty water supply in Dublin was spreading killer diseases like cholera and typhoid in the 1860s. As chairman of the city's waterworks committee, Gray came up with a radical engineering scheme to take water from the River Vartry in Wicklow and pump it to Dublin. Workers had to dig a four-mile tunnel through the Wicklow mountains using just picks, shovels and dynamite. They built a reservoir near Roundwood, which covered 409 acres and could store 2.4 billion gallons of water – enough for 200 days' supply for the city in the 1860s. Gray bought up land needed for the reservoir in advance with his own money so that speculators could not drive up the price. When the scheme got the go-ahead, he sold the land back at no profit to himself. It took a mere three years to build and it transformed the health and life expectancy of people living in Dublin.

8   Engineers Ireland and Irish Academy of Engineering joint submission to consultation process on water sector reform: www.housing.gov.ie/sites/default/files/migrated-files/en/Environment/Water/WaterSectorReform/Submissions/Organisations/FileDownLoad%2C31784%2Cen.pdf.

9   Department of the Environment water sector reform implementation strategy, 12 October 2012: 'Water Sector Reform Implementation Strategy' available at https://www.housing.gov.ie/water/water-services/policy/public-consultation-water-sector-reform.

14 The Secret Meter Surveys

1   Domestic water metering project pre-installation survey technical guidance document (July 2012). Obtained from the Department of the Environment under the Freedom of Information Act.

2   The guidance document explained it like this: 'It is important therefore that the location of the meter box is as close to the property curtilage line as possible. The reason for this being that should a meter record a leak then the location of this leak will be inside in the private property of the customer, over which the customer will have control.'

3   Draft Irish Water implementation strategy (June 2012) and final Irish Water implementation strategy (September 2012). Obtained from the Department of the Environment under the Freedom of Information Act.

15 The Crushing of a Protest Movement

1   Phone interview with Karen Doyle, 19 September 2018.

2   www.youtube.com/watch?v=k1ORsASwVNs.

3   The term had been coined in Ireland during the land wars in 1879. Captain Charles Boycott tried to evict tenants who had fallen behind on their rent in The Neale in Mayo. He was ostracised by the community, with his servants and farm workforce quitting and shops refusing to serve him. He had to leave the country the following year.

4   Interview with Mick Barry, 15 November 2018, Dublin. All quotes from Barry in this chapter are from this interview.

5   Group interview with John Lonergan and members of the Ballyphehane/South Parish Says No group, 1 November 2018, Cork. All quotes from John Lonergan, Donal O'Sullivan and Keith O'Brien in this chapter come from this source.

6   *The Irish Times*, 2 April 2012.

7   Josephine Feehily during public discussion on 'How (not) to do public policy: water charges and local property tax', 13 September 2018, Galway. See 'Response to Jim O'Leary': http://whitakerinstitute.ie/how-not-to-do-public-policy-high-lights-from-the-conference.

16 The Troika Time Extension

1   Pól Ó Conghaile travel blog, 23 January 2012: https://poloconghaile.com/time-to-bag-a-five-star-bargain.

2   John Moran evidence to the Oireachtas banking inquiry, 18 June 2015: https://inquiries.oireachtas.ie/banking/hearings/john-moran-former-secretary-general-department-of-finance.

3   *Ibid.*

4   Cabinet memo, 5 October 2012. Obtained from the Department of Communications under the Freedom of Information Act.

17 Irish Water Gets Its First Boss

1   Interview with John Mullins, 16 August 2018, Dublin. All quotes from Mullins in this chapter are from this interview.

2   Department of Communications briefing note for Irish Water establishment, 12 April 2012. Obtained from the Department of Communications under the Freedom of Information Act.

3   Domestic water metering programme briefing note for Minister Pat Rabbitte, 2 July 2012. Obtained from the Department of Communications under the Freedom of Information Act.

4   *Ibid.*

5   Oireachtas environment committee, 11 October 2011: https://www.oireachtas.

ie/en/debates/debate/joint_committee_on_the_environment_transport_culture_
and_the_gaeltacht/2011-10-11/3/.

6   Bord Gáis statement, 29 January 2013.

18 The Smartphone-wielding Protesters

1   21 July 2014: https://youtu.be/P3dFU6iKrN8.
2   Interview with Derek Byrne, 5 October 2018, Dublin.
3   https://youtu.be/d5KREHv3eWc
4   https://youtu.be/xsVIph2Z4Vs.
5   Interview with Frances Fitzgerald, 29 November 2018, Dublin.

19 The Irish Exemption from Water Charges

1   Interview with Noel Dempsey, 31 May 2018, Dublin. Unless otherwise noted, all
     quotes from Dempsey in this chapter are from this interview.
2   Interview with Micheál Martin, 10 January 2019, Dublin.
3   Water Framework Directive: https://eur-lex.europa.eu/legal-content/EN/TX-
     T/?uri=CELEX:32000L0060.
4   Noel Dempsey on RTÉ Radio's *Marian Finucane Show*, 24 October 2015.

20 The Meter Contract Controversy

1   Construction Industry Federation submission for budget 2019: https://cif.ie/
     wp-content/uploads/2018/08/CIF-Pre-Budget-Submission-Report-2019-LR.
     pdf.
2   *Irish Examiner*, 5 April 2014.
3   NewERA confidential report on domestic metering project, 12 July 2013.
     Obtained from the Department of Communications under the Freedom of Infor-
     mation Act.
4   *Sunday Independent*, 25 April 2010.
5   KPMG metering report, 25 June 2013. Obtained from the Department of Com-
     munications under the Freedom of Information Act.
6   Submission to Communications Minister Pat Rabbitte on consent for BGE/Irish
     Water to enter into capital commitments for Irish Water domestic metering pro-
     gramme, 4 July 2013. Obtained from the Department of Communications under
     the Freedom of Information Act.
7   Email from civil servant Andrew Conlon, 19 July 2013. Obtained from the
     Department of Communications under the Freedom of Information Act.
8   Submission to Communications Minister Pat Rabbitte on consent for BGE/Irish

Water to enter into capital commitments for Irish Water domestic metering pro-gramme, 4 July 2013. Obtained from the Department of Communications under the Freedom of Information Act.

9 Irish Water board minutes, 24 July 2013. Obtained from Irish Water under the Freedom of Information Act.

21 Meter Rush

1 *The Irish Times*, 31 July 2013.
2 Minutes of Department of the Environment management advisory committee meeting, 22 December 2011. Obtained from the Department of the Environment under the Freedom of Information Act.
3 Cabinet memo, 5 October 2012. Obtained from the Department of Communications under the Freedom of Information Act.
4 Bord Gáis outlined this in an Irish domestic water metering project document it sent to the Department of the Environment in July 2012. It said: 'Experience of the non-domestic meters programme gives rise to some concerns about filed crew competencies. We believe we need strong site supervision to address those concerns.' Obtained from the Department of the Environment under the Freedom of Information Act.
5 *Irish Independent*, 8 August 2013.
6 Phone interview with Mick Murphy, 19 December 2018.
7 Irish Water board meeting minutes, 16 January 2014. Obtained from Irish Water under the Freedom of Information Act.
8 Interview with Micheál Martin, 10 January 2019, Dublin.

22 A Neglected Water Service

1 Interview with Sean Laffey, 4 July 2018, Dublin.
2 Interview with Noel O'Keeffe, 1 November 2018, Cork.
3 The Ireland 2040 plan contains an initial €31 million in funding for fixing the faults in developer-provided water infrastructure.
4 Evidence of Jerry Grant at joint committee on future funding of domestic water services, 14 February 2017.
5 Interview with Sean Laffey, 4 July 2018, Dublin.
6 Irish Water was prosecuted by the EPA for the discharge of raw sewage at Kilmore Quay in 2017 and fined €5,000 in court. A new sewage treatment plant for Kilmore Quay is not due for completion until 2021.
7 Interview with Gerard O'Leary, 28 September 2018, Dublin.

8   *The Sunday Business Post*, 28 September 2014.

9   In 2018 the European Commission took an infringement case against Ireland for failing to deal with the THM problem and for failing to notify households of the threat from THMs in their public water supply.

10 Irish Water awarded an €80 million contract to J. Murphy & Sons to cover and upgrade the Stillorgan reservoir in November 2018.

23 The Twelve-Year Deal with the Unions

1   Interview with Eamon Donnelly, 15 August 2018, Dublin. All quotes from Donnelly in this chapter are from this interview.

2   Cabinet memo, 5 October 2012. Obtained from the Department of Communications under the Freedom of Information Act.

3   Interview with Noel O'Keeffe, 1 November 2018, Cork.

4   Cabinet memo, 5 October 2012. Obtained from the Department of Communications under the Freedom of Information Act.

5   Interview with Barry Cowen, 29 November 2018, Dublin.

6   Interview with John Mullins, 16 August 2018, Dublin.

24 The Dáil Walk Out

1   Draft memo for publication of second Water Services Bill, 26 November 2013. Obtained from the Department of Communications under the Freedom of Information Act.

2   Interview with Fergus O'Dowd, 7 November 2017, Dublin.

3   Dáil Leaders' Questions, 18 April 2012.

4   *The Sunday Business Post*, 17 August 2014.

5   Interview with John Mullins, 16 August 2018, Dublin.

6   *The Sunday Business Post*, 17 August 2014.

7   Parliamentary question from Barry Cowen to Environment Minister Phil Hogan, 19 November 2013: https://www.oireachtas.ie/en/debates/question/2013-11-19/457/.

8   Minutes of ministerial meeting in the Department of the Environment, 15 May 2013. Obtained from the Department of the Environment under the Freedom of Information Act.

9   Memorandum for the government on the 11th review mission for the EU/IMF programme of financial support for Ireland, 5 July 2013. Obtained from the Department of the Taoiseach under the Freedom of Information Act.

10 An 'Irish Water funding plan 2014' set by the NewERA semi-state watchdog

emphasised the urgency of the situation. 'On 1 January 2014 Irish Water will only have access to the remaining balance [€90m] of the National Pension Reserve Fund funding with which to fund its activities [which will be spent by week commencing 13 January 2014].' The government had to fast-track a planned payment of €240 million to Irish Water by 14 January 2014 so it did not run out of money.

11 Independent TD Denis Naughten was the only member of the opposition who stayed to question the government about the bill. 'I have the weight of the Opposition on my shoulders,' he said.

12 Interview with Brian Stanley, 23 October 2018, Dublin.

13 Interview with Micheál Martin, 10 January 2019, Dublin.

25 Turning Citizens into Consumers

1 Final Irish Water implementation strategy, September 2012. Obtained from the Department of the Environment under the Freedom of Information Act.

2 Submission from Siemens to the Department of the Environment during the public consultation process on water reforms, 24 February 2012: www.housing.gov.ie/sites/default/files/migrated-files/en/Environment/Water/WaterSectorReform/Submissions/Companies/FileDownLoad%2C31725%2Cen.pdf.

3 Minutes of meeting of senior officials group on economic infrastructure, 20 September 2012. Obtained from the Department of Communications under the Freedom of Information Act.

4 Cabinet memo, 5 October 2012. Obtained from the Department of Communications under the Freedom of Information Act.

5 Cabinet memo, 17 December 2012. Obtained from the Department of Communications under the Freedom of Information Act.

6 Bord Gáis presentation to Engineers Ireland, 7 March 2013: www.engineersireland.ie/EngineersIreland/media/SiteMedia/groups/regions/sout-east/South-East-Irish-Water.pdf?ext=.pdf.

7 Bord Gáis household information leaflet on Irish Water and water metering, February 2014: www.laois.ie/wp-content/uploads/Irish-Water-Publications_Public_Notices_Leaflet.pdf.

8 *Irish Examiner*, 13 September 2013.

9 *Irish Independent*, 11 October 2013.

10 Irish Water TV ad: www.mutiny.ie/home/our-work/irish-water-50sec-tv-%e2%80%a8%e2%80%a8recording-sound-mix.

11 Maria Graham speaking during public discussion on 'How (not) to do public policy: water charges and local property tax', 13 September 2018, Galway.

26 The Fateful Interview

1   Phone interview with Seán O'Rourke, 5 December 2018.

2   RTÉ Radio 1, *Today with Seán O'Rourke*, 9 January 2014.

3   Phone interview with Seán O'Rourke, 5 December 2018. All remaining quotes from Seán O'Rourke in this chapter are from this interview.

4   Interview with Barry Cowen, 29 November 2018, Dublin.

5   Interview with Micheál Martin, 10 January 2019, Dublin.

6   Evidence of John Tierney at public accounts committee, 15 January 2014: https://www.oireachtas.ie/en/debates/debate/committee_of_public_accounts/2014-01-15/3/.

7   John Tierney report to Irish Water board, February 2014. Obtained from Irish Water under the Freedom of Information Act.

27 Son of Garret versus Big Phil

1   Elizabeth Arnett presentation to Local Authority Management Association, 31 January 2014: http://lama.ie/31%2001%2014%20LAMA%20Presentation%20(3).pdf.

2   *Irish Independent*, 27 January 2014.

3   Interview with John FitzGerald, 14 June 2018, Dublin. All quotes from FitzGerald in this chapter are from this interview.

4   *Irish Independent*, 29 January 2014.

28 Labour Pains

1   Eamon Gilmore speech, 13 December 2013: www.dfa.ie/ie/nuacht-agus-na-meain/oraidi/speeches-archive/2013/dec/iieaaddressbythetanaisteonexitingthebailout/tanaiste-delivers-keynote-address-at-iiea---ireland-beyond-the-troika-programme-1.php.

2   Dáil debate on water reforms, 26 April 2012.

3   Interview with Eamon Gilmore, 21 August 2018, Dublin.

4   Email from Aoife McEvilly in the Department of Communications to colleagues, 11 April 2013.

5   Briefing note for cabinet sub-committee meeting on Irish Water, 15 April 2013. Obtained from the Department of Communications under the Freedom of Information Act.

6   Water sector reform programme presentation – from the Department of the Environment and NewERA, April 2013. Obtained from the Department of Communications under the Freedom of Information Act.

7   Gilmore, Eamon, *Inside the Room* (Merrion Press, Dublin, 2016), p. 270.

8   Interview with Brendan Howlin, 12 July 2018, Dublin. All quotes from Howlin in this chapter are from this interview.

9   Leaders' Questions, 11 February 2014.

10 Interview with Eamon Gilmore, 21 August 2018, Dublin.

11 John Tierney, Irish Water board report, February 2014. Obtained from Irish Water under the Freedom of Information Act.

12 Interview with Eamon Gilmore, 21 August 2018, Dublin.

29 The Water Meter Rebels

1   Group interview with members of the Ballyphehane/South Parish Says No group, 1 November 2018, Cork. All quotes from John Lonergan, Eddie O'Sullivan, Donal O'Sullivan and Keith O'Brien in this chapter come from this source.

30 Water Leaks

1   *Irish Independent*, 16 April 2014.

2   Interview with Brendan Howlin, 12 July 2018, Dublin.

3   Gilmore (2016), p. 271.

4   Interview with Joan Burton, 29 August 2018, Dublin.

5   Leaders' Questions in the Dáil, 16 April 2014.

6   *Ibid.*

7   Interview with Eamon Gilmore, 21 August 2018, Dublin.

8   *Irish Independent*, 21 April 2014.

31 Blue Rising

1   Letter from the chief governor of Ireland, Maurice Fitzgerald, to the sheriff of Dublin, 29 April 1244: https://chancery.tcd.ie/document/other/henry-iii/1.

2   Corcoran (2005), p. 9.

3   Report of the committee appointed for the better supplying the city with pipe water, 1775. Obtained from Diageo (the owner of Guinness).

4   Come Here to Me! blog, 5 July 2015: https://comeheretome.com/2015/07/05/arthur-guinness-and-his-right2water.

5   Interview with Derek Byrne, 5 October 2018, Dublin. All quotes from Byrne in this chapter are from this interview.

6   15 July 2015: www.youtube.com/watch?v=pgl3tx8vGWs&feature=youtu.be.

7   Interview with Michael Batty, 5 October 2018, Dublin.

8   Interview with Austin Dwyer, 5 October 2018, Dublin.

9   *Irish Daily Star*, 8 May 2014.

32 Can't Pay, Won't Pay

1   Phone interview with Phil Hogan by author during 2011 general election campaign, 18 February 2011.

2   Interview with Lucinda Creighton, 12 July 2018, Dublin.

3   *Irish Independent*, 2 December 2013.

4   Minutes of the Department of the Environment management advisory committee meeting, 26 April 2012. Obtained from the Department of the Environment under the Freedom of Information Act.

5   Interview with Edgar Morgenroth, 28 May 2018, Dublin.

6   *Ibid.*

7   Gorecki, Paul K., Lyons, Sean, and Morgenroth, Edgar, 'Affordability and the Provision of Water Services in Ireland: Options, Choices and Implications', 15 March 2013: www.esri.ie/system/files/media/file-uploads/2015-07/BKMNEXT 272.pdf.

8   The definition of water poverty used by the ESRI was a person who had to spend more than three per cent of their income on water charges.

9   Department of Housing reply to parliamentary question from Barry Cowen, 4 December 2018: https://www.oireachtas.ie/en/debates/question/2018-12-04/685/.

10   Interview with Joan Burton, 29 August 2018, Dublin.

11   www.esri.ie/system/files/media/file-uploads/2015-07/BKMNEXT272.pdf.

12   Interview with Edgar Morgenroth, 28 May 2018, Dublin.

13   Phone interview with Mick Murphy, 19 December 2018.

33 Hogan's Trickle-Down Threat

1   Interview with Brendan Howlin, 12 July 2018, Dublin. All quotes from Brendan Howlin in this chapter are from this interview.

2   Gilmore (2016), p. 272.

3   https://youtu.be/7WUtiWG927I.

4   www.thejournal.ie/phil-hogan-irish-water-omelette-eggs-1265690-Jan2014/.

5   Email from the Department of Communications civil servant to the Department of Environment, 19 November 2013. Obtained from the Department of Communications under the Freedom of Information Act.

6   Interview with Paudie Coffey, 21 June 2018, Dublin.

7   European Investment Bank statement on ESB loan, 17 November 2011: www. eib.org/en/infocentre/press/releases/all/2011/2011-171-esb-and-the-eib-agree-

a-eur-235-million-loan-to-fund-smart-investment-in-irelands-electricity-
networks.htm?lang=-en.

8   Interview with Eamon Gilmore, 21 August 2018, Dublin.

9   Interview with Gerry Horkan, 18 October 2018, Dublin.

10 Interview with Joan Burton, 29 August 2018, Dublin.

34 The Irish Water Power Struggle

1   *The Irish Times*, 9 February 2010.

2   Minutes of first Irish Water board meeting, 24 July 2013. Obtained from Irish
Water under the Freedom of Information Act.

3   Oireachtas environment committee, 11 October 2011: https://www.oireachtas.
ie/en/debates/debate/joint_committee_on_the_environment_transport_culture_
and_the_gaeltacht/2011-10-11/3/.

4   *Irish Mail on Sunday*, 19 January 2014.

5   Interview with Alan Kelly, 12 December 2018, Dublin.

35 Water Women

1   Interview with Denise Mitchell, 4 July 2018, Dublin. Unless otherwise noted, all
quotes from Mitchell in this chapter are from this interview.

2   25 September 2014: https://youtu.be/MYu9x0Pl0NQ.

3   Irish Water document on gender balance of staff. Obtained from Irish Water
under the Freedom of Information Act.

4   Shiel, Michael, *The Quiet Revolution: The Electrification of Rural Ireland* (Dublin,
The O'Brien Press, 2003), p. 123.

5   Phone interview with Seán Clerkin, 11 August 2018.

6   Phone interview with Damien Farrell, 28 November 2018.

7   Interview with Bríd Smith, 14 June 2018, Dublin. All quotes from Smith in this
chapter are from this interview.

8   *Village*, 13 April 2014: https://villagemagazine.ie/index.php/2014/04/dublin-
mep-candidates-4-brid-smith-people-before-profit.

36 Gilmore Out, Burton In

1   Interview with Eamon Gilmore, 21 August 2018, Dublin. All quotes from Gilmore in this chapter are from this interview.

2   https://www.youtube.com/watch?v=z1AQ2vzUKC0.

3   Walshe, John, *An Education: How an Outsider Became an Insider – and Learned
What Really Goes on in Irish Government* (Dublin, Penguin Ireland, 2014), pp. 228.

4   *The Sunday Business Post*, 8 March 2015.

5   Interview with Joan Burton, 29 August 2018, Dublin. All quotes from Burton in this chapter are from this interview.

6   Interview with Alan Kelly, 12 December 2018, Dublin.

37 The Water Wasters

1   Commission on Taxation report, 2009: https://researchrepository.ucd.ie/bit stream/10197/1447/1/Commission_on_Taxation_Report_2009.pdf.

2   Department of the Environment cost–benefit analysis on water metering, September 2011. Obtained from the Department of the Environment under the Freedom of Information Act.

3   Dáil debate on water reforms, 26 April 2012.

4   Bord Gáis household information leaflet on Irish Water and water metering, February 2014: www.laois.ie/wp-content/uploads/Irish-Water-Publications_Public_ Notices_Leaflet.pdf.

5   Interview with Edgar Morgenroth, 28 May 2018, Dublin. All quotes from Morgenroth in this chapter are from this interview.

6   Final Report on Household Water Consumption Estimates by Edgar Morgenroth, 21 July 2014: www.esri.ie/publications/final-report-on-household-water-consumption-estimates.

7   *The Irish Times*, 31 July 2013.

8   Jerry Grant of Irish Water later said: 'One of the great fallacies prior to metering was that the domestic consumer was using about 145 litres per person. We now know that is not right. We know that if we exclude the top seven per cent of households, usage is about 110 litres per person.' Evidence to joint committee on future funding of domestic water services, 14 February 2017.

9   Engineers Ireland explained the cost of the water service in its 2011 submission to the public consultation on water reforms: 'The bulk of the costs of providing a water service are fixed availability costs. In some cases the availability costs can be up to eighty-five per cent of the overall costs of water, yet pricing structures have to try to reflect these costs to some extent in a variable consumption charges'.

10 Bord Gáis Draft Irish Water implementation strategy (June 2012) and Bord Gáis final Irish Water implementation strategy (September 2012). Obtained from the Department of the Environment under the Freedom of Information Act.

11 Statement by the Commission for Energy Regulation (since renamed as the Commission for Regulation of Utilities) to author, 10 December 2018.

38 The Protesters' Flying Column

1 Irish Election Literature: https://irishelectionliterature.files.wordpress.com/2014/03/dfarrell4.jpg.
2 Phone interview with Damien Farrell, 28 November 2018. All quotes from Damien Farrell in this chapter are from this interview.
3 MacCionnath, Criostoir, 'They say cutbacks, we say fight back', MA thesis (NUI Maynooth, 2015), p. 90.
4 Irish Water board report, July 2014. Obtained from Irish Water under the Freedom of Information Act.
5 https://youtu.be/LquXqQ7YQ2s.

39 The Civil Servant Who Shouted Stop

1 Evidence of Martin Fraser at Dáil Public Accounts Committee, 3 May 2012.
2 Interview with Micheál Martin, 10 January 2019, Dublin.

40 The Right2Water Movement Begins

1 *The Irish Times*, 21 September 2005.
2 *The Herald*, 20 February 2015.
3 This was the opposite of what the country's senior trade union leaders like SIPTU's Jack O'Connor and IMPACT's Shay Cody believed. They were getting pay increases for workers and tax cuts through the social partnerships deals with the government. Ogle was anti-social partnership.
4 Ogle, Brendan, *From Bended Knee to a New Republic: How the Fight for Water is Changing Ireland* (The Liffey Press, Dublin, 2016), p. 57.
5 *Ibid.*, p. 62.
6 Interview with Dave Gibney, 21 August 2018, Dublin. All quotes from Gibney in this chapter are from this interview.
7 Phone interview with Brendan Ogle, 12 February 2019.

41 The Thin Blue Line

1 Phone interview with Damien Farrell, 28 November 2018. All quotes from Farrell in this chapter are from this interview.
2 Minister for Justice reply to parliamentary question from Paul Murphy TD, 6 October 2015: www.oireachtas.ie/en/debates/question/2015-10-06/425/.
3 *Ibid.*
4 *Irish Independent*, 24 November 2014.
5 Garda Síochána ombudsman commission annual report 2015. Available to

download from: www.gardaombudsman.ie/news-room/archive/garda-ombuds man-annual-report-2015-published.

6   Interview with Joe Higgins, 3 September 2018, Dublin.

7   Statement from An Garda Síochána to author, 26 February 2019.

8   Interview with Frances Fitzgerald, 29 November 2018, Dublin. All quotes from Fitzgerald in this chapter are from this interview.

9   TheJournal.ie, 17 February 2016.

10 Interview with Joan Collins, 14 June 2018, Dublin.

11 Interview with Dermot Connolly, 14 June 2018, Dublin.

12 https://youtu.be/O4a7EiWDokM.

13 Interview with John Brady, 8 November 2018, Dublin.

14 Garda Síochána Ombudsman Commission annual report 2015.

15 Statement by Garda Síochána Ombudsman Commission to author, 31 January 2019.

42 The Island that Said 'No'

1   Phone interview with Karen Doyle, 19 September 2018, Dublin. Unless other-wise noted, all quotes from Doyle in this chapter are from this interview.

2   The giant cranes were taken down in 2018 for safety reasons.

3   Interview with Mick Barry, 15 November 2018, Dublin.

4   Group interview with members of Cobh Says No to Austerity, 1 November 2018, Cobh.

5   Ibid.

6   Irish Examiner, 31 October 2014.

7   Group interview with members of Cobh Says No to Austerity, 1 November 2018, Cobh.

8   NBC News, 15 November 2014: www.nbcnews.com/news/world/water-unleashes-rebellion-relentlessly-rainy-ireland-n247551.

9   Group interview with members of Cobh Says No to Austerity, 1 November 2018, Cobh.

43 Noonan Pours Cold Water

1   Irish Independent, 7 October 2014.

2   The Irish Water bonuses came directly from Bord Gáis. John Mullins had negoti-ated a new pay deal with staff in 2012 to save €34 million over four years. Staff got a 'performance-related payment' if they did their job to an acceptable standard. In return, they agreed to a pay freeze, the abolition of allowances and the end of

annual salary increases based on length of service (better known as increments). Irish Water staff were hired under this Bord Gáis pay structure. It became a PR nightmare. The media had a simpler way of describing the 'performance-related payments'. They called them 'bonuses'.

3   Interview with Fergus O'Dowd, 7 November 2017, Dublin.

4   Phone interview with Jack O'Connor, 14 November 2018.

5   Interview with Eamon Gilmore, 21 August 2018, Dublin.

6   He had once told *Village* magazine of how former Taoiseach Brian Cowen had not been able to control the narrative to keep people with him. 'In modern politics, the twenty-four-hour news cycle is so immediate that unless your leader can have a narrative that people will subscribe to, you don't get the kind of social cohesion to plan forward.'

7   Interview with Joan Burton, 29 August 2018, Dublin.

8   Interview with Alan Kelly, 12 December 2018, Dublin.

9   Walshe (2014), p. 45.

44 The Socialist Triumph

1   Phone interview with Mick Murphy, 19 December 2018.

2   Interview with Paul Murphy, 17 October 2018, Dublin. All quotes from Paul Murphy in this chapter are from this interview.

3   This was a protest by 100,000 demonstrators in Seattle in 1999 against the opening ceremonies of the world trade talks. Riot police used pepper gas against them.

4   RTÉ News, 7 October 2014: www.rte.ie/news/player/2014/1007/20660902-jobs-housing-and-water-charges-dominating-in-dublin-south-west/.

5   Interview with Frances Fitzgerald, 29 November 2018, Dublin.

6   Interview with Denise Mitchell, 4 July 2018, Dublin.

7   Interview with Brian Stanley, 23 October 2018, Dublin.

8   TheJournal.ie, 5 October 2014.

45 Taking to the Streets

1   Interview with Dave Gibney, 21 August 2018, Dublin.

2   Email from Stephen Murphy to author, 11 March 2019.

3   'Right2Water Was it for this?', 11 October 2014: www.youtube.com/watch?v=8M4ZJ7tipjA.

4   Used with permission from the author.

5   Tweet from The Rubberbandits, 10 December 2014.

6   Phone interview with Karen Doyle, 19 September 2018, Dublin.

7   Interview with Rose Brien-Harrington and members of Cobh Says No to Austerity, 1 November 2018, Cobh.

8   *The Sunday Business Post*, 9 November 2014.

9   RTÉ Archives, 1979 PAYE tax marches: www.rte.ie/archives/exhibitions/1861-strikes-pickets-and-protests/469887-huge-demo-against-paye-in-dublin.

46 The Sacking Plan that Failed

1   https://youtu.be/ePdNDEIWdR0.

2   Interview with Joan Burton, 29 August 2018, Dublin. All quotes from Burton in this chapter are from this interview.

3   Leaders' Questions in the Dáil, 9 October 2014.

4   *Irish Independent*, 16 October 2014.

5   *The Irish Times*, 21 October 2014.

6   *Ibid*.

7   Leaders' Questions in the Dáil, 21 October 2014.

8   Interview with Alan Kelly, 12 December 2018, Dublin.

9   *Irish Independent*, 22 October 2014.

10 Alan Kelly statement on meeting with Irish Water, 22 October 2014.

11 Facebook post by water protester, 26 September 2014.

12 *Irish Daily Mail*, 17 February 2015.

13 Statement from An Garda Síochána to author, 26 February 2019.

14 Interview with Alan Kelly, 12 December 2018, Dublin.

47 The Garda Station Siege

1   *The Sunday Business Post*, 2 November 2014.

2   Phone interview with Ciarán Heaphy, 27 November 2018. All quotes from Heaphy in this chapter are from this interview.

3   www.broadsheet.ie/2014/11/05/pushing-back.

4   *Ibid*.

5   https://youtu.be/90s1cKbZV40.

6   A garda spokesman said the man who punched Inspector Hyland fled the scene without being arrested. There has been no arrest for this incident.

7   https://youtu.be/90s1cKbZV40.

8   Statement from An Garda Síochána to author, 26 February 2019.

9   RTÉ *Prime Time* blog on the water protests in north Dublin: www.rte.ie/news/primetime/2014/1107/657728-prime-times-mark-coughlan-the-water-protests-in-north-dublin.

10 *The Sunday Business Post,* 2 November 2014.

48 Watering down the Charges

1 Ogle (2016), p. 81.
2 Interview with Paudie Coffey, 21 June 2018, Dublin. All quotes from Coffey in this chapter are from this interview.
3 *The Irish Times,* 30 September 2014.
4 RTÉ News, 5 November 2014: www.rte.ie/news/player/2014/1105/20676629-labour-senators-vote-against-fg-as-confusion-continues-over-water (accessed April 2019).
5 Leaders' Questions in the Dáil, 5 November 2014.
6 Interview with Alan Kelly, 12 December 2018, Dublin. Unless otherwise noted, all quotes from Kelly in this chapter are from this interview.
7 Dáil debate, 19 November 2014.
8 There was an attempt to pretend the water meters were still relevant. It was called 'Beat the cap', which sounded like the name of a TV gameshow. If people used less than a certain amount of water, they could reduce their water charges. Irish Water's head of communications, Elizabeth Arnett, was sent out to explain this to a befuddled public.
9 Interview with Micheál Martin, 10 January 2019, Dublin.
10 Interview with Joe Higgins, 3 September 2018, Dublin.

49 Meter Attacks

1 Email from the Department of the Environment official to John Tierney, 17 November 2014.
2 Memo on metering protests from John Tierney, 17 November 2014.
3 RTÉ *Prime Time* water charges report, 12 November 2014: www.rte.ie/news/primetime/2014/1212/666444-prime-time-11-12-2014.
4 https://m.youtube.com/watch?v=yFlK6QcqVS0.
5 RTÉ *Prime Time* water charges report, 12 November 2014.
6 *Irish Examiner,* 7 May 2015.
7 *Irish Independent,* 19 September 2014.
8 Interview with Frances Fitzgerald, 29 November 2018, Dublin.
9 Fitzgerald brought up the water charge protests at the annual commemorative event for Michael Collins at Béal na mBláth in Cork in August 2015. She referred to the tough law and order stance Collins had taken when he got into the first Free State government. 'For Collins, disagreement was to be cherished, but

interference with the people, their safety and their property was unacceptable and was to be clamped down upon,' she told the crowd.

50 No Privatisation

1   Ogle (2016), pp 92.

2   *The Herald*, 24 November 2014.

3   Interview with Dave Gibney, 21 August 2018, Dublin. All quotes from Gibney in this chapter are from this interview.

4   Statement from An Garda Síochána to author, 26 February 2019. Gardaí have confirmed that Operation Mizen was never shut down but has been renamed as the Digital Intelligence Unit to monitor social media 'to ensure the safety of all involved in protests and public order incidents'.

5   Phone interview with Leo Varadkar, 5 January 2019.

6   Power, Martin J., Haynes, Amanda and Devereux, Eoin, 'Reasonable People v The Sinister Fringe: Interrogating the Framing of Ireland's Water Charge Protesters through the Media Politics of Dissent' (University of Limerick, April 2016).

7   Phone interview with Brendan Ogle, 12 February 2019. All quotes from Ogle in this chapter are from this interview.

8   www.youtube.com/watch?v=wv4Nyj2uZR0.

9   *The Irish Times*, 9 December 2014.

10 Phone interview with Eamon de Staic, 2 January 2019. All quotes from Eamon de Staic in this chapter are from this interview.

11 www.youtube.com/watch?v=OfEOLXR1gcA.

12 Five men from Rossport in Mayo were jailed in June 2005 for blocking the construction of a gas pipeline through their land by the multinational energy company Shell. They were released after spending ninety-four days in prison. The pipeline was rerouted due to their concerns about its safety. But the project remained hugely divisive.

13 It should be noted for the record that no garda was ever charged or convicted in relation to the policing of protests in Rossport or Jobstown.

14 Used with permission from the authors.

15 Phone interview with Donal Gibbons, 9 January 2019.

16 The Pink Ladies were a group of women in Dublin who wore pink high-vis vests bought from Centra stores as part of a cancer awareness campaign. They protested outside Coolook garda station about the policing of metering protests in November 2014. The pink high-vis vests were then adopted by more women involved in water charge protests.

17   https://youtu.be/Gc1Uv2OROl8.

18   *Ibid.*

19   Interview with Alan Kelly, 12 December 2018, Dublin.

51   Locked Up

1   Interview with Damien O'Neill, 24 October 2018, Dublin. All quotes from O'Neill in this chapter are from this interview.

2   Interview with Derek Byrne, 5 October 2018, Dublin. Unless otherwise noted, all quotes from Byrne in this chapter are from this interview.

3   'Derek Byrne Reads Irish Proclamation of Independence in GPO', 15 September 2014: www.youtube.com/watch?v=8XG_Yfvu_q8.

4   *Irish Independent*, 31 October 2014.

5   *Irish Independent*, 19 February 2015.

6   Interview with Michael Batty, 5 October 2018, Dublin.

7   Paul Murphy on *The Late Late Show*, RTÉ, 20 February 2015.

8   Interview with Paul Murphy, 17 October 2018, Dublin.

9   Interview with Alan Kelly, 12 December 2018, Dublin.

10   *Northern Standard*, 28 February 2015.

52   The Boycott of the Bills

1   Leaders' Questions in the Dáil, 13 May 2015.

2   Interview with Paul Murphy, 17 October 2018, Dublin. All quotes from Paul Murphy in this chapter are from this interview.

3   Letter from Maria Graham to John Tierney, 19 June 2015. Obtained from Irish Water under the Freedom of Information Act.

4   Letter from John Tierney to Maria Graham, 13 July 2015. Obtained from Irish Water under the Freedom of Information Act.

5   Interview with Tom Collins, 28 August 2018, Dublin.

6   Phone interview with Brendan Ogle, 12 February 2019. Unless otherwise noted, all quotes from Ogle in this chapter are from this interview.

7   Ogle (2016), p. 146.

8   *The Irish Times,* 8 July 2015.

9   Conference paper by Jerry Grant. Available to download from www.waternz.org. nz/Article?Action=View&Article_id=1607.

10   TheJournal.ie, 10 April 2015.

11   *The Irish Times*, 25 March 2015.

12   Interview with Mick Barry, 15 November 2018, Dublin.

13 Email from Alex White to author, 7 January 2019. All quotes from White in this chapter are from this source.

14 Noonan had been the health minister who had supported the state strategy to fight a court case taken by one dying woman, Brigid McCole, who had been infected with contaminated, state-supplied blood products. He later said sorry for his role. But when he was the Fine Gael leader in the 2002 general election, the party's vote collapsed and it lost twenty-three of its fifty-one TDs. Noonan resigned and Enda Kenny took over.

15 Interview with Joan Burton, 29 August 2018, Dublin.

53 Fianna Fáil Backs the Protesters

1 Leaders' Questions in the Dáil, 1 April 2015.

2 Leaders' Questions in the Dáil, 17 February 2015.

3 Walshe (2014), p. 44.

4 But whatever about the man with two pints, there was one constituent of Kenny's who wanted to pay his water bill. 'The Taoiseach has been contacted by X from Manualla [a village outside Castlebar] who has not yet received his water bill,' one of Kenny's staff told Irish Water. The bill of €19.73 was duly posted out.

5 Leaders' Questions in the Dáil, 21 October 2014.

6 *Ibid.*

7 Interview with Barry Cowen, 29 November 2018, Dublin.

8 *Irish Independent,* 26 March 2012.

9 *Irish Daily Mirror,* 25 May 2015.

10 *The Sunday Business Post*, 31 December 2017.

11 Interview with Micheál Martin, 10 January 2019, Dublin.

12 *The Sunday Business Post*, 26 April 2015. The water from the Vartry scheme was supplied to Dublin via a four-mile tunnel through the Wicklow mountains. The tunnel was identified as being in danger of collapse in a structural study in 1995. That would have cut off the water supply to 100,000 people in Wicklow and Dublin, but nothing had been done by the time Irish Water was set up. Irish Water eventually completed a new four-kilometre buried pipeline from Vartry to Callowhill to finally replace the Vartry tunnel in February 2019.

13 https://youtu.be/Con59NcZw8A.

14 Highland Radio, 24 July 2015: www.highlandradio.com/2015/07/24/taoiseach-enda-kenny-compares-small-glenties-protest-to-welsh-choir.

54 Siteserv

1 Interview with Catherine Murphy (now a TD for the Social Democrats), 24 October 2018, Dublin. All quotes from Murphy in this chapter are from this interview.
2 *Irish Independent*, 29 August 2015.
3 Interview with Denise Mitchell, 4 July 2018, Dublin.
4 Irish Water monthly metering reports to the Department of the Environment, August 2013–January 2017. Obtained from Irish Water under the Freedom of Information Act.
5 Department of Communications memo to Minister Pat Rabbitte to consent to the water metering project, 24 July 2013. Obtained from the Department of Communications under the Freedom of Information Act.
6 Dáil private members motion on the sale of Siteserv, 6 May 2015: www.oireachtas.ie/en/debates/debate/dail/2015-05-06/25/.
7 Leaders' Questions in the Dáil, 10 December 2014.
8 *The Sunday Business Post*, 19 July 2015.
9 Siteserv motion in the Dáil, 6 May 2015.
10 The commission of inquiry into the Siteserv sale is ongoing. Siteserv has publicly insisted that the sale of the company to Millington in 2012 was conducted entirely in full compliance with best corporate practice and governance standards.

55 Irish Water's EU Test

1 NewERA water sector reform programme financial model presentation to senior officials group, March 2013.
2 *The Irish Times*, 14 January 2015.
3 *Ibid.*
4 Interview with Joan Burton, 29 August 2018, Dublin.
5 Eurostat decision on Irish Water, 28 July 2015: https://ec.europa.eu/eurostat/documents/1015035/6761701/Advise-2015-IE-Classification-of-Irish-Water-Summary.pdf/fdbd9e8f-4823-40c5-9ae8-a08e19324635.
6 RTÉ *Six One News*, 28 July 2015.
7 Interview with Alan Kelly, 12 December 2018, Dublin.
8 Eurostat letter to Central Statistics Office, 24 July 2015: www.cso.ie/en/media/csoie/newsevents/documents/ClassificationofIrishWaterJuly2015.pdf.
9 O'Leary, Jim, 'How (not) to do public policy: water charges and local property tax' (Whittaker Institute, NUI Galway, 2018). Available at http://whitakerinstitute.ie/wp-content/uploads/2018/10/NUIG-Whitaker-Report-Water-Charges-LPT-Final.pdf.

10 Phone interview with Leo Varadkar, 5 January 2019.

56 The Hill 16 Protest

1 This was a tongue-in-cheek reference to Sinn Féin leader Gerry Adams' famous comment about the IRA during a tense time in the peace process in 1995: 'They haven't gone away, you know.'

2 *Irish Examiner*, 1 September 2015.

3 Interview with Derek Byrne, 5 October 2018, Dublin.

4 Phone interview with Damien Farrell, 28 November 2018. All quotes from Farrell in this chapter are from this interview.

5 Statement from Irish Water to author, 8 March 2019.

6 *The Sunday Business Post*, 6 December 2015.

7 Interview with Lucinda Creighton, 12 July 2018, Dublin.

8 Phone interview with Brian Leeson, 28 September 2018.

9 Interview with Damien O'Neill, 24 October 2018, Dublin.

10 Crumlin Says No member quoted during an interview in MacCionnath, 'They say cutbacks, we say fight back', p. 157.

11 Group interview with members of the Ballyphehane/South Parish Says No group, 1 November 2018, Cork.

12 *Ibid.*

57 The Final Days of Water Charges

1 *The Sunday Business Post*, 13 September 2015.

2 Interview with Paul Murphy, 17 October 2018, Dublin.

3 Interview with Joan Burton, 29 August 2018, Dublin.

4 *Sunday Independent,* 31 January 2016.

5 Interview with Alan Kelly, 12 December 2018, Dublin. All quotes from Kelly in this chapter are from this interview.

6 *Irish Independent,* 29 February 2016.

7 RTÉ *Prime Time*, 1 March 2016: www.rte.ie/news/player/prime-time/2016/0301 (accessed April 2019).

8 Interview with Simon Coveney, 19 October 2018, Co. Monaghan. All quotes from Coveney in this chapter are from this interview.

9 Interview with Noel Dempsey, 31 May 2018, Dublin.

10 *The Irish Times*, 25 March 2016.

11 Interview with Barry Cowen, 29 November 2018, Dublin.

12 Group interview with Keith O'Brien and members of the Ballyphehane/South

Parish Says No group, 1 November 2018, Cork.

13   *Ibid.*

14   Interview with Micheál Martin, 10 January 2019, Dublin. All quotes from Martin in this chapter are from this interview.

15   Interview with Derek Byrne, 5 October 2018, Dublin.

16   Phone interview with Leo Varadkar, 5 January 2019. All quotes from Varadkar in this chapter are from this interview.

17   Ervia relevant communications register, April 2016: www.ervia.ie/site-files/docs/who-we-are/group_-_relevant_communications_registerjan.apr.16.pdf.

18   RTÉ Radio 1's *Today with Seán O'Rourke*, 28 January 2016. A Fianna Fáil-led government had bought 7,500 electronic voting machines for €51 million in 2002 to replace paper ballots. But due to concerns they could be tampered with, they had to be sold off for scrap. It became a notorious example of wasting public money.

19   Dáil debate, 27 April 2016.

58   The Departure of John Tierney

1   Email from John Tierney to Irish Water staff, 8 November 2015. Obtained from Irish Water under the Freedom of Information Act.

2   Email from John Tierney to Irish Water staff, 16 January 2016. Obtained from Irish Water under the Freedom of Information Act.

3   *Irish Mail on Sunday*, 29 October 2017.

4   Short letter to author from John Tierney. His concluding comment was: 'Beyond that, I hope you can understand, I don't have anything else to add. I wish you the very best with your book.'

5   Email from Alex White to author, 7 January 2019.

6   Noel Dempsey address to the MacGill Summer School, July 2015.

7   Tipperary GAA statement on John Tierney, September 2016.

59   Flotsam

1   Statistics on water charges payments from O'Leary, Jim, 'How (not) to do public policy: water charges and local property tax' (Whitaker Institute, NUI Galway, 2018), p. 50. Available at http://whitakerinstitute.ie/wp-content/uploads/2018/10/NUIG-Whitaker-Report-Water-Charges-LPT-Final.pdf.

2   Interview with Micheál Martin, 10 January 2019, Dublin.

3   Interview with Eoin Ó Broin, 27 November 2018, Dublin.

4   *Ibid.*

5   TheJournal.ie, 28 February 2017.

6   Interview with Micheál Martin, 10 January 2019, Dublin.

7   Interview with Barry Cowen, 29 November 2018, Dublin.

8   Details of water consumption in metered households: www.water.ie/for-home/
     metering-explained/consumption-reports/. The Department of the Environment
     maintains that the actual water use now is 129 litres per person per day, in line
     with a recent report by the Commission for the Regulation of Utilities. However,
     this figure includes houses with leaks, which pushes up the average water use per
     person. When leaks are taken out, it reduces the water use per person to around
     the 109 litres per person per day, in line with the research done by Edgar Morgen-
     roth and Irish Water.

9   Irish Independent, 5 March 2017.

10   Irish Daily Mirror, 9 December 2016.

11   Statement from Elizabeth Arnett to author, 10 January 2019.

12   Statement from Jerry Grant to author, 8 January 2019.

13   Ibid.

14   Conference paper by Jerry Grant. Available to download from www.waternz.org.
     nz/Article?Action=View&Article_id=1607.

15   Phone interview with Leo Varadkar, 5 January 2019.

16   Interview with Paschal Donohoe, 12 October 2018, Dublin.

17   Interview with John Mullins, 16 August 2018, Dublin.

18   Interview with Joan Burton, 29 August 2018, Dublin.

19   Interview with Alan Kelly, 12 December 2018, Dublin.

20   Phone interview with Karen Doyle, 19 September 2018, Dublin.

21   Ibid.

22   Interview with Joan Collins, 14 June 2018, Dublin.

23   Phone interview with Damien Farrell, 28 November 2018.

24   Robert Watt speaking during a public discussion on 'How (not) to do public po-
     licy: water charges and local property tax' report, 13 September 2018, Galway.:
     http://whitakerinstitute.ie/how-not-to-do-public-policy-highlights-from-the-
     conference.

25   Baldoyle Anti-Water Meter Task Force posts its congratulations to Mia Brady on
     Facebook: www.facebook.com/baldoylesaysnotometers/photos/a.566599303460
     108/1084601768326523/?type=1&theater.

26   Interview with Derek Byrne, 5 October 2018, Dublin.

27   Phone interview with Pauly Dillon, 27 February 2019.

28   Ibid.

29 *Limerick Post*, 7 September 2018.

60 #Jobstownnotguilty

1 Phone interview with Jay Lester, 10 October 2018.

2 *Tallaght Echo*, 21 November 2015: www.youtube.com/watch?v=Ilx6_UzcWzE.

3 Phone interview with Mick Murphy, 19 December 2018.

4 Mick Murphy subsequently lost his seat on South Dublin County Council in the local elections in May 2019. Another Jobstown protester cleared in court, Councillor Kieran Mahon, was re-elected

5 Charge to the jury by Judge Melanie Greally, 26 and 28 June 2017.

6 The six men cleared were Paul Murphy TD, Cllr Mick Murphy, Cllr Kieran Mahon from Bolbrook Grove, Tallaght, Scott Masterson from Carrigmore Drive, Tallaght; Frank Donaghy, from Alpine Rise, Belgard Heights, Tallaght; and Michael Banks, from Brookview Green, Tallaght. The charges against a seventh man, Ken Purcell, from Kilatown Green in Tallaght, had been dropped during the trial.

7 Leaders' Questions in the Dáil, 12 July 2017.

8 Interview with Paul Murphy, 17 October 2018, Dublin.

9 Interview with Joan Burton, 29 August 2018, Dublin. Twitter and Facebook both said they had no comment to make. Statement to author, 17 May 2019 (Twitter) and 20 May 2019 (Facebook).

10 Interview with Joe Higgins, 3 September 2018, Dublin.

61 Still Water

1 Interview with Mike Quinn, 19 December 2018, Dublin.

2 Interview with Derek Byrne, 5 October 2018, Dublin.

3 Interview with John Gormley, 21 June 2018, Dublin.

4 Phone interview with Leo Varadkar, 5 January 2019.

5 Evidence of European Commission spokesman Aurel Ciobanu-Dordea at joint committee on future funding of domestic water services, 15 February 2017.

6 Phone interview with Leo Varadkar, 5 January 2019.

7 Interview with Alan Kelly, 12 December 2018, Dublin.

8 Interview with John Mullins, 16 August 2018, Dublin.

9 Phone interview with Leo Varadkar, 5 January 2019.

10 Interview with Noel O'Keeffe, 1 November 2018, Cork.

BIBLIOGRAPHY

Books

Bielenberg, Andy, *The Shannon Scheme and the Electrification of the Irish Free State* (The Lilliput Press, Dublin, 2002)

Corcoran, Michael, *Our Good Health – A History of Dublin's Water and Drainage* (Four Courts Press, Dublin, 2005)

Downing, J., *Enda Kenny, The Unlikely Taoiseach* (Paperweight Publications, Dublin, 2012)

Gilmore, Eamon, *Inside the Room* (Merrion Press, Dublin, 2016)

Leahy, Pat, *The Price of Power – Inside Ireland's Crisis Coalition* (Penguin Ireland, Dublin, 2013)

Lee, John and McConnell, Daniel, *Hell at the Gates: The Inside Story of Ireland's Financial Downfall* (Mercier Press, Cork, 2016)

Ogle, Brendan, *From Bended Knee to a New Republic: How the Fight for Water is Changing Ireland* (The Liffey Press, Dublin, 2016)

Shiel, Michael, *The Quiet Revolution: The Electrification of Rural Ireland* (The O'Brien Press, Dublin, 2003)

Walshe, John, *An Education: How an Outsider Became an Insider – and Learned What Really Goes on in Irish Government* (Penguin Ireland, Dublin, 2014)

Documents obtained under the Freedom of Information Act

Briefing note for cabinet sub-committee meeting on Irish Water, 15 April 2013

Cabinet memos

Cost–benefit analysis on the metering of households connected to public water supplies

Department of Communications briefing note for Irish Water establishment, 12 April 2012

Domestic water metering programme briefing note for Minister Pat Rabbitte, 2 July 2012

Domestic water metering project pre-installation survey technical guidance document, July 2012

Email from Department of the Environment official to John Tierney, 17 November 2014

Email from John Tierney about examples of metering protests to Department of the Environment, 17 November 2014

Email from John Tierney to Irish Water staff, 8 November 2015

Irish Water board minutes

Irish Water document on gender balance of staff

Irish Water monthly metering reports to the Department of the Environment, August 2013–January 2017

KPMG metering report, 25 June 2013

Letter from Maria Graham to John Tierney, 19 June 2015

Memorandum for the government on the 11th review mission for the EU/IMF programme of financial support for Ireland, 5 July 2013

Minutes of Department of the Environment management advisory committee meetings

NewERA confidential report on domestic metering project, 12 July 2013

Submission to Communications Minister Pat Rabbitte on consent for BGE/Irish Water to enter into capital commitments for Irish Water domestic metering programme, 4 July 2013

Water sector reform programme presentation – from the Department of the Environment and NewERA, April 2013

Other Sources

Gorecki, Paul K., Lyons, Sean, and Morgenroth, Edgar, 'Affordability and the Provision of Water Services in Ireland: Options, Choices and Implications' (www.esri.ie, 15 March 2013)

Hearne, Rory, 'The Irish water war, austerity and the "Risen people"' (Maynooth University, 2016)

MacCionnath, Criostoir, 'They say cutbacks, we say fight back', MA Thesis

(NUI Maynooth, 2015)

McMorrow, Conor, 'The Cowen government's water files', RTÉ Blog, 19 October 2015

O'Gorman, Aidan, Lynch, Alex, Bergin, Jack, Altermatt, Ruth and Hennelly, Thomas, 'A Report on The Policing of Protests in Ireland relative to Human Rights Standards and Good Practices Internationally' (University of Limerick, 2018)

O'Leary, Jim, 'How (not) to do public policy: water charges and local property tax' (Whitaker Institute, NUI Galway, 2018)

Power, Martin J., Haynes, Amanda and Devereux, Eoin, 'Reasonable people v the sinister fringe: interrogating the framing of Ireland's water charge protesters through the media politics of dissent' (University of Limerick, April 2016)

Trial Transcripts. The full transcripts of the trial of the Jobstown protesters are available at https://sites.google.com/view/jobstownnotguilty/trial

Newspapers

Belfast Newsletter
Irish Daily Mail
Irish Daily Mirror
Irish Daily Star
Irish Examiner
Irish Independent
Irish Mail on Sunday
Kilkenny People
Limerick Post
Munster Express
Northern Standard
Sunday Independent
Sunday Tribune
Tallaght Echo
The Herald
The Irish Times

The Sunday Business Post
The Sunday Times
Western People

Magazine Articles

Lowes, Tony, *Village*, 9 March 2010. Interview with John Gormley: https://villagemagazine.ie/index.php/2010/03/inside-the-mind-of-john-gormley

Correspondence

Email from Aindrias de Staic to author, 29 March 2019

Email from Eamon de Staic to author, 13 March 2019

Email from Stephen Murphy to author, 11 March 2019

Letter from John Tierney to author, November 2018

Statement from Alex White to author, 7 January 2019

Statement from An Garda Síochána to author, 26 February 2019

Statement from Commission for Regulation of Utilities (formerly Commission for Energy Regulation) to author, 10 December 2018

Statement from Elizabeth Arnett to author, 10 January 2019

Statement from Garda Síochána Ombudsman Commission to author, 31 January 2019

Statement from Irish Water to author, 8 March 2019

Statement from Jerry Grant to author, 8 January 2019

Statement to author by Department of the Environment (now known as Department of Housing, Planning and Local Government), 16 April 2019

Websites

Budget website: Budget.gov.ie

Come Here to Me! Blog: https://comeheretome.com/2015/07/05/arthur-guinness-and-his-right2water

Dáil debates: www.oireachtas.ie/en/debates

Department of Communications: www.dccae.gov.ie

Department of Public Expenditure and Reform: dper.gov.ie

Department of the Environment (later called Housing). www.housing.gov.ie

Department of the Taoiseach: www.taoiseach.gov.ie
Facebook: www.facebook.com
Irish Election Literature: https://irishelectionliterature.com
Irish Newspaper Archives: www.irishnewsarchive.com
Irish Water: www.water.ie
Jobstown not Guilty: https://sites.google.com/view/jobstownnotguilty/trial
Joe's Water Blog: www.joeswaterblog.com
NBC News: www.nbcnews.com
Oireachtas: www.oireachtas.ie
Pól Ó Conghaile travel blog: https://poloconghaile.com
RTÉ Archives: www.rte.ie/archives
RTÉ News: www.rte.ie/news
RTÉ *Prime Time*: www.rte.ie/news/player/prime-time
The Economic and Social Research Institute: www.esri.ie
The Journal: www.journal.ie
UCD: ucd.ie
YouTube: youtube.com

Interviews

Barry, Mick, 15 November 2018, Dublin
Batty, Michael, 5 October 2018, Dublin
Brady, John, 8 November 2018, Dublin
Brien-Harrington, Rose, 1 November 2018, Cobh
Burton, Joan, 29 August 2018, Dublin
Byrne, Derek, 5 October 2018, Dublin
Clerkin, Seán, 11 August 2018, phone
Coffey, Paudie, 21 June 2018, Dublin
Collins, Joan, 14 June 2018, Dublin
Collins, Tom, 28 August 2018, Dublin
Connolly, Dermot, 14 June 2018, Dublin
Coveney, Simon, 19 October 2018, Co. Monaghan
Cowen, Barry, 29 November 2018, Dublin
Creighton, Lucinda,12 July 2018, Dublin

Dalton, Joe, 1 March 2019, Dublin

de Staic, Eamon, 2 January 2019, phone

Dempsey, Noel, 31 May 2018, Dublin

Dillon, Pauly, 27 February 2019, phone

Donnelly, Eamon, 15 August 2018, Dublin

Donohoe, Paschal, 12 October 2018, Dublin

Doyle, Karen, 19 September 2018, phone and 1 November 2018, Cork

Dwyer, Austin, 5 October 2018, Dublin

Farrell, Damien, 28 November 2018, phone

Farrell, Vivienne, 1 November 2018, Cobh

Fitzgerald, Frances, 29 November 2018, Dublin

FitzGerald, John, 14 June 2018, Dublin

Gibbons, Donal, 9 January 2019, phone

Gibney, Dave, 21 August 2018, Dublin

Gilmore, Eamon, 21 August 2018, Dublin

Gormley, John, 21 June 2018, Dublin

Heaphy, Ciarán, 27 November 2018, phone

Heffernan, Seán, 24 September 2018, phone

Higgins, Joe, 3 September 2018, Dublin

Horkan, Gerry, 18 October 2018, Dublin

Howlin, Brendan, 12 July 2018, Dublin

Kelly, Alan, 12 December 2018, Dublin

Laffey, Sean, 4 July 2018, Dublin

Leeson, Brian, 28 September 2018, phone

Lester, Jay, 10 October 2018, phone

Lonergan, John, 1 November 2018, Cork

Maher, Chris, 14 July 2018, phone

Martin, Micheál, 10 January 2019, Dublin

McLaughlin, Martin, 15 October 2018, phone

Mitchell, Denise, 4 July 2018, Dublin

Morgenroth, Edgar, 28 May 2018, Dublin

Mullins, John, 16 August 2018, Dublin

Murphy, Catherine, 24 October 2018, Dublin

Murphy, Mick, 19 December 2018, phone

Murphy, Paul, 17 October 2018, Dublin

O'Brien, Keith, 1 November 2018, Cork

Ó Broin, Eoin, 27 November 2018, Dublin

O'Connor, Jack, 14 November 2018, phone

O'Dowd, Fergus, 7 November 2017, Dublin

O'Leary, Gerard, 28 September 2018, Dublin

O'Keeffe, Noel, 1 November 2018, Cork

O'Neill, Damien, 24 October 2018, Dublin

O'Rourke, Sean, 5 December 2018, phone

O'Sullivan, Donal, 1 November 2018, Cork

O'Sullivan, Eddie, 1 November 2018, Cork

Ogle, Brendan, 12 February 2019, Dublin

Quinn, Mike, 19 December 2018, Dublin

Rodwell, Crispin, 31 January 2019, phone

Smith, Bríd, 14 June 2018, Dublin

Stanley, Brian, 23 October 2018, Dublin

Stoat, Kit, 1 November 2018, Cobh

Varadkar, Leo, 5 January 2019, phone

ACKNOWLEDGEMENTS

During my work with the *Irish Examiner*, the Press Association, the *Irish Independent* and now *The Sunday Business Post*, I have been fortunate to have a first-hand view of many of the events documented in this book.

I always viewed the roll-out of water charges as a defining political and social issue in our country's history. But I had a nagging sense that there was a much bigger story than I had been able to report at the time. This book, therefore, is not an attempt to re-fight the battle over water charges but to dig deeper and find out what actually happened.

I have been fortunate to receive the cooperation of so many people who were at the heart of the Irish Water story. I am grateful to all who gave up their time to speak to me, often on multiple occasions. Where possible, I carried out interviews on the record. Some people did not want to speak publicly but were willing to provide their insights in private. This category includes special advisers, civil servants and political staff. TDs and senators from all parties in Leinster House also provided information and suggestions. They are too numerous to mention, but it all helped. I appreciate the cooperation I got from current and former members of Irish Water, Bord Gáis, councils, unions and An Garda Síochána, and from people involved in the many different water protests around the country. It was a pleasure to write about the musicians, the poets and the colourful personalities in this story.

The Freedom of Information Act was an invaluable tool in obtaining hundreds of previously unpublished documents, with the help of dedicated FOI officers in Irish Water, the Department of Housing, the Department of Communications and the Department of the Taoiseach. And the restoration of the FOI Act by the 2011–16 government allowed for the release of documents and cabinet memos that would have otherwise been off limits. YouTube and Facebook videos of the protests allowed me to capture real-time dialogue in a way that would not have been possible in the pre-social media era.

I would like to thank all the team at Mercier Press. Patrick O'Donoghue worked with me from day one to make the book possible, Noel O'Regan made excellent editing suggestions, Alice Coleman designed the cover and Wendy Logue and Deirdre Roberts looked after production and publicity. Thanks also to Jimmy Healy, who read the draft manuscript and provided great feedback, as well as Jennifer Armstrong, who did the proofreading.

My thanks to all my fellow journalists for their front-line reporting on Irish Water that helped to inform this book. I have been fortunate in particular to work with a great team in *The Sunday Business Post* over the past five years.

On a personal level, the experience of growing up in Milltown in Galway, which is served by group water schemes, gave me an early interest in the subject. My parents, Catherine and Oliver, bought us a BBC Micro computer, which is where I started off typing stories. They instilled a strong sense of the need for fairness, which I have tried to carry through in this book. I have always had huge support and encouragement from them, as well as my brothers, David, Barry, Damian and Colin, and my sister, Marie.

In school, I was fortunate to have two dedicated English teachers – Frank Mullen in St Benin's National School in Kilbannon in Galway and the late Padraic Nolan in St Jarlath's College in Tuam.

And, most importantly, I could not have written this book without my wife, Siobhán, who reviewed every draft chapter and provided endless helpful suggestions and feedback.

INDEX

ABOUT THE AUTHOR

Michael Brennan is the political editor of the *Sunday Business Post*. A native of Milltown, Co. Galway, he received a degree in journalism from DCU. After working with Midwest Radio and the *Irish Emigrant* newspaper in Boston, he joined the *Irish Examiner* in Cork, where he won the Young Journalist of the Year award in 2004. He later worked with the Press Association in Dublin, and for the *Irish Independent* for seven years as political correspondent and then deputy political editor. He joined *The Sunday Business Post* as political correspondent in January 2014 and was promoted to political editor in May 2016.